THEM

WHITLEY STRIEBER

CONTENTS

Them
by Whitley Strieber

"Whatever this is, it is more complex than we can possibly imagine."
  —Col. John Alexander

"The human species is too young to have beliefs. What we need are good questions."
  —Anne Strieber

"Every day, life feels mightier, and what we have the power to be, more stupendous."
  —Emily Dickinson

This book is dedicated to the memory of Anne Strieber, without whose courage, dedication, and insight, Communion and all that has followed could not have happened.

ACKNOWLEDGMENTS

If I acknowledged the support of all who deserve to be named here, this would be a book of acknowledgements. I say this because every person who has lived the close encounter experience, whether in civilian or military life, has played a part in *Them*.

I would like to thank so many friends who have generously shared their knowledge and wisdom with me, most especially Col. John Alexander, Richard Dolan, Dr. Christopher "Kit" Green, Linda Moulton Howe, Mitch Horowitz, Leslie Kean, Dr. Jeff Kripal, Dr. Garry Nolan, Dr. Hal Puthoff, and Dr. Jacques Vallée.

I would also like to remember the people who met the visitors at our cabin: Lorie Barnes, Raven Dana, Dora Ruffner, Peter Frohe, and those who cannot be named.

As well, I would like to express my gratitude to the family who took me in when the situation in my home became too unsettling for me to work.

PREFACE

From *Whether* to *Why*: Confronting Whitley Strieber's *Them*
by Mitch Horowitz

Whitley Strieber does something unprecedented in *Them*. It is so simple that, like most radical theses, we wonder why we didn't attempt to see it this way earlier.

The author pursues the question of "visitor" phenomena from the perspective of the reported beings themselves. With this simple shift in focus—supported by historical and medical record, critical testimony, technological evidence, and thousands of encounter experiences (including his own)—Whitley upends nearly everything about the current UFO narrative, including its never-ending loop of "he said, she said" contentions over secrecy and coverups.

Since the publication of *Communion* in 1987, rejectionists, satirists, and skeptics have abused Whitley. Terms like "crackpot"—inadequate and divisive—come easily to their lips. I have worked with Whitley for more than twelve years; we are friends, collaborators, and interlocuters. We have occasionally argued, as friends do, and reconciled. At every point, I have found Whitley, as both a man and an author, ethical, hardworking, reliable, and profoundly capable. He has done the things in life that many people aim to: raise a family, care for a spouse (in this case with terminal brain cancer), and maintain a household. He is good-humored and self-effacing. He delivers criticism directly but diplomatically. People at risk of psychosis or chronic "fibbing" hit the rocks at a certain point. He has not.

Simply put, the "greatest hits" of both ufology (with its tendency to posit endless whitewashes) and rejectionism (with its tautological excuses and shoot-the-messenger devices) form a framework that we as a seeking community must finally exit. *Them* is an offramp.

Rationalist philosopher David Hume (1711–1776) proffered a simple, but often misunderstood, formula for evaluating miracles: counter claims ("bugs on the windshield," "drones," "delusions," "tricks of light," "coverups") must finally, and following sustained analysis, appear more tortuous than the proposed class of phenomena itself. That is the threshold we are on, as Whitley explores in *Them*.

Them will not satisfy ardent critics. It does not always satisfy me as someone with critical sympathy for the visitor thesis. But the book would have proven a source of satisfaction to the father of empiricism, William James (1842–1910), who placed great stock in testimony or what rejectionists mislabel anecdote. Testimony, over time, becomes a record. We routinely use it in medical science. For me, the most enthralling element of *Them* is Whitley's analysis, based partly in zoology, of the innate difficulty, if not impossibility, of different species sharing understanding. Elementary forms of communication are decipherable but not questions of meaning. This, the author reasons, may pose the greatest barrier to our approaching the visitor question.

Why are they interested in us? Do they need to learn from our empathy? Are they issuing a warning over human survival? Are visitor phenomena bound up with extra-physical or near-death experiences? These are among the questions he considers.

Prior to Darwin, it wasn't that we lacked evidence for biological evolution. We had fossils, bones, and organic data. What we lacked was a unifying theory. Darwin brought that. In a sense, Whitley does something similar in *Them*. The book will be debated, as it should. But of this I have no doubt: It is among the most important interpretations of visitor phenomena since Jacques Vallée's *Passport to Magonia* appeared in 1969. Jacques's book popularized the interdimensional thesis of UFOs. *Them* provides *a psychological* thesis.

By considering what the visitors may want, and the difficulties of our understanding them (and perhaps they us), Whitley, finally, moves the debate where it must go: from asking *whether* to asking *why*.

Mitch Horowitz is a PEN Award-winning historian whose books include *Occult America* and *Uncertain Places*. He published three of Whitley Strieber's nonfiction books—*The Key, Solving the Communion Enigma*, and *The Super Natural* (coauthored with Jeffrey J. Kripal)—at Penguin Random House.

FOREWORD
DEEP SECRETS AND DEEPER STRANGENESS

by Dr. Jacques Vallée

Them is about aliens and it is about us. It builds on everything the deeply inquisitive mind of Whitley Strieber has experienced and investigated throughout his life. His readers have followed him across this dangerous landscape before, and we've heard his critics challenge the veracity of his observations. This new book is evidence of the credibility of his research. But *Them* is much more. *Them* is a two-part dissertation on the deeper nature of the phenomenon. In part 1 it gives a long-denied voice to the private words of his most trusted readers, the close encounter witnesses themselves; and part 2 is the result of his long investigation into the official lies and the political sleight-of-hand that has distorted the record, obscuring the true nature of the data and making an objective, urgent scientific study well-nigh impossible in the United States.

Whitley is uniquely positioned to observe both of these theaters, and he is particularly gifted to extract their deeper essence.

There is an unprecedented drama unfolding in the lives of many families—our own neighbors. For many years I have been privileged to follow the work of Whitley—and especially of his late wife Anne

—as they saved, catalogued, and finally secured (at Rice University) the testimony of thousands of such witnesses. This book can only bring out a small but representative sample of the drama they have experienced but it puts an end to the suggestion that Whitley's imagination alone has been fomenting some sort of myth: *This is real.* It touches many families with no prior experience, or indeed interest in the phenomenon. Science has no explanation for it, in spite of all the "experts" posturing on TV or before Congress. Yet ignoring it doesn't represent an acceptable intellectual approach.

The contrast between the direct, honest reporting from ordinary witnesses and the contrived statements of officials in positions of authority is the most striking feature in part 2. This is not only insulting to common people reporting important experiences, it is plain wrong, a misuse of authority to mislead the public, and in some cases a violation of the proper application of classified information rules.

The fact that modern science, the legal system, and our complicated administration have no convenient channel for a comprehensive study, doesn't mean that witnesses of the reported drama should be ridiculed or ignored. This book cites fact after fact to build the case for in-depth realignment of public policy with public need.

A major shift in American attitudes toward the phenomenon has taken place in the last few years. We can only hope it will lead to a similar shift in open research, but it might just as easily bury the inconvenient data even deeper within the catacombs of the official world, as it has done before. Yet the facts have been restated here, more clearly than ever. Some of us, like Whitley, will continue to face the unknown entities and to trust the only genuine guides we have to make sense of *Them*: the witnesses themselves.

Jacques Vallée
  Paris, 12 January 2023.

INTRODUCTION
AN INCREDIBLE AND CONFLICTED SITUATION

To more people every day, it is coming to seem as if there is somebody here besides us. More than one somebody, quite possibly. Given that there are now official admissions that certain videos produced by the military contain images of objects of unknown origin, it would seem appropriate to take another look at the close encounter narrative. But let's not keep turning over old, tired pages and continue to engage in a debate that cannot now be settled. Let's try something new.

If we do have visitors of some sort in our midst, on one level they seem to be trying to communicate with us. There is also friction and violence, and sometimes they do not treat us as we believe we deserve to be treated. There is exploitation as well, and danger both to civilian and military close encounter witnesses.

This book is an attempt to look at this situation seriously and deeply by exploring the way human lives and society have been and are being impacted. It does not address the argument about whether or not our visitors are aliens. There is no concrete proof of that. Rather, I am going to proceed *as if* the close encounters thousands upon thousands of people experience have some basis in reality—not necessarily that what we perceive is what happens, but that *something* happens that cannot be explained. I don't want to argue about the nature or presence of our visitors, but rather to explore how our relationship with them—whatever they are—actually works, and from that hopefully gain insight into their motives and minds.

Behind all the denial and the refusal to address the obvious human issue of the close encounter testimony, there is fear. In part, that's why I have titled my book after a science fiction movie, the 1954 film *Them*. It is about the appearance of giant ants in the Mojave Desert a few years after the detonation of the atomic bomb at the Trinity site. It perfectly reflects the fear of the alien that, in the real world, dominates our approach to the UAP/close encounter unknown. (I will use UAP rather than UFO throughout this book because Unidentified Aerial Phenomenon is more inclusive of this vast, complex and largely unknown phenomenon than is Unidentified Flying Object.)

It's time to look at that clearly enough to get past it once and for all.

Our visitors are hidden behind a wall of secrecy. In part, this is because of the fear. In part, it is because of mistakes that have been made and the corrosive effect of admitting them. But it was not the fault of our defense and intelligence community that the secrecy became institutionalized. Our visitors manipulated them into it, as we shall see.

Nevertheless, secrecy in general is out of control, and when it comes to the subjects of UAP and close encounters, urgently so. In 1989, Erwin Griswold, Solicitor General of the United States under presidents Lyndon Johnson and Richard Nixon said, "there is massive overclassification and the principal concern of the classifiers is not with national security, but rather with government embarrassment." Perhaps the central reason for the classification of so much material about UAP encounters is exactly that—fear of embarrassment. It isn't trivial, though, not at all. The embarrassment I am referring to involves the inability to handle a very disturbing situation that is of immediate concern to every human being on this planet.

It is always assumed that UAP secrecy originated as official policy.

That is not correct. Our visitors are very secretive, and by their actions they have made sure that our policy would follow theirs. They have placed our official world in a position where it has no choice but to keep their secrets for them. I will show how they have done this, and discuss what we can do to change the situation.

Before I continue, I'd like to briefly explain why I use the term "visitors" and not "aliens." The first reason is that they come and go in our lives. They never linger long. The second is that we have no idea what they are or where they are from, and "visitor" is a neutral term.

The modern encounter experience began with a sighting of unknown craft in the sky near Mt. Rainer by pilot Kenneth Arnold on June 24, 1947. There followed many more sightings, and in the 1960s close encounters began to be reported. From the beginning there was denial on our side and secrecy on theirs.

But why? Why didn't they just land and show themselves in 1947? Better put, as there are many signs that they have been here for a long time, why have they chosen to disguise themselves in such a way that we mythologize them rather than letting us see them for what they are ... whatever that is? If they are aliens from another planet, wouldn't they simply land? If we were able to go to another inhabited planet, wouldn't we?

Good questions to explore.

Human beings have frequent encounters with our visitors, and not just alone and in the night. Group encounters are common and encounters happen day and night. Most people who have them are never exposed to memory recovery techniques such as hypnosis. Prior to the publication of *Communion,* they were also not much exposed to the now very extensive presence of contact stories in the culture, and the letters in this book will reflect that lack of contact with media about the phenomena that the authors experienced.

Even though people are often put under tremendous pressure and suffer extensively from encounters, the public reaction is generally indifference, hostility, or laughter, and the official one denial or silence. Writing in the *Spectator* on December 17, 2022, Sir Martin

Rees, the Astronomer Royal, summed up the attitude that anyone who reports a close encounter experience must face when they attempt to take their information to officials, intellectuals, and scientists: "Some people claim to know the answer already—and many of them like to write me green-ink letters. I respond usually by asking: if aliens had made titanic journeys across interstellar space, would they just meet one or two well-known cranks, maybe make some corn circles, and then leave? And I urge them to write to each other, not to me."

Sir Martin's comment is painful to read, but it is not his fault that he was inspired to make it. He is only responding to the verifiable evidence he has available, which is all any responsible scientist can do. That he has not been exposed to better data is tragic. This data is not classified. It is readily available but has never been gathered. I don't refer just to witness testimony. There are neurological techniques that offer the promise of more objective insight into what events, internal or external, imagined or real, that may lie behind that testimony. There are also physical objects—implants—that have never been studied in any consistent and scientifically sound manner. This should have been done years ago, but a scientific community dependent on granting that might be removed if studies of "fringe" topics are undertaken, has understandably been unwilling to do that. Why a human experience so extensive as close encounter would even be considered "fringe" is beyond me. It seems to me that it is a mistaken cultural stance that has been induced by social engineering of some sort.

Be that as it may, why, after over fifty years and hundreds of thousands of reported encounters, is there no conventional hard evidence? Not so much as one single definite and verified photograph of one of our visitors. No verifiable connection between close encounters and UAP. No image of a person being abducted.

Remarks by Undersecretary for Defense for Intelligence and Security Ronald Moultrie, made in a press conference on December 16, 2022, reflect this apparent lack of evidence. When asked if the Department of Defense possessed anything that suggested the presence of "space aliens" on Earth, he replied, "no, we have nothing." As I will discuss in part 2 of this book, he might not be lying, but also, unless people like distinguished engineer Dr. Robert Sarbacher, who told me personally in 1986 that he was working in an official capacity on otherworldly materials found at the Roswell crash, were pathological liars, we did have such things at one point. The reason for this disconnect is that the history of the UAP/alien phenomenon has been catastrophically damaged by the extreme secrecy associated with it. Senator Daniel Patrick Moynihan, who took an interest in the situation, used to call secrecy "a disease," and, like Solicitor General Ganz, warned that it "keeps mistakes secret." I wouldn't go so far as to call it a disease, but the concealment of mistakes and embarrassments is a basic reality of the system.

In March of 2022, UFO researcher John Greenewald Jr.'s Black Vault website, which is the world's leading repository of officially sourced UAP-related information, obtained a report from the Defense Intelligence Agency under the Freedom of Information Act entitled "Anomalous Acute and Subacute Field Effects on Human Biological Tissues." Dated March 11, 2010, it discusses the negative effects of close encounter, which include many things long reported by witnesses who have routinely been ridiculed in the media and dismissed as publicity seekers. The document shows that, in fact, the intelligence community was well aware that these encounters—including abductions and unexpected pregnancies and numerous injuries of different types that will be discussed in this book—were real and were dangerous. And yet that community did nothing to offset media mistakes. On the contrary, the mantra of denial added to the problem.

If the abductions are real, then human eggs, fetuses, and semen are routinely being taken. I personally had semen forced from my body through the use of an electroejaculation device of a type that was used to assist men with sexual dysfunction prior to the invention of drugs like Viagra. During my struggle, my rectum was torn, leaving me with an injury that to this day occasionally causes discomfort. Instead of any sensitivity being shown to me in the public space because of the rape, I was made into an international joke—I became the "rectal probe" man.

I hope that this book, by bringing more clarity to the fraught and difficult subject of close encounter, will lead to greater understanding of the mystery, and with it more humane treatment of the witnesses.

The letters I have chosen to analyze are from the "Communion Letters Archive" now housed within the Archives of the Impossible at Rice University in Houston. In an act of true prescience, my wife Anne decided to save the thousands of letters that we were receiving after *Communion* was published. She hired a secretary and spent years opening them, reading them, and cataloging them. She kept the ones containing detailed descriptions, which the archive now houses. If the visitors are real, then this is among the most important archives in the world, a crucial key to our chances of understanding them and their reasons for being here. If not, it will have another use as the largest collection of modern folklore ever assembled.

When the letters are analyzed, it will be seen that, in some cases, it cannot be that the encounters they describe are hallucinatory or imaginary. A number of them involve multiple witnesses and daytime encounters, and none of the authors had hypnosis or other attempts to stimulate memory. Nor are their stories repeats of the experiences that I published in *Communion*. Most of the narratives aren't just different from mine, they are radically so—which means, of course, that the authors were telling their own stories, not reworking mine.

Somebody created the complex events described by these witnesses. Was it some aspect of the human mind? Possibly, but while there is a logic to them, it is not our logic. As we move through them, it will become evident that the mind of our visitors is not informed by human logic, or even a human experience of reality.

Now that we know that governments have been lying about the unexplained nature and unknown origins of unidentified flying objects for generations, I am not going to be trusting the explanations that they have provided in the past. That game is over. Instead, I am going to look beneath the false dismissals to the original stories that they were intended to hide.

Our visitors' single most robust and consistent policy is secrecy. Nevertheless, we can discover much about our relationship with them by using existing tools of research into and analysis of the data that is already in the public space, as well as access close encounter witnesses directly for study. But if scientists and academicians are going to be able to obtain grants, the official opposition to advancing this research has to end. Right now, there isn't a single major funding source that would provide money for UAP research, let alone research into the close encounter phenomenon.

When, in 2017, a story appeared in the *New York Times* revealing that U.S. Navy pilots had made video of unexplained objects while on patrol, the initial response of some scientific commentators was to make the same claim that they had been making for years: they must have been reflections on cockpit windows.

It fit the facts so poorly that it was simply ignored—finally. For years, though, accurate and credible reports were dismissed with this and other shibboleths. There may have been hidden motives. For example, *Aviation Week & Space Technology* editor Philip Klass, whose publication's success depended on a good relationship with the U.S. Air Force, was a leading denier.

The intellectual community should long ago have realized that the silence of and denials by the military did not mean that the situation was as they claimed. Given the wealth of testimony, science and the academy should have more seriously entertained the idea of exploring the evidence that is already abundantly available outside of the official world.

Even though many different types of evidence are available right now, only a few people outside the tiny but dedicated ghetto of UAP investigators have tried to take advantage of it. Aside from some groundbreaking studies involving the effects of contact on the brain, which will be discussed in a later chapter, there is nothing, and certainly nothing anywhere in the peer-reviewed literature. As matters currently stand, even if such a study were done, the prejudice is so fundamental that a peer committee who could view it objectively might not be obtainable.

In part, this is due to our visitors' clever use of social control, but in part it is emotional, and that's the part we can change. People naturally feel threatened by the idea of an unknown intelligence in our midst that's possessed of mysterious powers. This has caused our intellectual leadership to react with a silence that is frighteningly similar to that of the Inca's advisors when they faced Francisco Pizarro and his handful of Spanish soldiers. That was a fatal silence, and this could be, too, if we do not look past our emotions to the reality of the enigma.

Taking the close encounter narrative seriously does not mean embracing the idea that aliens are here or, as a matter of fact, that anything outside of the human mind is at play. We can now be reasonably sure that there are objects in our skies that we don't understand, but whether or not they are connected to the close encounter reports is unproven. Better to explore more deeply before drawing conclusions, especially falling into the trap of debating a proposition before all the facts are known. Taking this approach will enable us to find out if contact is more dreamlike or hallucinatory, or if there seems to be coherent policy behind it, by which I mean a clear indication that something is wanted of us that would suggest that the beings that I and others encounter are real and not figments of our imagination. If we do this logically, we will either expose details of relationship that do suggest that they are a real presence of some kind, or we will not.

The first place to go to pursue such an endeavor is not secret documents or the whispers of "insiders." It is witness narrative, both civilian and military. That said, it's also time to get past the question of whether or not people are lying or are the victims of false memories generated by hypnosis which has, in fact, been performed on only a relative handful of close encounter witnesses compared to the vast number of people who have found themselves—and, as often as not, their families and friends along with them—face-to-face with the visitors.

On September 9, 2022, the U.S. Navy replied to a Freedom of Information Act Request from John Greenewald Jr. that it does indeed have more UAP videos, but it said that it would not release them. The Navy said, "The release of this information will harm national security as it may provide adversaries valuable information regarding Department of Defense/Navy operations, vulnerabilities, and/or capabilities." Gregory Cason, the deputy director of the Navy's FOIA office, added, "No portions of the videos can be segregated for release." In a later chapter, we will discuss exactly what this sort of statement means. As for the U.S. Air Force, it has remained silent on the matter and, as will become evident, has reason to do so.

In November of 2021, the Department of Defense announced the creation of the Airborne Object Identification and Management Synchronization Group (AOIMSG). In July of 2022, it became AARO, the All-domain Anomaly Resolution Office and, after the National Defense Authorization Act and the Intelligence Authorization Act for Fiscal Year 2023 passed in December of '22, it became the Unidentified Aerospace-Undersea Phenomena Joint Program Office, with responsibility for collecting data from six intelligence organizations, among them the Defense Intelligence Agency and the National Geospatial-Intelligence Agency, the Air Force, the Space Force, and the Navy. I believe that it has been formed because of the significant increase in UAP activity that has been recorded worldwide over the past few years. There is no mandate for it to make public reports. Also, while there is a secure process for anyone who has signed secrecy agreements related to UFOs/UAPs to AARO and Congress regardless of the level of classification, there is no avenue for them to engage in public disclosure.

NASA is now also involved. The press information about its investigation, which began in October of 2022, states that its program is intended to "gather data on events in the sky that cannot be identified as aircraft or known natural phenomena." According to a CNN report, NASA also said that "there was no evidence that UAPs are extraterrestrial in origin." Given that they are starting with this assumption already in place, it may be that their conclusions will end up sounding like those in the Air Force's 1968 *Condon Report*, which stated that "UFO phenomena do not offer a fruitful field in which to look for major scientific discoveries." Such a statement was defensible then—just—but it is not defensible now.

On June 25, 2021, the Department of Defense released a "Preliminary Assessment" concerning UAP. It said little, but it did confirm that some of the imagery and other data collected remained unexplained.

In October of 2021, James T. Lacatski, a participant in the Advanced Aerospace Weapon System Application Program (AAWSAP), published a book, *Skinwalkers at the Pentagon: An Insider's Account of the Secret Government UFO Program,* co-authored with journalist and broadcaster George Knapp and Colm Kelleher of Bigelow Aerospace Advanced Space Studies. *Skinwalkers at the Pentagon* lifted the lid on an extensive group of programs being run within the Defense Intelligence Agency that explored not only many aspects of technological questions like UAP propulsion systems but also the abduction phenomenon and other contact-related phenomena. The book was mocked in a few venues for including discussion of what are known as "paranormal" events, on the obviously flawed assumption that something that is witnessed as a ghost or a werewolf or whatever must not exist at all because such things "can't be real." To say that a perception didn't happen because the description of it seems impossible is absurd. Unless someone telling a strange story is intentionally lying, then something has happened. Whether or not their description is accurate is another question.

On November 10, 2021, Avril Haines, Director of National Intelligence, made the following comment at the Our Future in Space event at Washington National Cathedral: "Always there's also the question of 'is there something else that we simply do not understand, which might come extraterrestrially?'"

There are different factions in the intelligence community and in Congress, some advocating a more open approach to the subject, others wishing to close it down. As of this writing, the faction wanting to keep the secrets is regaining control, if it ever lost it.

In part 2 of this book, we will discuss the reasons that the official world has ended up boxed into keeping the visitors' secrets.

If contact is underway, the stakes are the highest in human history. If we get it right, there exists the very real potential for us to become what amounts to a new species—in effect, a new mankind. Profound, extremely strange and irreversibly negative changes in the human condition are also possible.

And yet, as I sit here writing this, I reflect on the fact that I cannot point to a single definite piece of hard evidence of the physical existence of a visitor such as the one depicted on the cover of my book *Communion*. Why not? Why the bizarre combination of a vast store of contact testimony and not a single scrap of evidence?

Something is wrong.

PART I

WHAT HAPPENS IN THE SHADOWS

"Is that somebody there?"
Whitley Strieber in *Communion*

CHAPTER 1
ENCOUNTER: THE CRITICS SPEAK OUT

T here was widespread criticism of *Communion* at every level of society, but there was only one group of critics that really concerned me. This was the visitors themselves. Ever since 1988, I've known a bit about what they think, but it was not until I sat down in the letters archive at Rice that I discovered that there was more.

The archive is stored in file boxes organized by date. I had a box brought out for me and began looking through it. Almost the first letter I pulled out was one from a man who had seen some of the visitors looking through a copy of the book in a bookstore in Bayside, New York.

Shortly after it was published, the military history editor at William Morrow and Company, Bruce Lee, had stepped into a bookstore in Manhattan to see if the book was selling. He saw two people in overcoats and hats looking through a copy. Edging closer, he watched their reactions to what they were reading.

He was shocked to discover that not only were they paging through it with extraordinary speed, they were laughing and talking about how I'd gotten one thing and another wrong. Then they stopped. They looked up at Mr. Lee. He found himself confronting huge black eyes. Immediately, he got his wife and told her that they had to leave the store. As they went out, the two strange entities followed them. He watched them go off down the street ... and not be glanced at twice by a single passerby. One might think, "Oh, of course not, it's New York." But there is another reason, which is known as misdirection. Stage magicians have used it for years. To see how effective a tool it is, one has only to watch "The Monkey Business Illusion" on YouTube. So the two visitors who walked off down the street without being noticed were simply taking advantage of the human mind's tendency to focus its attention on what it expects to see.

At first, when I heard Mr. Lee's account of what had happened to him, I was extremely upset. I felt that all my effort had been wasted. The visitors thought my book was ridiculous. Anne, however, had a different idea. "They reacted, and in a way that we can't deny actually happened. They've honored your effort but also challenged you to work harder and understand more."

Perhaps.

In early April of 1990, we received a second letter from a witness who had already told us part of his encounter experience, but who, after reading the Bruce Lee story, had more to add. His letter is marked by Anne with the number 1 and an exclamation point, meaning that she thought it exceptionally important. Of the letters she had saved, it is number 3,843. I had not seen it prior to visiting the archive.

It is important because it is a description of an encounter that is strikingly similar to what happened to Mr. Lee. As Mr. Lee's was detailed in *Transformation,* the follow-on to *Communion* in 1988, I cannot say that the letter was written before Lee's account was public knowledge. Anne must not have thought so, however, as she had previously spoken with the author, another of whose letters she had run in the newsletter that we were publishing in those days.

THE LETTER: VISITORS IN A BOOKSTORE

On March 2, 1987, I was briskly walking on the east side of Bell Boulevard in Bayside, heading south at 39th Avenue towards Waldenbooks bookstore to see if they got *Communion* in yet. In front of me, I approach four persons who are staggering, very boisterous, laughing loudly, and acting rowdy. They are dressed funny for such a warm day. They are wearing woolen skull caps, huge scarfs around their necks and faces, and have on these enormous sunglasses. The little that I can see of their faces appear to be painted white. I determine that they are drunk. It makes me feel ill at ease and uncomfortable, and I stop, waiting for them to pass Waldenbooks. They stop in front of the bookstore, blocking the door and then hang out there, joking and laughing loudly. I now cross the street as I do not want to be near them. I then decide to walk around the block. On my return, they are no longer there.

I enter the bookstore and go to the desk. The clerk has her back to me and is as far as she can be from her desk. I inquire about *Communion*. She has a look of fear in her eyes, and I wonder what's bothering her. She informs me that the book is "over there, where those four are standing."

I walk over. They are in pairs, each sharing a book. They are briskly going to different parts of it, back and forth, quietly laughing and commenting to one another, "This isn't so," over and over. One group comments to the other, "Check out this page." and they laugh. I reach in front of them to get a book, and their heads turn toward me, and I notice the skin on their heads is very white, and in the space between their faces and sunglasses, I see their huge eyes.

I walk in fear twenty feet to the other side of the room. They become boisterous. I stand there watching them.

About one minute later a young couple enter the store. The man, in a suit and tie asks about *Communion*. He walks over to the visitors and politely asks them what they think of the book. They turn their heads toward him. He returns to the counter, taps his companion on the shoulder, and says in a low, fearful voice, "Let's get out of here, fast." They leave.

The visitors then continue to scan the book for about another five minutes, giggling and laughing. They then turn to leave and walk by me in pairs two abreast. My head is bowed. I am looking straight down because I don't want them to know that I noticed them. I am scared.

As they pass me, and I am just becoming relieved, the one on the right rear breaks rank, turns, and come directly to me. The other three, walking slowly toward the door, do not notice that he has done so. He passes me, pausing briefly and laughing in a low voice. It's like a taunting laugh. As he turns and repasses me, he brushes his arm against me. I think he is trying to knock me down, but it is gentle. I realize now that the visitors can set us up and play with us. After being touched in this manner, I get a message that they mean no harm.

ANALYSIS

As I don't recall seeing this letter, it may be that Anne remembered how much Bruce Lee's story had upset me and chose not to show it to me. The fact that it came to hand, seemingly at random, during a brief visit to an archive containing so many thousands of letters is typical of the whole experience. I can't explain it and I don't intend to speculate. When you live a life involved with the visitors, it's how things work. In any case, the letters are currently cataloged only by date, so my finding it, as far as our understanding of reality is concerned, can only be attributed to chance.

It's a perfect place to begin our exploration of what the visitors have revealed of themselves in their encounters with us. First, they're not angels or mythological beings charged with mysterious grandeur. Neither are they demons, leaking the very stench of evil out of their pores. While grand and terrible entities are certainly part of our experience of the numinous and the unknown, it's not clear to me that anything like that is involved here.

In this particular case, what I see is somebody putting on a display that is almost certainly intended to be communicated to me. First, a friend has the experience. Then we get a letter from another man who also had it and who, as will be seen shortly, had earlier participated in an extraordinary sighting that another of our friends had. As we will see again and again, there is a peculiar weave in what our visitors do, one that challenges us to make the crucial connections.

In the first of these two cases, there is a slightly sinister tone—when the two visitors look at Bruce Lee, he is frightened enough to leave. Similarly, when the second witness does the same, they challenge him then give him a subtle reassurance that they mean no harm. But is that true?

In both cases, the realization that they weren't human was a large part of the reason for the fear response. But the larger part of it was those eyes.

The huge eyes of our visitors are among the most powerful motifs in modern culture, and our response to gigantic eyes is deeply engrained in us. It is reflected in the "eye god" statuary of the distant past, and even in modern times in the hypnotic eyes of some politicians and celebrities. The gigantic eyes of the visitor on the cover of *Communion* triggered a flood of memories in people around the world. They also triggered awe and fear. A question must be asked: When we look at these eyes, are we looking at the physical eyes of aliens, who have naturally evolved in that way, or at something that has been designed to overawe us, even something that is in some way part of us? While it is easy to assume that such strange looking creatures must be from somewhere else in the universe, there is not enough evidence to close the question. In my experience, coming face-to-face with one of the visitors is almost like encountering a living mask. But what does it conceal? If they are telepathically connected, it could be an entire race. That would certainly explain the sense of awe that is involved.

Gods with huge eyes are commonplace in early human cultures, and Julian Jaynes, in *The Origin of Consciousness in the Breakdown of the Bicameral Mind*, theorizes that "eye-idols" once triggered auditory hallucinations and were used as memory aids by people who had not yet evolved modern consciousness, which generates its own internal monologue. Could it be, therefore, that the gigantic eyes of the visitors return us to some earlier state of mind, generating in the process the same overwhelming feeling of power that might have awed ancient peoples when they stood before the glaring effigies of the past?

This is typical of the sort of contradiction that is inherent to contact. If they are from within us or from our world in some way that, perhaps because of how we perceive and think, we cannot understand clearly, then what we are looking at here is a sort of mirror, but one that is balanced on a strange shadow-line between mind and matter.

On the other hand, if they are, in the final analysis, entities from another world, our fixation on their eyes could have to do with the age-old mammalian challenge of the eyes, which exists in many forms in many different species and is highly developed in the primates. Never look a gorilla in the eye, as an example, and if you look deeply into the eyes of another person, you will soon feel some very complicated emotions. Looking into the huge and therefore intimidating eyes of unknown beings would be *very* challenging. (I can assure you that this is true. It feels as if they are looking into you more deeply than you can look into yourself. It is humbling and terrifying.)

But what of the way they acted both with Bruce Lee and this correspondent? It felt sinister to both men, not because they were threatened, but simply because of those eyes. Their actions toward our correspondent seemed to be almost a parody of a tough gang of kids who are letting a possible victim off easily, then relieving his fear that they might do him harm.

Both Bruce and our correspondent reported that the visitors were paging through the book very rapidly. The latter even says that they mentioned specific pages, but maddeningly for me, he didn't specify them.

I was disappointed when Bruce told me that they'd been laughing at my book, which is probably why Anne never showed me this letter. She thought that they were honoring me by acknowledging my effort at all. As she pointed out, they've never done that for another book, movie, or anything we have said or done about them. All well and good, but I'd still love to know what they thought was wrong and what made them laugh.

But there is more to explore here than the reaction to the book. What we have are two instances, vanishingly rare, of visitors moving openly through the human world. When Bruce Lee saw them, they were dressed in overcoats and hats and wearing glasses. They chatted and laughed as they walked out behind him. They were completely at ease. They knew how to stroll casually off down a crowded street. They were confident that nobody would notice what they were.

The ones in Waldenbooks had a different approach. They seemed not to care who knew what, but they were careful to use similar disguises so that their different appearance wouldn't be immediately obvious. Their disguises were so minimal and so obvious (it was not cold enough for overcoats and scarfs) that it seems to me that they wanted to be noticed. In other words, they wanted the letter to be written just as the first two had wanted Bruce Lee to take his story back to William Morrow & Co., and thus to me.

Our correspondent's first sight of the visitors on the sidewalk is of "four persons who are staggering, laughing loudly, and acting rowdy." He then notices their inappropriate dress and that their skin seemed "painted white." A year later, I was to notice that same odd whiteness in one I saw in a public place and thought to myself that it looked as if they were wearing mortician's wax. (This event will be discussed in part 2.)

When they stopped in front of the bookstore he was going to enter, he crossed the street. When he returned, they were nowhere to be seen. When he went into the bookstore, the clerk had her back turned and was standing as far away from her post at the counter as she could. When he walked over to get *Communion,* he saw that the four who were in front of the bookstore were now standing in groups of two paging through the book. As was true of the couple in Manhattan, they're turning pages and laughing. When he saw their eyes over the sunglasses, he was frightened.

They then "become boisterous." Were they trying to put him at his ease or intimidate him, or were *they* nervous? If they were human, we would probably see them as teenagers, self-conscious and uneasy, and trying to hide it.

He watched them for a few minutes as they continued to scan the book. They then put the copies they're reading back and walked out, passing him. But one of them "breaks rank" and went close to him, "laughing in a low voice." Once again, a sense of self-consciousness is projected. When he brushed his arm against our correspondent, he initially felt that he's going to be "knocked down," but the touch was actually gentle.

Afterward, our correspondent felt played with but was left with the impression that they "mean no harm." It's exactly the sense one would get seeing a menacing-looking man on the street at night, who then passes by with a pleasant "good evening."

Neither of these stories describe people with whom it would be impossible to live. On the contrary, if this is how they're going to appear when and if they're walking among us, they will soon be integrated into human societies worldwide.

But there's more to it than that. As Bruce Lee noted when he saw the two visitors walk off down the street without being noticed, the visitors are good at misdirection, and this next story illustrates an absolute mastery of the art.

You are on a jam-packed highway, headed home during the evening commute. Something in the sky attracts your attention. You look up.

A giant plane is about to crash right into your car.

CHAPTER 2
ENCOUNTER: CALL OF THE MORLOCKS

This second story involves two witnesses who never met one another but who jointly had one of the strangest experiences I have ever come across. I was introduced to one of them when I was doing research on *Communion*. The other is the same correspondent whose story figures above. (As will be seen, many of these stories—in fact, most of them—involve more than one witness.)

The fact that this event involved huge objects and happened on a crowded highway, and yet went unnoticed by all but a few of the thousands of passersby, is truly remarkable. The event should have been a sensation, reported on every newscast in the country. That it wasn't shows just how masterful our visitors' control of the situation is. The array of tools they have to control our perception and memory suggests that they have engaged in contact with less advanced species before.

When I first heard the story from a friend when I was doing research for *Communion*, I thought of the H. G. Wells novel *The Time Machine*, with its cannibalistic Morlocks coming up from underground to kidnap and eat the innocent, surface-dwelling Eloi. (In those days, I was still profoundly traumatized by the *Communion* experience.) In Wells's powerful imagination, humanity in the far future has evolved into two distinct forms that are locked in a grotesque symbiosis. The Morlocks provide the Eloi with their every need, rising to the surface from time to time to harvest them for food. The Eloi live in a state of hypnosis, forever bound to the Morlocks, never understanding the grim truth of their beautiful slavery.

But why do I bring this story up? Another way to put the question is, why didn't the very many people present notice this fantastic event?

First, let's look at the description of the event as experienced by my friend. This is from *Communion*:

"In August 1986 a man had a remarkable experience while driving toward Great Neck, Long Island, on the Grand Central Parkway. It was 9:30 p.m., and the sky was overcast, with a three-thousand-foot ceiling. The man suddenly saw an enormous airplane coming toward him so low that it looked like it was about to land on the parkway. It had two bright lights in the nose, lights that seemed to shine beams directly into his eyes. There was a red light at the tip of one wing and a green one at the tip of the other. As he passed under the plane he looked up and saw that there were rivets in the undersurface, which was streaked as if it had scraped along the ground. He saw four engine pods with whirling propellers. The nose of the plane was flat and there was no horizontal stabilizer. The man slowed down and leaned his head out the window, looking up at the bizarre craft. It seemed almost to be standing still and the propellers made no noise at all. Soon he was past it and taking the Great Neck exit, which makes a horseshoe around a small hill. Above this hill he saw what appeared to be an advertising sign made of many small lightbulbs. It had an angle in it, suggesting that it was attached to two sides of a building. It was flashing, but the symbols were incomprehensible. As he rounded the horseshoe and saw the sign from another angle, he realized that there was no building there. Then he concluded that it must be a plane. But it suddenly shot off to the southwest, rising into the overcast with blinding speed.

"He is a leading perceptual psychologist with encyclopedic knowledge of just exactly how the brain perceives things, and what misperceptions mean. What's more, he has a near-photographic memory and eyes so superb that he can see the moons of Jupiter unaided. He is also highly intelligent and exceptionally emotionally stable, having had many hundreds of hours of psychoanalysis as part of his clinical training.

"Anybody can have a hallucination or a misperception. But this highly qualified man feels certain that what he saw was actually there. Interestingly, other drivers did not react to it at all. I wonder if that might not be because they *believed* an illusion that this man's mind was too highly trained to mistake. Most people saw a plane and an advertising sign. But this acute, trained mind saw beyond the camouflage to what was really there—a device of unknown origin and purpose.

"How interesting that such an outrageous perceptual joke would be played on a skilled perceptual scientist—who himself has superb perceptual equipment. Or perhaps the visitors were indifferent, and chance played the joke. Then again, maybe it wasn't a joke at all. What about the light shining in his eyes—did they use it to learn something from him, or induce him to act in some drama of importance to their enigmatic designs?" (I might add, here, that the other witness also experienced a light being shone on him.)

The other witness was not a scientist, or at least, he doesn't describe himself as such in his letter. As he is now deceased (both men are), I cannot say what he did in his life, but his letter does contain a very clear description of what happened on that evening.

THE LETTER: ON A NOT-SO-LONELY ROAD

May 6, 1988

I have procrastinated until now, nonetheless, it is torture for me to write this, and I don't know why.

Please refer to page #292 of your book, *Communion*. I read it in July 1987.

The sequence of my observation of events and thoughts on the Grand Central Parkway:

I am going eastbound, the next exit being New Hyde Park Road. I see a small bright light, stationary in the distant sky. This light is very high in the distant sky and now it's approaching straight ahead. I've never seen a plane here before. I'm thinking, could it be a UFO?

Ten seconds later there is a loud, deafening roar and what appears to be an airplane with very bright lights. It is dipping lower and lower very swiftly.

My God, it's coming in so low and fast, it's going to crash into me! I should be dead in one second, At least I won't suffer.

There is a loud roar.

There are two lights shining straight ahead, and now one bright beam has been turned on me. I am enveloped in a blinding light. I am staring at it in awe and disbelief. I'm alive! The craft is standing still in front of me. This is when I realize this is not a plane and could be a UFO. After eight seconds I can't take the bright light anymore and I look down for a fraction of a second. I look up and lean forward in my seat. The light beam goes off and there is a clicking, sliding sound, like a slide being put into a projector. Through the window I see a figure standing there. I strongly feel that this is being done manually by that person. The craft moves up a little bit.

Now there is a beam of light coming from the bottom of the craft straight down on me. I can see the front of the craft and also part of the bottom.

There is a loud roar.

The craft starts to pass very slowly, about ten feet over me. The color of it is grayish brown. There are small, dim lights.

I see grooves and streaks and thin white scratch lines criss-crossing through.

Now there is a very low whirling, churning sound that sort of sounds like that of the Staten Island Ferry when it is docking, when the motors are cut.

It is huge, like an aircraft carrier.

I see the two recessed propellors in front and two more in the rear.

I have never seen anything like this in my life.

There is a loud hum, then a whoosh and a swishing sound.

It is gone, I don't see it in my rearview mirror. I turn around in my seat, looking through my rear window and out my driver's window. It is gone.

I get off the next exit to find a cop; briefly upon turning off the exit I see a small craft on my left on top of the grass. I am being tailgated and honked at; I can't stop. I have to go on.

Sequence of observations and thoughts and events on the Grand Central Parkway overpass at Searington Road:

I see what appears to be an advertising billboard on my right.

It appears to be a circus-type billboard that has multicolored, rotating and blinking orange and purple lights with white balloons. There is a short person standing nearby in a clown suit, and three other short persons that are whitish looking with masks. They are standing sideways and their eyes are almost twice human size. The billboard has a white trail of gasses or steam or vapor issuing forth.

The car in front of me, which I'm not sure of, but I think is a light faded blue Chevy Vega, drives up over the curb and stops, which is what I wanted to do. I stay on the road and stop alongside. I want to ask these circus people if they had seen the UFO fly over. I feel the man in the car ahead of me thinks likewise. After he stops, he turns his lights out and car off. He is about 5'8" tall and wearing a blue polo shirt and gray slacks. He gets out of his car, pauses, and walks briskly toward the billboard. The clown goes back to the billboard and then the three others approach him (the man) anxiously as if something is wrong and there seems to be a sense of urgency to this. The man is talking and gesturing skyward with his arms. This had to be about the UFO, because if he wasn't there first, that's what I would have been doing myself. Then suddenly numerous (ten to fifteen) excited midgets, apparently in glad anticipation to see this man, are climbing down from the rear and right side of this billboard and jumping off. Then they rush up to the man, bouncing as they walk, like our astronauts on the moon, and then very swiftly and efficiently encircle him. I suddenly realize that none of them are humans except the man who got out of his car. Their skin is very tight and very white and very wrinkled. It has the appearance of either a thin plastic covering or a coat of white paint. There is no facial or head hair on them.

I reach over to roll my right window down, planning to talk to them.

In unison, the nonhumans then stop and look straight at me with a mean, angry look. Now their eyes appear to be five times human size. Their eyes are glossy shiny light brown. In a thought transference I get the message in English with a male voice, "Don't bother us, we're busy." I hesitate and then there was another thought transference, as they glare at me, "Go away or we'll hurt you."

I am now scared. I drive slowly away while observing the craft. At first I figure this must be an observation or monitoring post. It looks like a building or machinery. After I pass it, it looks like an erector set in the rear.

Afterthoughts:

I tell my daughter and son-in-law about it the next morning. They do not believe me.

I see no report of this in the press or on the radio. Because of the above I decide not to report this and to blank it out of my mind, figuring that no one will believe me.

I did just that, but when I read page 292 of your book I was stunned. This brought back my memory of it all over a period of days.

When everything I described occurred, I was well rested after having four days off from work. On a scale of 1 to 10, I was a 10 physically and emotionally. I was not or had not been drinking or on drugs or tired.

Please refer to my enclosed photographs. (Ed. note: there are no photographs included with the surviving letter. Had they shown images of the entities or devices described, they would have been saved.)

I feel that most people thought they only saw a plane and an advertising sign because they weren't curious enough to bother to think and look for anything further. Perhaps they didn't bother because it was too traumatic already. I have faced many dangerous situations. A friend of mine saw a UFO in the 1960s and another friend in the 1970s, but I doubted UFOs unless and until I saw one for myself. All these years I have been scanning the skies for one, but when it really happened I wasn't ready to accept it.

ANALYSIS

Like my friend, our correspondent was also going eastbound on the Grand Central Parkway when he saw a "small, bright light, stationary in the distant sky." Then, seconds later, "there is a deafening roar and it appears to be an airplane with very bright lights." It's coming lower "so fast it looks like it's going to crash into me. I should be dead in one second." But that doesn't happen. Instead, "now one bright beam has been turned on me. I am enveloped in a blinding light. ... The craft is standing still in front of me." The light is so bright that he looks away. When he looks up again, "the light beam goes off and there is a clicking sound. ... Through the window I see a figure standing there." The gigantic craft is directly overhead and a "huge beam of light" is "coming down from the bottom of the craft straight down onto me." As both men experienced this light and both also saw and remembered the bizarre scene, it can be inferred that the light may have been enabling them to see what others could not.

The object is very low, appearing to the witness to be about ten feet above his car, still lit, but with "small, dim lights." Just as the other witness reported that the underside was "streaked, as if it had run across the ground," this witness sees "grooves and streaks and thin white scratch lines" on the hull passing just overhead.

Like the first witness, he finds that it is very suddenly gone. He wants to stop, but he can't due to the traffic and so moves on. Next, he sees what "appears to be an advertising billboard" on his right as he drives along the Grand Central Parkway overpass near Searington Road. "There is a short person standing nearby in a clown suit, and three other short persons that are whitish looking with masks." He notes that their eyes are "almost twice human size." He notices a car in front of him which he recalls as a "faded blue Chevy Vega." I once rode in the other witness's car, which was an old compact, but I do not recall the exact make. The Vega then drives up onto the roadside and stops.

After *Communion* was published and the first witness had read it, he told me that reading the account as I had written it caused him to remember more. (At the time, we had not received the account of the second witness.) He had pulled off the road and gotten out of his car. He did this because he saw a group of people standing in a circle below the flashing advertising sign, and he wanted to ask them if they knew what was going on. As he was walking up to them, what he described as a dwarf came up to him and said in a harsh voice, "Get out of here." This was all he needed to convince him to get back in his car and drive away. He was quite frightened.

The second witness reports that the man "gets out of his car, pauses, and walks briskly toward the billboard," and then the three other short figures approach him "anxiously as if something is wrong and there seems to be a sense of urgency to this." The stories now diverge in important ways. The first witness remembered being ordered off, but this is how the second describes the situation: "The man is talking and gesturing skyward with his arms. ... Then suddenly numerous (ten to fifteen) excited midgets, apparently in glad anticipation to see this man, are climbing down from the rear and right side of this billboard and jumping off. Then they rush up to the man, bouncing as they walk ... and then very swiftly and efficiently encircle him."

As we shall see, these people are not the only ones who will be described as "bouncing" as they move. In the story called "Visitors in the Trees," what appears to be a similar sort of individual is described as having a bouncing walk. This would suggest that these were actual, physical individuals from some place that has stronger gravity than Earth—that is, a planet that is physically larger. This small fact is one indication that, for all its strangeness, in the end this story may be about physical people from another planet in the physical world —in other words, alien contact in the classic meaning of the phrase. I am not advocating this as fact, only saying that subtle similarities like this between accounts are among a number of clues that do suggest it. And yet, at the same time, many other possibilities remain in play.

This bouncing walk brings up a question. Could a planet enough larger than Earth to cause its inhabitants to walk in our gravity like we do on the moon also sustain life? A paper entitled "Potential long-term habitable conditions on planets with primordial H-He atmospheres" that was published in *Nature Astronomy* in June of 2022 showed that liquid water could exist on very large planets with hydrogen-helium atmospheres similar to that of Earth in her earliest phase of evolution, as long as they were far enough from the stars they orbited. Over time, they might possibly, as Earth did, evolve an atmosphere able to sustain life.

Are we, then, looking at visitors from a larger planet with stronger gravity?

My psychologist friend remembered that the little men who came up to him took a hostile attitude toward him. They did not approach him in the "glad anticipation" that the second witness perceived. But the second witness also noticed how they "swiftly and efficiently encircled him," exactly as if they were trying to limit his movements.

As the second witness watches, it becomes clear to him that "none of them are humans except the man who got out of his car." He describes their skin as being "very tight and very white and very wrinkled. It has the appearance of either a thin plastic covering or a coat of white paint."

He then reaches over to roll down his right window. His motive is to talk to them. "In unison the nonhumans ... look straight at me with a mean, angry look. Now their eyes appear to be five times human

size. Their eyes are glossy shiny light brown. In a thought transference I get the message in English with a male voice, 'Don't bother us,
we're busy.'" When he hesitates, they glare at him and he hears a
voice say in his mind, "Go away or we'll hurt you." (As will be seen in
part 2, when we discuss the military experience of the phenomenon,
they can certainly do that.)

This is an instance of the telepathy that isn't supposed to exist.
But it might not be entirely true that there is no known medium that
can carry voices into the brain. The U.S. Army had something called
Project MEDUSA, which could project sound into the brain using
microwaves. I cannot offer documentation, but I don't see any reason
why such a technology couldn't be evolved to the point that it could
project words, and having heard such words spoken by the visitors at
one point (discussed in *Transformation*), I wouldn't be in the least
surprised to find that they possessed the technology. Project
MEDUSA was revealed in December of 2006 in response to a
Freedom of Information Act request by Donald Friedman. The document released doesn't state that voice communication to the brain
using microwaves has been achieved by us, but it does say that
microwave hearing is a phenomenon described by human observers
as the sensations of "

buzzing, ticking, hissing, or knocking sounds that originate
within or immediately behind the head. There is no sound propa-
gating through the air like normal sound." It goes on to describe the
frequencies involved.

In any case, both witnesses were warned away, and both left.
Whether or not the man the second witness saw was the first one is
impossible to determine. But it is possible to conclude that some sort
of operation involving a group of visitors and a group of people was
being carried out alongside that crowded highway, and most
passersby were not noticing.

In the close encounter experience, there are many reports of
people being "called" to encounters with the visitors. One such
example that has been publicized is the story of Canadian close
encounter witness Corina Saebels. She was with a friend when they

both felt called to take a drive at night. During this drive, they found themselves stopping by the roadside where they encountered small creatures with "green, glowing eyes." They then experienced an abduction. They were left with burns and other injuries that required medical attention. Corina has described this in her book *The Collectors* and in an interview on my podcast *Dreamland* in February of 2008. There are many other such stories in the literature.

It's fair to ask, what may be going on here? Just how deeply are we involved with our visitors? If they are indeed from another planet or another realm of reality, are they somehow related to us—Morlocks to our Eloi?

There is no way to tell the objective of the astonishing meeting alongside the Grand Central Parkway, held in such odd conditions, at once clandestine and yet so blatantly public. It is fantastic that more people didn't notice but also fair to ask, why not? Something like the monkey business illusion could have been involved, and I think that such misdirection might be what the visitors often use to seemingly disappear, become invisible and otherwise confuse witnesses. Many magicians can do stunning things with misdirection. As the visitors appear able to read minds, they might have a powerful ability to misdirect. (This does not speak to what they are. It is very easy to assume that, because of the way their appearance is described and how correspondents react to them, that we are talking about extraterrestrials. Let's never forget, across this whole text, that there is nothing as yet proven regarding their origin.)

What can be going on, then, that openly public events can take place— who knows how often—that are ignored by us just as the hypnotized Eloi ignored the Morlocks when they emerged from their subterranean lair?

Was the huge sign, like the great sirens in *The Time Machine*, there to call certain people to certain meetings? If so, were they conscious of this, or did they come more like the Eloi, drifting as if in a dream?

And why? Why all this subterfuge and misdirection? If we were a spacefaring race who found an intelligent but immature species trapped on a dying planet, wouldn't we simply land and set about helping them?

If we could, we probably would. But if we acted too hastily, we might cause so much confusion that our chance of being of help would be lost forever, and we would have to stand by, our only card played badly, and watch them die.

We are experiencing this confusion right now here on Earth. In fact, we are so confused that it is difficult to determine who is here, let alone what their motives may be. My life is dedicated to getting past this confusion, which, for most of us, leads to disbelief and dismissal. In the minds of those sworn to protect us from threats, though, it is like a wall.

Given the abductions, there is certainly some sort of threat involved. But our correspondent was not devoured, at least not physically. Are there other things about us, though, perhaps worth more than calories, that somebody else might want to harvest? The reports of those abducted would suggest that sexual material is one. There are more, too, as we shall see.

If they are predators, have they evolved an adaptation that puts us into a state of hypnosis or created technology for this purpose? If so, is that hypnosis, then, life itself?

It's not my desire to be histrionic here, or to carelessly evoke the brooding sensibility of horror stories, but I do think we need to face the possibility that our visitors' motives might be far more complicated than we have thus far even speculated. We know that they want us to survive. Otherwise, why the vast warning cry about the state of the planet that has been impressed into the minds of virtually the entire close encounter witness community or the documented visits to nuclear weapons facilities, some in the U.S. and some in Russia, which point to a concern about nuclear war? Add to this the possibility that they are engaged in human seed banking or some sort of artificial reproductive program, and it's obvious that we are valuable to them.

The Morlocks didn't support the Eloi in order to facilitate their spiritual growth or cultural enrichment. Just as we are the dependents of our living protein resources, the cattle, the chickens, the fish, and so forth, the Morlocks were dependents of the Eloi. Can it be that our visitors have a similar dependency on us—not, I don't think, for protein, but for some other form of nutrition not yet understood by us? This next case will begin our journey of exploration into that very question.

CHAPTER 3
ENCOUNTER: THROUGH THE NIGHT WINDOW

When I first read this letter years ago, I was reminded of something Anne had said when, a few months after the *Communion* experience, she was hypnotized under the care of Dr. Robert Naiman: "Whitley has to go. They come for Whitley." It would seem that I am not alone when it comes to this business of being taken ...

THE LETTER: JINGLE JINGLE
...

Sometime in the fall of 1973, I believe that I had just turned thirteen years old. A total of six teenagers in two rooms would make for many interesting stories on its own, but nothing like the story I am about to tell. I shared my room with my sisters. We would chat amongst ourselves until Mom and Dad would become enraged at the noise of giggling. Threats of impending punishment were a nightly ritual. We would will ourselves into slumber to avoid the temptation to speak.

It seemed that I had been asleep for hours when I heard a noise that sounded like jingle bells. Jing, jing, jing, I kept hearing it, but it was not a noise coming from a dream that I was currently involved in. I wasn't aware that I had been dreaming at all when I noticed the noises generating from somewhere outside my window. I had listened to the jingling for a few minutes before deciding to look out the window to check it out.

As I think back, I am intrigued by my completely calm response to what I was looking at. Directly in the middle of the yard where the swimming pool used to be was a large metal saucer-like vehicle. It was almost as if the occupants had thought that the cleared terrain had been prepared for them to utilize as a landing pad. The vehicle was much smaller than what I would have guessed.

I noticed a hatchway appear from where there was previously a seamless place. It just appeared out of nowhere like an invisible orifice. There were four or five small kids who walked out of the ship onto the lawn. They were much smaller than I was and were no threat to me. I would estimate that they were probably the size of a five- or six-year-old. They were wearing body-hugging dull silver/gray suits that seemed to cover them completely from head to toe.

I noticed two of them take something from nowhere. I quickly saw that it was a ladder of some sort. I perceived it to be a rope ladder with metal hooks on the ends. I became amused at the simplicity of the tools in which a seemingly advanced group of beings were forced to use to enter my domain. I heard the metal ends of the ladder as they gripped tightly on the windowsill directly in front of my face. I saw them with my own two eyes right in front of my nose. My heart started racing as fear began to consume me. It was really happening. I not only saw it, I heard it as well.

I saw the fingers of the first to reach my window as they reached up to pull themselves up by the ledge. These were not people fingers. There were only four of them and they were a different color. They seemed to have a bulbous look to them. It was when the head started to peep up over the ledge directly two inches in front of my face that I lost it. The head was donning no helmet. It was completely hairless with wrinkles like frown marks across the brow line. The color was that of a dead person, kind of ashen. It was about to pull itself up to where we would be eye to eye when I became so terrified that I was no longer able to witness this scenario any longer. I flew out of the room screaming. I couldn't understand why no one was waking up.

ANALYSIS

A bedroom full of teenage sisters, much giggling as always, parental threats from down the hall, whispered conversation, then—at last—sleep. A bit later, though ... well, not that.

Deep in the night, one of the girls is awakened by what sounds like sleigh bells, a sound that would be familiar to anybody who has attended a traditional séance, in which the spirits are said to ring bells that are left for them on a table in the séance room. This is one of many subtle hints that recur across the whole arc of the close encounter experience, of a connection between the dead and our visitors ... unless, of course, "connection" is the wrong word because they are one and the same.

Intrigued by the persistent sound, she gets up and looks out the window. In retrospect, she's amazed that what she saw didn't shock her because hanging over the lawn "as if it was a landing pad" was a "metal, saucer-like vehicle." It seems very small to her: "much smaller than I would have guessed." Quite often, witnesses report that entering what looks like a small ship leads to a large room, or even a vast interior. Could it be, then, that they aren't ships at all but something else—portals, perhaps, to another world—or even a part of this one that is hidden to us? As NASA is presently exploring the idea of warp drives, which would briefly bring two different points in the universe into contact with one another and enable instantaneous movement between them, the idea of connections between distant points in the universe doesn't seem as impossible as it once did. In 2013, NASA engineer Harold "Sonny" White showed that such a drive would be possible and would not require the gigantic amounts of energy previously thought. In the August 13, 2013, edition of *The New Scientist*, he commented, "I did some work in 2011 and 2012 as part of the 100 Year Starship symposium and discovered ways to reduce the energy requirements by many orders of magnitude, so for a 10-metre diameter spacecraft with a velocity of 10 times light speed, I can reduce the negative energy needed." Specifically, the amount of energy necessary can be reduced from the mass-energy of a planet the size of Jupiter to something the size of the *Voyager* spacecraft, about 700 kilograms.

Of course, it's a long way from calculations to an actual drive, but if we are indeed talking, here, about somebody from another planet, they might well have accomplished this long ago. The point is that Dr. White's work shows that it *can* be accomplished and, therefore, that travel between stars is probably quite feasible.

It might also explain why their vehicles seem to function outside of the laws of physics—they aren't flying at all, or even vehicles, but points of contact between worlds.

If so, then when our correspondent observes a hatchway open where there had previously been no evidence of any door, what is she actually seeing? It appeared "like an invisible orifice." Four or five "small kids" walk out onto the lawn. As they appear to be the size of children of five or six, she doesn't feel any sense of threat, at least not at that moment. She next notices that they are not wearing children's clothes but rather silver-gray suits.

Then two of them pluck an object out of nowhere. To her, it appears to be a rope ladder with metal hooks on the end. She has now understood that these are not children, but the low-tech ladder coming out of the high-tech flying saucer has confused her. What can this be about?

She soon finds out because, as she continues to peer out the window, she hears the metal ends of the ladder latch onto the windowsill "directly in front of my face." Then she sees the fingers of the first one to reach the window, right there, inches away from her. They were "not people fingers"; there were only four of them and they seemed bulbous to her. (Our visitors have been described by others as having broad fingertips.) She reports that "the color was that of a dead person, kind of ashen"—a hint, perhaps of some sort of connection with the dead? But what in the world would aliens have to do with the souls of the dead? And, in any case, do "souls" even exist? Here, we come face to face with the problem I discussed in the introduction: we have never been able to detect any sort of nonphysical consciousness using any known form of detector—but, of course, prior to James Clerk Maxwell's proposal of electromagnetism in 1864, we had no idea that radio waves might exist, and nothing that could detect them. It should not be forgotten that the absence of an ability to detect and measure something does not mean that it cannot exist.

Nevertheless, we have convinced ourselves with increasing cultural force since the beginning of the Enlightenment in the eighteenth century that there is no soul. The belief is now so powerful that even those of us who do think we have a soul cannot actually experience any sensation of this part of us.

Now that they are close, her heart starts racing. As the entities come up the ladder, she feels consuming waves of terror. First the fingers. Then a head appears. It is hairless, with a wrinkled brow. It is not human. Its color reminds her of the skin of a corpse. As the entity pulls itself up, she turns and races screaming out of the room.

But then something quite impossible happens: nobody else wakes up—and there the memory ends. This blank may conceal the greatest mystery that mankind now faces, or has ever faced, and we will see it again and again over the course of this vast story. This distortion of memory happens again and again in the close encounter experience, to the extent that neurologists and memory experts should be very careful when they assume that they are encountering natural memory when dealing with close encounter witnesses. They are, in fact, dealing with controlled memory, which suggests that our own memories are being manipulated to create an impression of contact that our visitors want us to believe, or perhaps, if their motive is altruistic, one that we can understand.

Between 1997 and 2000, the British Defence Intelligence Staff produced a report of an investigation into, among other things, the effects of close proximity to UAPs. Known as the Condign Report (different from the U.S. Air Force's Condon Report of 1969), it was eventually released by the Ministry of Defence in response to a request made under the terms of the British Freedom of Information Act.

In it, there is reference made to "plasmas" that, when approached, can cause witnesses to emerge with memories of events that did not happen. Reading the report, it's clear that the word "plasma" is being used to avoid the culturally toxic "UAP."

It should be noted that the report doesn't claim that close encounters do not happen. Instead, it amounts to an official admission that plasmas exist and can be approached, and it agrees with the wealth of other observations that close encounters can alter memory.

While it's certainly possible that this particular witness had a nightmare and nothing more, it is also possible that somebody did indeed approach her in the way she remembers—or, more accurately stated, in the way they wished her to remember.

It's as if they let her remember their approach normally then turned off any memory of subsequent events and never allowed her family to remember anything at all, or didn't approach them.

This would be consistent with the entire body of the experience. I think that it's reasonable to conclude that whoever is here is creating a theatrical presentation about themselves in our memory and therefore in our collective imagination.

Are they doing this to hide something from us, or trying to use memory as a way of communicating with us? Given that this book must rely on witnesses' memories in its effort to construct a picture of our visitors and to understand their motives, the book must reckon with the editing process that seems to take place in the minds of all who come into contact.

When she saw what was coming in the window, the young girl, alone at night in a houseful of sleeping people, ran screaming, and very understandably so. There her memory ends.

But is this entirely a mystery? Can we learn more?

Oh yes, most certainly. We can learn more about missing time and what it might contain, and some great secrets. But before we reach those mysteries, let's see if we can find out more about what is lost with that disappeared time.

CHAPTER 4
ENCOUNTER: WHERE DID THAT TIME GO?

After a quiet night in their settled life, a long-married couple awakens to what promises to be another normal day. They dress and have their breakfast. Not wanting to be late for work, the husband hurries. The wife, a longtime teacher, is not working today. Her plan is to clean house, which she starts doing about an hour later. Then—

THE LETTER: A DISAPPEARED DAY

In 1976 I was vacuuming my living room floor at about noon. Suddenly I felt quite ill and thought I was going to vomit, so I sat down on the couch to see if the sick feeling would subside. I then saw that I was not alone; there were three strange little people standing alongside the couch, just looking at me. I froze with fear, as I had never seen anything like them before, not even in the movies.

Two of them were short and fat, about four to four and a half feet tall, with broad faces and enormous black eyes, but with only a hint of where a nose or mouth might have been, almost like a pencil drawing. They had wispy bits of brown hair at the back of their heads, and they didn't have blue suits on like the ones you described in *Communion*; instead, they were wearing brown shrouds. These, I knew instinctively, were the workers. The other was female, thin and about five feet tall. She wore a black shroud and had black wispy hair at the back of her head. Her face was very elongated, with huge, dark, piercing eyes, and once again just a hint of where a nose or mouth would have been.

The tall thin one started to speak to me with her mind and told me I was to go with them. I answered with my own mind that I wouldn't go. Somehow, telepathic communication seemed perfectly normal at the time, and I felt quite comfortable communicating that way. This doesn't mean that I wasn't frightened—I was beside myself with fear. She kept saying, "You must come with us," and I kept refusing. She then said I could go free, and I got up off the couch and crawled along my hallway to the front door. When I got there, they pulled me back with their minds until I was on the couch again. They let me go again, and the result was identical, except that this time my husband was standing at the front door. I clung to him, and I will always remember how the sweater he was wearing smelled.

They pulled me out of his arms and back to the couch and once again told me it was useless to fight, as I had to go with them. The two workers seemed to be busy doing something all the time this was going on, but I have no idea what it was. The next thing I was aware of was the sound of my husband's car pulling up to the house. I heard him come through the front door and down the hallway, and at this point, I noticed that the visitors were gone.

When my husband walked through the door, I didn't believe it was him at first; I thought it was another trick. It took me about fifteen minutes to really believe that they were gone and that my husband was home. My next shock came when I found out it was 5:30 p.m. It seemed like it should be 1:30 p.m. at the most.

I wonder, where did that time go?

ANALYSIS

This woman wrote to me for the same reason that most of the others did: she had a bizarre encounter with somebody who had the same large, dark eyes that I had depicted on the cover of *Communion*. When Anne first handed me this letter, she said, "We really do not understand ourselves."

I think that it was a critically important insight. Rather than say, "This woman remembered being abducted by aliens," we are better off asking, "Why did this woman end up with this memory, and what does it mean about the human experience?"

She finds herself confronted by beings who looked very much like the ones I saw during my abduction—they had the same enormous eyes.

Just like the girl who saw the visitors coming in her window but remembered nothing else, this woman only sees her visitors for a short time. The letter gives us more information than the one from the girl conveys because it reveals how she resisted and how they overpowered her. As the girl ran screaming, she may have also been overpowered by the application of a mental force of some kind that we do not understand—at least, not on a conscious level.

"I froze with fear," the woman writes. She hears—not verbally, but in her mind—a clear and commanding female voice: "You will come with us." She replies mentally that she won't go. The demand is repeated, and she continues to refuse. She reports that, while it was happening, this wordless communication seemed normal.

Does this, then, mean that this was actually a familiar situation for her? We have no way to tell, but as we have seen, a primary characteristic of the close encounter experience is that mental communication, which we cannot use in our ordinary lives, now feels normal. For me, this raises a huge question about what our relationship to these entities actually is. How could we find such exotic communication so natural when we participate in it, unless it reflects a capability that is normally hidden inside us but can be triggered by somebody who knows how to do it?

It is also clear from both of these letters that memories may be distorted, edited, and removed. A speculation that will recur throughout this book presents itself here: are we dealing not with rare experiences at all but rather with a common one that is rarely remembered? And if the latter is true, then are we, indeed, Eloi? The Morlocks were human beings who had evolved into cannibals, but as we're not being physically eaten, is there evidence that something else may be being harvested from us?

Because of the distortions that are fundamental to this whole story, it is going to be impossible to answer a question like that definitively.

Finally, the strange woman with the huge eyes tells our correspondent that she is free to go. She then tries to escape. But she is not in any sort of a normal state. Her situation is so dire that she reports that she "crawled" along her hallway to the front door.

When she reaches the door, they "pulled me back with their minds" and she found herself once again on the couch. Yet again, they let her go, and this time her husband was standing in the doorway. "I clung to him." She could even smell his sweater, but she soon realized that there was nobody there—he was an illusion. They once again pulled her back, telling her that it was "useless to fight."

Maybe it was, but if so, then why did they have to struggle with her at all? They had to force her to bend to their will. Eventually they either turned her consciousness off as if with some sort of anesthesia or later removed her memories of what happened when they worked their will on her.

We cannot say exactly what happened either to her or to the girl, but perhaps, if we dig a bit, we can arrive at some better-informed speculations.

Let's discuss a couple of possibilities. First, if this was a new experience for her, then her fear and resistance are easily explainable. But if not, and on some level she knew what they were going to do with her, then the mystery about ourselves and our predicament grows deeper and more ominous. Why does this happen, and why do we fear it so? In my own case, I knew very well what was happening to me. There was no "missing time," and what was done was the extraction of semen. This was accomplished through the use of an electrostimulation device that was inserted into my rectum to force an erection. Our correspondent did not say whether or not she experienced sexual penetration of any kind, but if, say, an egg was stolen from her, that would certainly be one reason to suppress her memory of her experience.

As mentioned in the introduction, there has already been something bordering on an official admission that sexual events take place during close encounter experiences. The 2010 report on "Anomalous Acute and Subacute Field Effects on Biological Tissues" mentions abductions, sexual contact, and anomalous pregnancies. Our correspondent was not pregnant when she was abducted, nor did she become so afterward, but it seems perfectly possible that an unwanted sexual intrusion of some sort is what lies hidden in the gap of missing time. If this was what happened, the wiping of her memory is understandable. Many thousands of us remember such things and have to bear these memories. Do we have children elsewhere, or is something else done with our sexual material?

I think of the huge eyes and the overpowering mind and this woman, who died never knowing where she had been taken or why, or what, if anything, she had lost on that harrowing afternoon. For this is a story not just of the loss of a precious part of each of us who is affected but also of the loss of humankind's innocence. We are waking up to the likelihood that not only are we not alone, but whoever is here might not see us as we see ourselves. On the contrary, some of their actions suggest that they might even regard us more like a crop to be tended, growing in a field that is our Earth, but in their eyes important for reasons that we don't understand and absent the rights that we accord ourselves.

It is also becoming clear that this fierce, patient, and determined presence is, whether by intention or not, waking us up to itself. Looking around us at the condition of our planet, I can well understand why our visitors might have chosen to take action. There is no time left to sleep in the womb of Earth. The infant mankind is too large for her to hold. Her waters are broken, we are in the process of leaving the birth canal and coming out into a new life, which if individual births are any example, is going to be quite a shocking experience.

Our poor correspondent, of course, does not see any of this, or perhaps has simply been made to drink the legendary milk of Nepenthe, the bitter opium of forgetting, and sent back to her life.

Her next memory is of hearing her husband drive up. When he comes through the front door, she is immediately suspicious. Another trick? It takes her some moments, but she finally realizes that it really is him. She then discovers that it's 5:30 in the afternoon. It should be about 1:30. She has been in a state of complete unawareness for *four hours*.

The last sentence in her letter is, "Where did that time go?"

One of the most common ways that the close encounter experience is dismissed is as a sleep disturbance. Whatever this was, it was not that—it happened in broad daylight to somebody running a vacuum cleaner.

The years passed, and she eventually did, too. Her privacy was abused by a UAP researcher in her home country, who put her name out in public, causing her great anguish. She died without ever finding out what happened to her. But *something* did. Was it a waking dream? If so, then why did she see two different kinds of entities that have been reported by many others but were unknown to her at the time? Collective dreaming? Is that possible? There is no evidence of such a phenomenon but plenty of evidence suggesting that abduction by unknown presences is real.

Hers is far from the only encounter that has taken place in the middle of the day. But how is it that something that can happen in broad daylight remains so hidden? To expand on the theme of *The Time Machine*: Are encounters actually not "alien" contact at all, but an unknown part of nature and of what it is to be human? If so, then perhaps what is rare is not encounters like this but recall of them.

Are we being harvested by Morlocks or birthed by midwives? Or given the complexity and vastness of reality and of the presence that has directed its attention toward us, perhaps, in some way, both?

Another question arises: Did they *want* her to see them take her and remember their power—or was it an accident, perhaps the vacuum cleaner drowning out some hypnotic command? Either way, her letter represents a step beyond the previous one, which is why I've placed it here in our story.

There are tens of thousands of close encounter reports every bit as vivid as the ones being discussed here. But as the Condign Report points out, people who have been in close proximity to UAPs may remember things that "did not happen."

It has been demonstrated experimentally that false memories are not difficult to create. So might something very different be going on here than what is being described? I would certainly think so, but I would add that strange physical injuries, disappearing and aborted pregnancies, and the implantation of metallic objects into witnesses are provable. To an extent, all three things have already been proven but not in an orderly, scientifically rigorous manner.

In May of 1989 an implant was placed into the pinna of my left ear. The attempt to remove it was documented on video, and what the doctor observed was not normal. When he touched it with his scalpel, it moved from the top of the pinna of my left ear down into the earlobe.

I was awake when it was put in. I was overpowered by two people —not aliens—and it was inserted under the skin without leaving an entrance wound. (I have discussed this event extensively, most recently in *A New World*.)

Given this personal experience, I would advocate strongly that something unusual is being done to people. I would not go so far as to assert that I know what it is or who is doing it, though, and above all, I cannot assert that the close encounter stories we have reflect exactly what happened to the people reporting them. I feel that most of the cases I'm discussing here are at least somewhat accurate descriptions of what actually happened— because in all of them, either the person was awake or quickly woke up when the event started, or there was more than one witness, or both.

Still, though, I cannot assert anything for certain except the ambiguity of it all.

Dr. Michael Persinger (1945–2018), who spent his career from 1971 until his death exploring various methods of affecting perception by stimulating the temporal lobe, was able, using magnetic fields, to experimentally induce hallucinations that test subjects experienced as anything from the presence of aliens to a visit from God.

He discovered that, when a person's head is placed between two strong alternating electromagnetic fields, a glow appears in their peripheral vision, caused by stimulation of the retina. Transcranial magnetic stimulation is used in the diagnosis of brain conditions by exciting nerve axons in the motor cortex. Magnetic field therapy can also help treat conditions like depression and addiction.

Dr. Persinger was of the opinion that magnetic fields were the underlying energy that enabled experiences such as telepathy, psychokinesis, and the abduction experience, which he regarded as an illusion caused in the brain by the same sort of force field that generates earthquake lights. But the fact that Dr. Persinger could induce hallucinations that appear to be alien contact doesn't mean that all the experiences reported outside of the laboratory setting are fundamentally illusions. It only means that they can, to a degree, be simulated in the lab.

That the close encounter experience goes beyond any hallucination is eloquently—and frighteningly—demonstrated by the next letter. Here, we find not an abduction at all but perhaps a failed attempt at one. Or was it a failure at all? It could as easily have been a warning: that the labyrinth that is our world, the human reality in which we wander, forever facing ourselves anew, bears also a darkness that, in the words of the old Catholic prayer to the Archangel Michael, "wanders the world seeking the ruin of souls."

CHAPTER 5
ENCOUNTER: AN ENTITY OF TOTAL EVIL

This next story involves the projection of fear. It is an example of the ability that our visitors have to transmit emotions almost as a beam of energy, as if some kind of emotional flashlight has been turned on and pointed at the victim.

My initial impression, when Anne showed me this letter, was that it described a relatively common sleep disorder known as "exploding head syndrome." But its shared nature and extraordinary duration mean that, if it is that, it is by far the most extreme case ever recorded, and the only case of extensive involvement of two fully awake people.

It's the wee hours of the morning. A man has been working late. When he finally gets home, he's exhausted. He undresses quietly to avoid awakening his wife then slides into bed beside her.

This is his report of what happened next.

THE LETTER: EXHAUSTED
AND AFRAID ...

My younger brother owns a recording studio, and as I am an amateur pianist, arranger, and composer, I frequently use the studio to make demonstration tapes. Even a three-minute recording can take several days to put together, and on this occasion, I stayed overnight the first night, finished recording about midnight, then headed home on the sixty-mile drive back to my place.

When I got home, it was about 1:45 a.m., and I undressed and slipped into bed without waking my wife. I rested my head on the pillow, feeling very happy about the results of the recording session and looking forward to playing the results for my family on the stereo the following morning.

I reckon my head had been on the pillow for less than thirty seconds when, for want of a better word, it exploded—the only way I can describe that shocking sensation is that I thought a bomb had blown me to pieces and that "I" was nowhere and had ceased to be. After a few seconds, the vacuum of what used to be me was filled by an entity of total evil. This evil thing so terrified me that I wanted to start fighting, until I became conscious that I was unable to move my limbs. Although I was screaming to my wife to wake up and help me, my lips barely moved and the screams were whispers. Eventually, maybe a minute or two later, my bodily control returned, and with it real screams. My wife awoke immediately and did her best to comfort me. I realized that my pillow was wet with tears.

After I gained control, I explained to her what had happened. She switched on the bedroom light and made us some coffee, and we sat up in bed talking quietly about what might have occurred. I became calmer. I knew the whole thing had not been a dream because I'd never fallen asleep. We both put it down to a rather violent out-of-body experience, perhaps even an attempted "possession" by some entity. We were alarmed, but everything was OK, and since she had to go to work in the morning and I had the housework and paintings to paint, we had decided to turn off the light and get some sleep when we both said, "What's that noise?"

We heard a low humming sound. A quick glance at the clock told us it was 2:30 a.m. The humming soon changed to a deep, fast throbbing. It didn't sound like a plane, or a truck, or a car. It got louder and stopped right over the roof of the house, directly above our bedroom. There were no flashing or glowing lights, just a very loud thumping sound right over our double bed. We froze; what on earth could be on the roof?

Before I could volunteer to go outside and see what was going on, all our nice little stories about OBEs and possession were shattered, as something invisible grabbed me by the chest and started pulling with amazing force. I felt like my soul, not my body, was being pulled up vertically toward the loud throbbing noise, and although I thought it would be futile, I screamed for her to lie on top of me. When she did this, the sensation of pulling eased a little.

I was screaming and struggling against an invisible "beam," with my wife lying on top of me in my bed at 2:30 a.m. What a sight we would have presented if someone had walked in! It might have seemed funny later, if it hadn't gone on for another two hours. Throughout the night the children, who slept directly across the hall from us, never woke up. "They" pulled, I resisted, she hung on, and the engine throbbed, until finally it went away. Exhausted and badly shaken, we fell asleep.

ANALYSIS

This many-layered and complex story at first seems terrifying and threatening, but it also illustrates an important reality: we do have the ability to resist these bizarre attacks, if an attack this was. Despite the hours of struggle that were involved, in the end nothing dire happened to the witness. Perhaps this is because whatever the dreadful presence was had no choice but to leave with the dawn. If so, then it wasn't following the usual pattern of interaction with our visitors, who as we have seen and will see again, can and do appear during the day.

Let's unpack the story, layer by layer.

The witness finishes a long session at a recording studio then drives home late at night. He has been working hard and is exhausted. He doesn't mention seeing or hearing anything unusual on the drive or as he arrives at home. It would seem, though, that somebody or something had noticed him. But why this particular man, and why this particular event?

In all the thousands of letters we received, this is the only one that describes such an attack. Letters detail a variety of approaches, kidnappings, meetings, all sorts of interactions, but this is the only one we received where the witness reported what would be classically characterized as an attempt at possession.

He slips into bed, puts his head on the pillow, and an instant later experiences a remarkable and devastating sense of being more than killed. "I had ceased to be." His impression is that his head has exploded, and he is now in a black nowhere, effectively more dead than dead.

He has the sense that his body has been emptied of self. But that's only a fleeting impression. Next, he is "filled by an entity of total evil." What is so odd about this statement is that we don't "feel" evil or good like moods or emotional states. Evil acts and thoughts, the appearance of people who look dangerous, frightening words and so forth, cause us to feel threatened. But we don't "feel" evil and good like we might feel hot or cold. Something that projects evil is replacing him in his body. He is being stolen from himself.

He attempts to struggle but cannot move. When he tries to scream, all that emerges is a whisper. What he is experiencing is sleep paralysis, a well-known feature of hypnagogia, the transitional state between waking and sleep— probably as a result of being exhausted after his long drive. However, his hypnagogic perceptions are atypical, and what will shortly unfold has nothing to do with hypnagogia or, as far as I know, any documented form of sleep paralysis. I have been unable to locate a description of any other hypnagogic experience that involves being hollowed out in such a dramatic way or feeling oneself replaced by something that radiates evil like a horrible glow. As is normally the case with sleep paralysis, he soon regains control of his body. His desperate whispers turn into real screams. His wife awakens and sets about comforting him.

They turn on the light, the wife makes coffee, and they sit up in bed discussing his nightmare. He argues that it wasn't any sort of dream because "I'd never fallen asleep." This is normal for hypnagogia, which takes hold as we drift off, not after we are already asleep.

There is nothing normal about what happens next.

The husband and wife are now wide awake. They are medicating themselves with caffeine. Nevertheless, they decide to try to go back to sleep. This contradiction probably reflects a deeper fear that they are not expressing. They want both to be alert to whatever is frightening them and also to return to their normal sleep state. Or is something else going on? Does their desire to stay awake conflict with another desire, possibly not originating within them, which cannot be fulfilled unless they are in more unguarded sleep?

Coffee or not, they turn off the light and settle down. Both of them now hear a low humming sound over the house. This has now become a multiple-witness event, and it seems appropriate to explore the degree to which unusual perceptions can be shared. Two people are highly unlikely to share a hallucination. It's not impossible, of course, and we will discuss folie à deux in the context of another multiple-witness event in a later section.

A bit of modern folklore concerns "walk-ins," which are said to be souls that take the place of a body's current inhabitant. This haunting idea was popularized by Ruth Montgomery in her 1979 book *Strangers Among Us.* No substantive evidence is offered in the book, which postulates that certain evolved souls enter bodies to use them in an effort to help mankind reach a new level of being. They are called starseeds, and there is a voluntary aspect to the exchanges. When the starseeds take over a body, its current inhabitant is sent off to a sort of resort for souls. Reassuring, if so, but not quite what is happening here. Hardly.

This reads like something out of the demonic possession literature—but is such a thing really possible? To believe that it is, one must also believe that disembodied entities exist, and that at least some of them do terrible things, among them stealing bodies from their rightful occupants.

I corresponded with this witness after we received his letter. He did not mention any feeling of an unwanted presence now lurking within him. I also spoke to and corresponded with the witness who had been taken from her living room, and she also had no sense that anything about her had been changed. Then again, if some bizarre sort of exchange had taken place—if that is even possible—the new inhabitant of the body would be unlikely to reveal that fact, or might not even know.

If the secret of missing time is that souls may be traded out of bodies, then what are we?

Beyond those speculations, there is a bottom-line question here, and it is an important one: can we determine *anything* definite about what happened to this couple? If stories of such things as possession and walk-ins intersect in some way with encounter memories, then it is certainly a matter for deeper study, one which would bring our whole experience of this elusive and yet intrusive presence into greater focus. This would be in large part an academic pursuit, a matter of seeking into myth for resonances that might illuminate current witness testimony. But that isn't all that would be of value. Unless science and the academy seek toward the same goals in the context of broader acceptance of the existence of the mystery, little will be accomplished.

To explore what science might do with a story like this, let's take a look at how the brain conducts its business.

In it, sensory collection and evaluation works like this: the thalamus detects input from the sense organs and sends it through the sensory cortex to the hippocampus, where it is compared with past experience. The amygdala then connects this previous experience to the current input and establishes whether there is a potential threat. If so, the hypothalamus is activated and a fear response is triggered. If not, then a whole array of other responses may come into play. Is this food, an object of desire, a matter of curiosity, and so forth?

The thalamus collects input from all the sense organs in the body except smell. Odors are evaluated somewhat differently, but the result is the same: if a threat is detected, the hypothalamus will trigger a fear response.

All of this activity is electrical, and the particular quality of an emotion does generate a specific and measurable frequency.

Given this, can emotional states be affected by applying different frequencies to the brain, thus altering the way it is processing perceptions at a given time?

There are many methods of mind control, such as Silva mind control and neurolinguistic programming, and many books on the use of such techniques. There is also hypnosis and other methods of suggestion to control thoughts and actions and to plant thoughts in the mind. But these do not involve altering brain activity using some sort of electromagnetic stimulation, which may be closer to explaining what happened here.

Books such as *Trance Formation of America* by Cathy O'Brien and Mark Phillips and Donald Bain's *The Control of Candy Jones* make claims involving hypnosis and the control of victims using hypnotically buried triggers, but not the use of distant signaling.

The CIA's massive, years-long and notorious MK-ULTRA program sought to develop techniques of mind control, some of which did involve experimentation with mood- and perhaps thought-changing radio frequencies. Neurologist Dr. José Delgado, who was allegedly part of this program, developed a device he called a stimoceiver, which involved the transmission of FM frequencies to an electrode implanted in a subject's brain. It was successfully tested on animals, and a dramatic video made in 1964 shows Dr. Delgado controlling an enraged bull with it. Experiments on human subjects followed—patients were chosen who had "neurological disorders, including temporal-lobe epilepsy and related episodic behavior problems," and whose illnesses had proven intractable to other treatments. Dr. Delgado wrote, "Radio stimulation of different points in the amygdala and hippocampus in the four patients produced a variety of effects including pleasant sensations, elation, deep, thoughtful concentration, odd feelings, super relaxation, colored visions, and other responses." Did those "other responses" include anything like fear or a sense of being attacked by something profoundly evil and conceivably of being detached from the body?

After the exposure of the MK-ULTRA program, Delgado returned to his native Spain to avoid lawsuits filed by people who believed that he had caused them harm with his experiments. But the fact that remote control of emotions using the FM frequency was publicly demonstrated during the 1960s leads to another question: Was this developed further? The answer is yes, but what has followed is not necessarily sinister. Brain-machine interface device research and development has progressed dramatically, especially in the last few years. Google and other companies are actively working on devices that can be worn or chips implanted that allow direct interface between computers and brains. In July of 2022 a brain-computer interface device was implanted at the Mount Sinai Medical Center in New York. The device was injected through the jugular vein into a blood vessel in the brain of a patient with amyotrophic lateral sclerosis in the hope that it would enable him to transmit thought commands to computers. The system has already been implanted into four patients in Australia, and the developer, Synchron, is working to increase the power and reduce the size of the devices.

But this involves either a wearable device that adds information via radio frequencies or implanted devices that do the same thing. It does not involve anything that would affect the fear response or create the impression—or illusion—that body and soul are being separated.

But radio frequencies are not the only means of affecting brain activity. Light can also be used, and a paper published in the 21 March 2022 issue of *Nature Biomedical Engineering* describes tiny injectable photothermal transducers that can affect certain neurons in the hippocampus, motor cortex, and other areas of the brains of mice. There is no reason that the same procedure could not be extrapolated to humans. Once the transducers are injected, affecting the brain with such a system requires a specialized light source, and if the subject leaves the light, the effect will end. But that's given current techniques. If more advanced versions of any of these systems exist, it seems probable that a sense of separation of the consciousness from the body could be induced from a distance. Would it be an *actual* separation, though? Can that even happen? This is where our ability to obtain verifiable and repeatable evidence fails. Thus we cannot know—which is unfortunate because if what happened to this man was something in the nature of an experiment and it is repeated on a larger scale, it is going to cause mayhem.

In our society, research is proceeding in the direction of both enabling wireless contact between brains and computers and affecting brain states from a distance—but not without anything being added to the brain, and not without a source that is close to the subject. Of course, it's always possible that secret research has gone farther. When I had the implant placed in my left ear, quite unusual means were in use, and while I may have glimpsed something else in the room, all I actually saw were the two people who first rendered me helpless by unknown means then inserted the object right through the skin. It is still there.

As I have discussed it quite extensively elsewhere, I will mention here only that, by the way they got into our house—bypassing an armed alarm system and leaving a powerful free-floating magnetic field in our garage— they also demonstrated a sophisticated ability to control magnetism. Could this mean that somebody *does* have the ability to induce states similar to what Dr. Persinger created, and to do so at a distance?

If so, then why? That question goes right to the heart of the whole enigma. Why any of it?

We have now established that efforts to affect thoughts and emotions have been carried out both by the Central Intelligence Agency on humans and by university groups on animals; a number of commercial enterprises are working on brain-computer interaction; and (from my own experience) that an advanced implant technology, apparently in human hands, existed in 1989. What we have not determined is how any effects could be induced in an individual without some sort of physical access to the brain.

To explore further, let's get back to the couple, now wide awake in their bedroom. They've had their coffee and they are calming down. They decide to turn off the light and get some sleep. But before they can do so, they both hear a noise, a low humming sound. The sound changes to a "deep, fast throbbing" that stops immediately over their bedroom.

They are not body-asleep/mind-awake at all. Their perceptual systems are in a normal state of awareness, or very close to it.

A moment later, as our correspondent reports, "something invisible grabbed me by the chest and started pulling with amazing force." He feels that it's his soul that it's trying to capture, not his physical body. Desperately afraid, he screams for his wife to lie on top of him. But why does he do this? By protecting himself with her body, isn't he putting her in harm's way? Or does he know, on some unacknowledged level, that getting his wife to do this would be protective? If so, then that would be because we do indeed know more about such experiences than we want to acknowledge.

Battle is now engaged. The sound throbs, his soul is dragged, he and his wife cry out. This goes on for hours, until dawn. Only with first light does the sound rumble off into the distance.

In another such case, an individual was in bed at about 11:00 p.m. when he thought that his cat had climbed onto the bed. But when he tried to stroke it, he got the shock of a lifetime.

What he saw was "a black void" that began rotating, brushing his face as it did so. Soon, the rotation caused a whooshing sound, then it rose to the howl of a powerful wind. He got the impression of a great fury and then felt "a pulling sensation" on his chest. It felt is if the thing was trying to pull his soul out of his body. Enraged, he leaped out of the bed. The thing then disappeared.

Like the woman vacuuming her living room, neither of these witnesses ever got any answers. I am not trying to find fault when I say this. On the contrary, I don't see how science, or even life itself as we now understand it, could provide useful answers. Dr. Persinger was able to induce states that mimic the appearance of ghosts and aliens, but that doesn't prove that there isn't some unknown force that can generate these experiences, only that they can be simulated by the application of magnetic fields to the brain.

Close encounter does more than figuratively explode the heads of witnesses. It does the same to everything those witnesses believed to be true about what we are and the way our world works. It leaves many of them questioning whether or not this even *is* our world.

Another witness described this sort of attack to me a little differently: "It was as if my mind exploded into a billion pieces." To this man, the feeling was like "the universe was inside me." A few nights later, though, things were very different. He heard something in the hallway. When he turned on the light, what "looked like a skeleton covered with rotting flesh" came flying down the hall, a fiery sword over its head. It was followed by a sound like howling wind. The man then collapsed. He was found by a friend, who helped him to his feet. So this experience has relevance to neurology, psychiatry, and religious studies, where the mythological implications of the flying skeleton might be explored. As to the outcome of such studies, perhaps we would find somebody there, either a presence independent of us or one hidden behind a door within us that the pressures of our time, from the danger of nuclear annihilation to population pressure to environmental collapse, is slowly opening.

Abduction experiences could conceivably be the result of an intrusion by aliens. When it happened to me, that is what I came to think. But if so, then what are stories like these?

Of course, there is a vast literature of demons and demonic possession, but not so much about entities that radiate a sense of evil. Evil is a quality of something that is done—a theft, a murder—not a tangible radiation like light or sound. Nothing "radiates" evil. But that is what these people are describing.

It is as if emotion can be made to propagate like radio waves. But what could do that? Surely emotional states cannot be projected like death rays into a victim's consciousness. Unless, of course, they can.

If the throbbing machine was there to steal the poor guy's soul, why would it terrify him with an "evil ray"? Far more effective to lure him with a "goodness ray." Then he would have willingly sailed into the trap, one would think.

In fact, the machine or entity was simultaneously dragging his consciousness out of his body while threatening him in such a way that he used every means he could think of to resist it, including the loving support of his wife.

Like the strange beings who insisted that the vacuuming woman go with them and overcame her resistance with a sort of mental rape, the throbbing sound source was making a demand of him that he desperately wanted to resist. Given the stealth that our visitors are capable of employing, it also seems to have been making certain that he *would* resist—just as had the entities who captured the woman.

Why do this? Unless the two incidents were both accidental revelations of something that was meant to be hidden, then it can be reasonably hypothesized that some sort of mechanism for overpowering the human will may have been being tested in all three of these cases.

In the first case, the young girl panicked and ran but remembers nothing afterward. In the second, the woman experienced a blackout and may or may not have been taken somewhere. In the third case, an overt attempt was made to remove what felt to the victim like his soul. It failed, but that doesn't mean that the test wasn't successful. Failure can often be more instructive than success.

For most of us, if "the soul" has any meaning at all, it is abstract. We do not think of it as a part of the person, like an organ, perhaps, that can be altered, even removed. This is because it's a rare human being who has any convincing evidence that it exists as part of them. We look to the past for belief in the soul, but even at full tide during the medieval era, the sea of faith was always as much a sea of doubt. If we did believe in the soul—could sense it like we sense a hand or feel a sigh—we would have a very different history and this would be a very different world. There would be no belief systems in perpetual violent confrontation with one another. Prayer would be a precise technology, not the blind and desperate bargaining that we engage in now. If we knew with absolute certainty that consciousness survived, both fear of death and the grief of loss would be very different affairs. Our entire understanding of ourselves and the world around us would be profoundly different, more insightful, and almost certainly less belligerent.

From the beginning, we have doubted not only our souls but also our gods. The reason is simple: gods don't answer prayers, except by chance, and, like Job, we are unable to understand why they are arbitrarily cruel and transgressive. We have always sacrificed to them in order to receive favors and protection. When our sacrifices failed to bring about the result we wanted, we either increased the value of the sacrifices, as the Aztecs did, or rebelled against the gods, smashed their statues, and looked for new ones, as the Romans did when they replaced their pantheon with Christ.

We have a long history of mistaking natural forces for deities then turning on them when they don't listen to us. But the fact that our gods are inventions doesn't mean that a nonphysical part of us doesn't exist.

Judging from these encounters with apparent soul thieves, we should take the possibility of the soul much more seriously than we do. If the experiences were real in some absolute way, then it can be conjectured that at least some of our visitors are here because of our souls and that their motives may not be in our interest.

If the soul records experience, for example, it might provide a rich sort of food to somebody whose life is starved of this commodity. In fact, if our visitors are outside of the stream of time looking in —if such a thing is possible—then the ability to taste of the continuously unfolding surprise that is the human journey might be irresistibly delicious to them. Also, though, what if souls are changed out all the time, and the current inhabitant sometimes doesn't wish to leave? Then, perhaps, force must be used, which would explain the insistence of the beings that menaced the lady in her living room and the force applied to the man in his bed, not to mention the reason that the young girl ran screaming when she realized what was happening.

If capture of souls is something objectively real, then the attempt to extract the man from his body may have been a test conducted by somebody who is learning how to do it. If so, I would think that many of us, or even all of us, will learn one day how that test came out. But will we want to know?

We want contact to be something positive for us. But I think that we are best off never forgetting that we live in a very large structure that is teeming with stars and even more so with planets. If it is full of intelligent living forms, there must be a vast number of different aims and motives, and for a species like ours, which does not itself have the ability to travel the stars and thus little knowledge of what might be out there, there must be many different sorts of vulnerability.

As long as we prefer to believe that our visitors don't exist, we are going to remain passive to their presence, and this always makes me wonder about the motive behind the debunking. Is there a hidden agenda of some sort being consciously followed by at least some of the deniers, or is the debunking a cultural artifact that arises out of the sheer improbability of the situation. Anybody who looks into it even superficially must see that as so many people are reporting strange experiences, something must be happening to them. And as the number of reports is so large, surely their cause should be investigated. But as that has not been done and is not being done, the general public remains unaware of the situation and therefore completely helpless before whatever is causing it. The people who face the visitors alone in the night deserve to know why it happens and what, if anything, can be done to help them.

Judging from the accounts we have seen so far, one would think that our visitors have things to hide. And yet it's all strangely contradictory. If you want to hide an event like the one that transpired under the sign by the roadside in Queens, why site it there? Why use a brightly lighted sign at all, much less send a huge object along the route of a crowded highway at an altitude of a few feet? And why allow the young girl and the vacuuming lady to remember anything? And why leave the man whose soul was attacked alive to tell the tale?

It is obvious that, whatever is happening, it is no ordinary experience, not a known hallucinatory state, for example. But is it an actual, physical experience? People sometimes have protracted experiences, even extending over their entire lives, yet there is not one known case of a visitor sitting down across a table from a human being and talking, whether physically or not. It simply does not happen.

People ask why they don't communicate, and justifiably so.

It may be because they can't. This next story suggests that not only may they be having that problem, but they may be experimenting with ways to overcome it.

CHAPTER 6
ENCOUNTER: VISITORS IN
THE TREES

Throughout this book, I have been shifting between positions regarding what our visitors are. The ambiguity of the situation allows no other approach. For this next letter, I will be working from a supposition that they are a real, external presence of some kind, possibly from some other planet. However, given the extraordinary strangeness of the situation, also hypothesizing that, even if that is true, it may be only part of their story.

With this in mind, we will now take a look beneath the surface of an elaborate daytime encounter involving an entire family. What happened to them demonstrates two things: first, that our visitors *do* want to communicate with us; second, that although the gulf between us is truly a wide one, it can be crossed. For this to happen, both sides will have to come to understand more about each other's abilities, needs and limitations. This letter demonstrates what our visitors propose to do to facilitate the process.

We got the letter in the early 1990s, but I did not understand it until just a few months ago, in February of 2022. The reason is not mysterious: it has taken me years of thought, research, and contact to have (hopefully) useful insight into the way the minds of our visitors work. Reading the accounts of others; talking to thousands of them;

learning about the physics of reality, the brain, psychology, and mythology; and, above all, having as much relationship with our visitors as I have been able to manage has taken me to the point that I am able to see a few things that seem to make sense.

It's just after dinner at a fairly isolated rural home. The wife and mother is in the kitchen washing up. She sees something mildly unusual but thinks nothing of it.

That will change.

THE LETTER: A BLUEPRINT FOR COMMUNICATION

The event I'm going to relate happened at our house, in a sparsely populated part of the countryside. The house has two stories and is built on a steep hill, so that when you look out the windows on the second floor, you can see into the tops of the trees that grow next to the house.

At about 9:00 p.m., what I thought was a large car with bright headlights rolled down our gravel driveway. I was washing the dinner dishes while looking out the kitchen window, which overlooks the circular driveway, but I didn't see any car there, so I thought nothing of it and went on up to bed.

We slept until about 7:00 a.m., and when I was back at the kitchen sink after breakfast, I looked out the window to see a woman in a red windbreaker jacket enter the stables. She was wearing white pants and was holding a long stick in her hand. I told my daughter to go see who it was, but when she returned, she said no one was there. I then saw a man jump off the pumphouse nearby, which is eight feet tall, and run off toward the trees. He was small, with brown hair, and seemed to bounce in a way that had no relation to gravity.

Next, I left to do some marketing, and when I returned, my husband walked up to me and said, "There are people in the trees!

We've been trying to talk to them, but they won't answer." My husband and I walked up to the front porch, where we saw the children calling up at the treetops, "Come down, we won't hurt you." I looked and saw that whoever was up there had constructed some sort of platform.

We went upstairs to look out of the bedroom window at the beings we had been trying to talk to from below. The second story windows are just at the right height so that we could view them on a level plane. The trees they were in are right outside this window, about sixteen or twenty feet away, so we could see the beings clearly.

I said to my daughter, "Do you see what I see?" She said, "Yes, Mom, there's two of them. What's that thing coming out of that one's head?" I noticed that there was some kind of beautiful beaded antenna sticking out of the left side of the head of one of the beings. One of them looked slightly Asian, and the other seemed more Caucasian, but smaller and with a brown mustache. One of them had on a remarkable piece of jewelry—it was a band striped in different metals of all colors: silver, gold, platinum, green, red, purple, and black. We could only see them from the chest up since the branches and leaves covered the rest of their bodies. I got the feeling they were monitoring everything: our yard, the air, perhaps radio waves.

Since they continued to ignore us, we went downstairs and outside again. I felt brave and wanted to find out more about what was going on, so I went and got our Rottweiler dog. Holding him by the collar, I explored underneath the trees. This caused a commotion, and I saw ten or twelve pairs of legs, all wearing white pants, scamper away from me up the hill. I let go of the dog, and as I approached the house, I saw a woman who was the same type of being you describe in your books. She was dressed in a kelly green jumpsuit and was too long and thin to be a human being. She was climbing among the branches of one of the trees next to the house. I said, "You have no right to do that without my permission; you should have asked." I instantly realized how silly this accusation sounded, and I quickly opened the front door and went back into the house.

Back upstairs, at the bathroom window this time, I was able to get a closer look at her. She was unlike anything I've ever seen. Her arms were long and unbelievably thin, and she had some sort of fawn-colored soft leather flight cap on, of the type that pilots used to wear in the old-fashioned open cockpits of early planes. She was also wearing goggles from the same era, although the lenses were shaped to fit her large, slanted eyes. I can't recall that she had a mouth, or much of a nose. She had soft-looking gloves on, and her jumpsuit was closed down the front with some sort of metal fasteners. She looked like she was engaged in filming and aimed a black video-type gadget directly at me. I immediately jumped into the shower and jerked the curtain shut as fast as I could, whereupon my husband walked in.

I said, "Did you see her?" and he said no, so determined to learn more, I left the bathroom and went out of the house, across the front yard, and into the rundown paddock area of the property. There I saw the most incredible being that I have ever seen. It was almost inde-scribable—a silver, crystal, moving mass of energy and light with the exact same striped band of jewelry that I described before on it, perhaps where a neck would be. I stood three feet away from it, awestruck.

The children and I are a little bit vague about what happened during the rest of the day. We remember that at about 4:00 p.m. two of our friends arrived, and I told them to come and see the people in the trees. I insisted that they come upstairs with me and look out the windows, but we saw nothing.

The next morning, as we headed for the beach, we noticed that the birds were back in the trees again. There had been none there the previous day. My daughters and their girlfriend and my husband and I all talked about our adventure while at the beach. Jini had seen the man with the mustache, as well as some of the other beings. My daughters Dana and Ruth verified their height; Jini showed me with her hand how tall they were (about five feet). My husband took the stance of denial, postulating that we'd all somehow had similar hallucinations. Since then, he's acknowledged their presence but is reluctant to discuss it.

I got very ill after that visit. The following week I lost thirteen pounds. I needed two liters of intravenous fluids the following Friday. On Saturday I was better, after a week of sore throats, fevers, restless nights, and nauseous days. My littlest one has ground her teeth down and pulls the covers entirely over her head every night, but we're more calm about it now than we used to be.

ANALYSIS

It took me many years to understand that this seemingly arbitrary group of strange experiences is actually well organized and has a very definite aim. As we shall see, it moves toward that aim in careful steps, starting with something completely innocuous and ending with an exposure to a spectacular apparition that, bizarrely, might be human.

I have speculated previously that these events might be more common than we realize. Missing time is, after all, a frequent part of the ones we do remember. Judging from Bruce Lee's experience and the event in Queens, people can physically witness these events and not even notice, simply because they are too strange to register.

On the first reading years ago, I did not see what in this letter is clear to me now. What I see now is a carefully organized journey to a powerful final event, and one that offers great promise for the human future, even prophesying a complete change in the nature of man. It is, perhaps, a prediction about what we will become after the culture we live in now has fallen.

The letter describes a journey. The witness is led on a carefully graduated path of encounters, each one stranger than the last.

The ancient Greek story of Ariadne leading Theseus through the labyrinth of the Minotaur works somewhat like this and can be used to reveal the hidden meaning of the contact and the promise of freedom that it represents.

Ariadne led Theseus out of the Minotaur's labyrinth and landed with him on the island of Naxos. There, he left her behind and traveled on to Athens. She became the wife of Dionysus, god of joy. Her name means "most holy." In our culture, holiness has become abstract. We might remember that it emerges out of old words that mean "whole" or "intact." The unviolated. That which has not fallen, by which was meant, in earliest times, not only not fallen from divine grace but also from understanding.

We can interpret this darkness as the material culture that was invented in the northern hemisphere, and the Minotaur's labyrinth as all the violence and fear and desperation that it produces. On offer here, then, is a very different worldview, for what this letter records is a path out of the labyrinth.

Let's see if we can follow the thread. First, though, let's identify the participants. We'll make them characters in a little play that is the experience itself. The presence, or visitors, we will call Ariadne. The family involved in the contact will be the Theseuses.

The first event is just very slightly unusual: as Mrs. Theseus is washing up after dinner, she notices the headlights of a car in the driveway. As the lights go away, she assumes it's someone turning around and doesn't investigate. What has happened, in effect, is that the thread that Mrs. Theseus is to follow has been gently placed in her hand.

The second event is more focused than car lights in a driveway: The next morning, now in broad daylight, comes the appearance of a physical entity. After breakfast, Mrs. Theseus is again at the kitchen sink when she notices a woman wearing a red windbreaker and white pants enter their stable. Mrs. Theseus understands jackets. She understands pants. She sees another human being. She sees what she thinks is a stick. It may have been nothing but that, but I might note that there are a number of appendages described in the story. Like each experience, each appendage is stranger than the last. But why? What can it mean?

What can be said with assurance is that this encounter is being created by a very good mind, but one that would appear to come from a different cultural background. In the culture of the people who are doing this, the connection between the increasing complexity of the encounters and the increasing strangeness of the appendages would quite probably be obvious.

This may seem like a small thing, but as all communication is built out of mutually understood details—language, logic, assumptions—those details are particularly important when mutual understanding is limited or nonexistent. They must be identified clearly and their meaning understood as well as possible, or the communication is never going to succeed in generating a shared meaning.

Mrs. Theseus will have no trouble remembering these first two events because her brain can still draw on previously verified knowledge to construct a coherent perception out of what her optical anatomy is delivering to it: first, an ordinary car turned around in the driveway; now an ordinary-looking woman has entered her barn.

When something is being perceived, the brain spends much more time searching through its memory banks to find previous examples that match the perceptions than it does transforming into accessible imagery what the optic nerve is delivering. The brain depends on previous experience to understand current input, which is one of the core reasons that contact is so very hard to remember clearly. When current input can't be compared to anything in the memory banks, the brain reacts very unpredictably. Such events do not persist in memory long and often leave a residue of anxiety that has no apparent cause.

It would appear that the presence that is managing contact understands this, and we can think of this understanding of human brain function as the thread that Ariadne has placed in Mrs. Theseus's hand.

The extended Theseus family—all of us—are preparing to enter both the mystery of contact and our own darker inner mystery, the

Minotaur's labyrinth itself. When we finally confront that monster, we will find that he has another name, which is us.

The stranger in the barn needs to be investigated, but as she doesn't appear to be threatening, Mrs. Theseus, who is busy, calls on her daughter to go down and look around. But there's nobody there. Not surprising. Meeting somebody in the barn wasn't our guide's point. What was important was the acquisition of a second witness. As events become stranger and stranger, a corroborating witness is going to be essential. Without it, the witness will soon forget everything that is about to happen. Our ET Ariadne clearly understands this.

She can now draw us a little further toward the freedom that lies beyond the labyrinth of our dying world and the fears that shadow our lives.

Mrs. Theseus comes to the third turning in the labyrinth: confrontation with something that is truly impossible. She sees a small figure on her pump house—still human but noticeably strange.

Moving the strangeness level a bit higher, the little man jumps off the pump house. But it's eight feet high. And yet he survives an impossible fall and now goes further by bouncing off as if gravity didn't apply to him as much as it does to other people. (This is the same bouncing step that was described by the Queens witness when discussing the movements of a similar small individual.) Our correspondent is now engaged with the first level of extreme strangeness. She is beyond the border of normal human experience.

Will the Minotaur of fear of the unknown now roar, or will her fears remain quiescent?

As the impossible man demonstrates vulnerability by running off toward a stand of trees, she remains calm. Our figurative Ariadne, by causing the first impossible act to be carried out by this nonthreatening form, makes sure that Mrs. Theseus won't drop the thread. She watches, but he doesn't reappear. So she decides that the most reasonable thing to do is to continue with her normal activities. She goes to the grocery store.

Just as well. Ariadne is also a weaver, remember, and has some important weaving to do just now.

While Mrs. Theseus is at the store, her fourth turning of the labyrinth is prepared for her. Mr. Theseus and the kids notice what appear to them to be people climbing around in trees near the house. When she returns, Mr. Theseus reports this to her. He further says that he and the children have been calling to them to come down. A high strangeness event has been rendered unthreatening by the presence of husband and children and their calm response. Nobody has gotten a gun, called the police, or anything like that. They simply want to engage with the strangers.

Once again, Mrs. Theseus isn't frightened into dropping the thread. That is not to say that there's no stress involved. As we shall see, there is great stress involved. It's just that our skillful Ariadne is preventing Mrs. Theseus from feeling it just now, and therefore forgetting the entire episode or going into denial about it. The Minotaur of fear still sleeps, and the multiple-witness corroboration means that the brain has a means of cataloging the incident. Others see the beings, so whatever they are, the brain concludes, they must be there. Mrs. Theseus will remember.

But does this also mean that aliens live in trees? I don't know and it doesn't matter. What we can conclude is, whoever this is, there is certainly one clear message: as we don't go up in trees and they do, they live, at least to some degree, as we do not.

With all these witnesses supporting one another, Ariadne can now safely raise the strangeness level higher. We move to the fifth turning in the labyrinth.

Mrs. Theseus now also looks up into the tree and sees not just people but what she describes as "a platform" that has been constructed among the branches.

But what is this? It's not a treehouse, but it clearly doesn't appear strange enough to be described in any extraordinary way. In fact, its ordinariness grounds the whole experience even as its presence in the wrong place advances the strangeness.

As ordinary as it is, this discovery is so odd that it could have been frightening. It could even conceivably have caused Mrs. Theseus to finally panic, that is to say, for the Minotaur within her to roar and cause her to drop the thread.

But that is not what happened. Instead, she made a crucial decision—one that we are all in the process of making right now. With her daughter beside her, she chooses to follow her curiosity rather than her fear. They thus make the decision to ascend the stairs—that is to say, to climb Jacob's ladder.

A new world begins to open before them.

As the tree is only fifteen or twenty feet from the house, they can see what's happening clearly, and what they see is astonishing: two people are there, one wearing a bizarre antenna and the other a magnificent—and magnificently strange—necklace.

The appearance of this appendage is an absolutely crucial moment in this story, for it prefigures the last and most important event: a vision of what human beings will be like when we have at last escaped from the labyrinth of the Minotaur, and perhaps what we already are like—the grand truth of us—with which we have lost contact.

The journey will now continue into perceptions for which the brains of the Theseuses—as will be true of all of us—will have few points of reference to draw on.

Having made the decision to ascend, Mrs. Theseus moves toward the sixth turning in the labyrinth. She now sees something that is completely outside of her experience—but it isn't there by itself. Instead, it's attached to the head of one of the people in the tree, but also somebody she's seen before in a "normal" state.

It should not be forgotten that the antenna is attached to a human being and the necklace is being worn by one. What this means is clear enough: these strange and wonderful things are in some way connected to us. Later, we will see how.

We have now arrived at the all-important seventh turning in the labyrinth. And is that not light we see ahead—faint but there? Could we be at last about to escape the Minotaur, who has ruled our lives essentially forever? Not quite, for that isn't the exit. The admission of contact is the beginning of the journey out of the labyrinth we live in now. And yet, that admission is not—must not—be a simple thing. We have spent so much time denying the reality of the presence that we are not presently prepared, as the rest of what happened to the Theseuses will make clear.

Mrs. Theseus next spots an extremely thin woman with huge black eyes and wearing a green jumpsuit climbing in another nearby tree.

This new being cannot be seen as one of us. We have now moved from unexpected car lights through a woman in a windbreaker to a gravity-defying dwarf to humans with odd appendages climbing around in trees to the appearance of somebody who is not of our race at all.

Does it also suggest that we are at the point, in the wider world, of similar contact? We can only wait, work to continue to prepare ourselves at every level, and hope that, if that thread is put into our hands, we don't drop it as we have done before, a subject to which I will return.

Make no mistake, though, contact with beings like this is not the end of our journey. We search the skies looking for aliens. This is not the goal, though. The entities people see—from the alien to the ghostly, the bedlam-strange and even those who are seemingly human—they're Ariadne to our Theseus, and our destiny is the same as his, to leave them behind.

Mrs. Theseus tells the strange woman that she has no right to be there. When, during the *Communion* experience in December of 1985, I found myself engaged with a similar individual, I said, also, "You have no right." She replied, "We do have a right." But why? There are so many possibilities, but in the end, there can be only a few that are real: they may have been given the right by somebody perceived to be in control, perhaps government or even religious leaders; they may think that those who have encounters gave it to them personally, and given that so much of the experience unfolds in amnesia, perhaps we did; it could be that they need something from us for their own survival, or ours, or both.

In any case, they are here and they are doing as they wish, but also agree that a right is necessary or the answer would have been silence or perhaps, simply, "It doesn't matter."

Mrs. Theseus now ascends once again to get a better look at the creature. This is exactly what so many close encounter witnesses end up doing—what I did, so many years ago, when I elected to walk out into the woods at night to reengage with the people who had abducted me. I was too curious to hide. As, in fact, more and more of us human critters are.

Her reward is to get a detailed sighting of somebody with long arms as narrow as sticks and wearing a light tan leather flight cap and goggles molded to fit her big, slanted eyes. She wears gloves, and her jumpsuit is closed with metal fasteners. That is to say, she may look very odd indeed, but what is being demonstrated to the observer is that, along with the differences in appearance, there are similar physical needs—thus the recognizable clothing. She says with her gear that she is a pilot or some sort of flyer.

Now an experiment is conducted. The entity turns and points what looks to the witness like some type of video device at her. Her reaction is to jump back from the window. Just as a person unschooled in photography might be uneasy about having their picture taken, our witness senses some sort of attack here. But is her curiosity stronger? Will she drop the thread?

Ariadne waits.

And she goes for it. She wants more. She's not alone: I have heard a thousand witnesses say in one breath how badly they were treated and in the next how much they wanted to learn more. In fact, that's me, too.

And now, the beginning of a new octave, the eighth turning in the labyrinth. Mrs. Theseus leaves the protection of the human world by going outside despite the fact that she has seen an alien there.

She then sees beyond the body and beyond life as we know it, into another, shining life that appears in the form of a crystal mass of what looks like silver light but is wearing the same elaborate necklace that one of the two people in the tree wore. Is this, then, the person who wore the necklace, but now appearing in a form truer to its own reality—and ours? We must not forget that the necklace was worn by a human being, and the fact that the two people wearing the strange objects were from different parts of the world means that this is about all of humankind, an indication of the actual and completely extraordinary journey of total transformation that is on offer here.

There is also something else about this remarkable image, which is its complexity. It is difficult for the brain to generate novel complex images. In fact, they do not often appear spontaneously outside of psychedelic experiences and, more rarely, dreams, but this family group was not on psychedelics and the witness was awake when she saw this imagery. Was it a hallucination or in some way part of objective reality? We can only preserve the question.

She walks up to it. Stands a few feet away. It gradually floats off. The encounter that started with the car lights has concluded with a crystalline entity that in no way resembles a human being or, for that matter, any sort of creature, as we understand that term. Thus Mrs. Theseus has been taken through seven levels of contact and been exposed to the entirely different reality—incredibly beautiful—that awaits beyond.

The family compares notes. All the children had seen one thing or another. The husband either doesn't recall anything or is unwilling to discuss the subject.

Please note the difference between what happened to Mrs. and to Mr. Theseus. She was handed the thread of ever stranger experiences, one after another. Mr. Theseus had only a few glimpses. She was provided with a carefully designed experiential foundation that would support the retention of ever stranger memories. He was not.

Later, while on an outing, the family discusses what they have seen. The children recall observing the strange people; at this point, Mr. Theseus does, too, but theorizes that it was a shared hallucination. We all live with this level of denial, in our own minds and in our culture. I will not argue against it. Those who live in it need to, or that's not where their minds would be. For them, the Minotaur is not asleep. It is roaring threats and warnings from the depths of their labyrinth. Fear generates anger and it generates stress, and that is why we deny this reality, ignore it, probably shoot at it, and generally confuse ourselves trying to fit it into our established beliefs about the way the world works.

Despite all the efforts that were made to keep Mrs. Theseus from burying the memory due to a total lack of precedent experience in her life, or panicking over the strangeness of what she was observing, a week later she is having a severe stress reaction. She feels so bad that she goes to hospital, where it is found that she is seriously dehy-drated, so much so that she's put on intravenous fluids. Ultimately, she loses over ten pounds.

Such a reaction could be due to various types of radiation expo-sure, but as the family was fine when I met them at least two years after the letter was written, I doubt that this was the cause. Stress, also, can generate these symptoms. A further indication that it was stress is Mrs. Theseus's report that her youngest child also began to grind her teeth at night.

This is all part of the message, I think: we are not in for an easy time. Admitting the new into our understanding of the world, let alone our interior universe, is an extremely difficult and stressful task. It cracks the foundation of what we know and threatens to turn the solid footing of our understood world into the shifting sand of the unknown.

What we have observed here appears to have been an experiment in contact. Was it, really?

It seems so. It may be so. And if so, then we can expect sooner or later to see figures that do not appear to us to be human. When we do, though, it will be important to try to forget the human-alien dichotomy. There is intelligence in this universe, and we are all part of it. One humanity, then. Many different races. All seeking the same outcomes that we do but traveling down different paths.

Careful analysis not only of the Communion Letters archive, but of the whole enormous literature of contact—this huge deposit of improbable story—will enable us to familiarize ourselves with that logic ... to make it the basis for a grammar of communion with the mind behind it.

Looking at the story of Ariadne and Theseus, we can see not only our own future in contact and beyond but also a possible motive of our visitors. Ariadne marries Dionysus—that is to say, she embraces joy and becomes holy for it.

The only words the visitors ever said to me in clear spoken English have been two: "have joy." And for all the darkness and the danger, and despite all the confusion that it brings, ultimately this whole experience is about that holy thing.

Our visitors will experience it when we finally leave them behind in this reality, just as Theseus left Ariadne behind on Naxos and set out on his own. They seek for us to leave them behind and take the journey of Theseus to Athens, the city of the philosophers and their legendary stone of truth, called gold because it is eternal.

The whole vast experience of sightings, disclosures, revelations, discoveries, and contact is Ariadne extending her thread to all of us.

Shall we take it? Do we attempt to leave the labyrinth of our history and our lives that, for all its horrors, is also the only home we have ever known or can imagine?

She will linger here for a time, but my sense of it is that this does not mean forever. There is no guarantee that we will take the thread. The vast majority of us don't even know it is being offered. Those of us who do are divided in our views. Is this dangerous? Is it valuable? Is it even real, or are our visitors really Sancho Panza to our Don Quixote?

There is only one way to find out: we must take the thread.

CHAPTER 7
ENCOUNTER: A NEW YOU

At first this extraordinary story seems like nothing more than a fairly typical description of a strange event and a dream that was connected with it. But the event was not witnessed by one person in isolation, and multiple witnesses always gives high strangeness stories more credence. And, for reasons that we shall see, the dream under discussion here cannot have been anything ordinary.

For such a big story, it is deceptively compressed, just a few hundred words, so when we analyze it, we'll divide it into its separate elements. But for now, let's read the few words as they were written.

THE LETTER: A LIGHT IN THE WINDOW

I will begin by saying that I was between ten and eleven years old in 1953 and lived in a rural area. My sisters and I all slept in the same room. One night my mother came hurrying into the bedroom to wake us up. She told us to look out the window. We did, and there was a large, hot, glowing globe in the sky. It floated any way it wanted to go. My mother was a little scared and told us to be quiet, but as I remember it now, it was already very, very quiet outside, like a vacuum. I was watching this globe float around when I suddenly became very drowsy. Here is where my conscious memory ends, until lately, when I started reading *Communion*. The "buried" visit now emerges:

I am eleven years old; I can see "him" floating outside my bedroom window. He is only three to four feet tall. He has a skinny gray body, a large head, large slanted eyes, a line mouth, no nose, ears, or hair. I feel eyes that can "film" everything. I heard in my head, "You have been chosen. We will not harm you." Then there was blackness. Next, I am floating through our living room upright, about six inches off the floor. Beings are floating with me. As we float past my mother's room door, I look in her bedroom and see between three and six beings that are glowing from their bodies with a pure white light. They are clustered around my stepdad. He had been crippled since he was five years old. The beings are very interested in his legs. They are holding one of his legs in their hands. I am thinking to myself at seeing this, "They can heal Pop's legs!" They did not, of course, but I believed they could. Then there was blackness again.

Next, I am sitting up on a "doctor's table" with my legs hanging over the side. I feel relaxed and curious and excited. "My friend," as I believe this being was, is at my feet, scraping the bottoms of them. That tickled me, so I pulled my foot back, and he laughed with his eyes and in my mind. They scraped skin off of my arms and feet.

They took a little hair off my head and cut my nails. I asked questions in my mind, but before I could verbalize them, they answered back very softly but directly, "We are making a new you." I asked him, "Are you like angels?" and he replied, "Not as you have been taught." My friend said it was time for me to go, and I would forget their visit. Extreme sadness, longing, and sorrow passed through me, and I cried real tears and begged them "not to forget me" and "Why did I have to forget them?" His answer was "Because there are those who will tamper with your mind." Then there was blackness.

I think added to all this was a flash memory of a big screen and seeing I know not what! It was something about a promise of returning to see me again, and a half-remembered conversation about a "bad time on Earth." Then I was floating back into my living room and there, lined up like zombies, was my whole family! I thought to myself, why do they all look like that? Then there was blackness a final time.

Back when I started remembering the visit, I asked my sister if she remembered anything strange about our farmhouse. She acted as if I had opened a long-forgotten dream. I didn't tell her anything about what I was remembering on my own, but the memory made mine even stronger and very, very real. She saw the globe; she saw the face in the bedroom window. I made her describe the face, and it matched the one I saw perfectly. She remembers my mother telling her to get away from the window "or they will see you." Where was I when mother said that, since we were all in the same room? Was I gone, already taken? I don't know. I do know that these visitors are real, and that they are here. I have strange thoughts about "cocoon" type human bodies in a "white mist," who will wake up when it's time.

I have felt love, compassion, protection, somewhere from these beings. I see "my friend" with his arms around my shoulders, when I cried about going home. In this there was a pure, joyful, and wonderful feeling of being chosen (abducted). There is also a raw, terrible fear that if they do come back, I would simply go insane or have a cardiac arrest; they have probably been in and out of my life like threads on a weaving loom.

I had a dream not long ago about the farm: I dreamed the "government men" came to the farm and made me mad and took my souvenirs that the "alien" gave me. They had men in white suits all over our farm, and the "lady doctors" wanted to give all of us shots; she said it was to "feed us." I politely told her I wasn't hungry.

My mother sent me a letter one time before she died about a "vision" she had of "Earth's demise." It was total carnage, she said, but we would survive it. In her vision she asked if her children would survive; "whomever" answered "Yes."

About two years ago I spent some time at my daughter's house. It is in a wooded area. I had a dream while there: In my dream I got up and went into my grandson's room and took his hand, and we went outside in the dark, which I would never, never do. We seemed to float to the front gate, out by the road. We stopped for a moment, and all these "funny-looking children" came out of the woods to meet us. I thought they were so ugly! I "thought" to my grandson, "Don't play with those children, honey; they're too different." Anyway, we were escorted to a saucer-shaped thing at the dead-end circle of the road, and a door was opened in it with a ramp going up. The light inside was intensely bright and "my friend" was there at the door. I then woke up!

Approximately four weeks later my grandson asked me a funny question: "Mamaw, what does an alien look like?" I was flabbergasted; what did he know of aliens? I asked him to draw one on his own, and he did. It's similar to the ones I remembered.

ANALYSIS

These thousand words compress a big and revealing story into a small space. First, there is the sighting of the brightly lit object outside the window. The event is initiated by the mother, who will play a very different role in the last part of the communication. At the window, she is playing a role that is often seen in the close encounter experience, which is that of facilitator. Some people do this consciously, others do not. As we saw in the previous letter, when the senses deliver perceptions that the brain can't relate to previous experience, our ability to remember them is reduced, even to the extent that they may be forgotten completely in a very short time. Sometimes, as shown by the monkey business illusion, events might not be recorded at all. And we know as well that our visitors can manipulate human memory.

We did learn from the "Visitors in the Trees" letter that those on the other side of these events understand our memory problems, but also that it is going to take great care on their part to overcome them. I suspect that it might be easier for them to repress our memories than to enable us to come away from encounters with accurate ones. If I am correct, then this will be central to the challenge of establishing a relationship with us that communicates the same meaning to both sides.

This correspondent then notes another effect that's familiar to many close encounter witnesses: the surroundings have become extremely silent. When the visitors are nearby, animals often become motionless. Birds stop, even frogs and crickets. Is it that time itself is stopping, or is it a sort of waiting ... or are the animals aware of something we cannot detect?

Now the abduction begins: "I suddenly became very drowsy."

Her natural memory stops there, but when she later asked her sister whether she also remembered the experience, her sister responded that she saw the globe and that their mother told her to get away from the window. This illustrates a type of contradictory behavior that is characteristic of close encounter. If the mother is afraid for her children, why draw them to the window in the first place? Had she been behaving normally, she would perhaps have closed the blinds and sat watching over her kids, not woken them up and paradoxically encouraged them to look at something she didn't want them to see.

It would seem that one part of this woman is afraid for her kids, while another is playing the facilitator role.

The event happened in 1953, but it was not until the correspondent read *Communion* in 1988 that she remembered anything more. When the book's catalytic effect worked, she first recalled that she could see what she describes as "him" floating outside the bedroom window. (Her sister, when asked in 1988, also remembered this face.) She is then told that she has been chosen and that she won't be harmed.

Chosen for what, though?

The same thing, I would think, for which all of mankind has been chosen. It is not easy to define it, but it is the reason that our visitors are here. They want us to survive, but as I've suggested, altruism is not the only reason. We have been chosen for something. As we dig deeper into these letters, we will gain some insight into what this may be and, then when we examine the military reaction to contact, come to understand the instinctual basis of resistance. (I am not insisting here that we shouldn't resist. Perhaps we should. But we should first understand what is wanted from us before we make that decision.)

As the girl floats out of the house, she sees the visitors examining her crippled stepfather and comments that she thinks that they could probably cure him but don't. This is very often the case, and I have wondered how different our world would be if they did intervene. But that happens only very rarely, and there will be other instances in this story where there is an absence of intervention. The fact that it is so rare should sound a warning bell for people who expect a "landing" that will change our world and perhaps save it. Given how elusive our visitors are even in the lives of close encounter witnesses, I don't see any reason to expect the cavalry to show up like that. In fact, what is happening is that contact, still far from becoming a state of communion, is unfolding by very slow accretion. I have the sense that, until we understand them more clearly and on our own terms, they are not going to engage very completely with us. When they do, as we are seeing across the arc of the enormous story of contact, it is often a difficult and challenging experience.

There now occurs a description that would have made sense in 2000, but not in 1988 and certainly not in 1953. The girl finds herself on an examining table having skin scraped off the bottoms of her feet. They also take fingernail clippings, some hair, and scrapings from her arms.

When she feels curiosity about this, she hears in her mind, "We are making a new you," a statement that would seem to mean only one thing: they are DNA sampling in order to create another human being from her stem cells, or an outright clone.

I asked biologist Dr. Garry Nolan about generating DNA from skin scrapings. He replied, "It is not possible with any current tech to do this from dead cells. Plus, fingernails and hair do not contain DNA to any appreciable extent."

The key here is "dead cells," and the question that immediately comes to mind is, "Were all the cells collected dead?" If not, then a method called somatic cell nuclear transfer can be used to generate stem cells out of skin. The nucleus of a skin cell—the part of a cell that contains DNA—is implanted into an egg cell that has had all of its own genetic material removed. This results in an unfertilized egg cell with a skin cell nucleus. It can be made to produce embryonic stem cells that could conceivably lead to the generation of a clone. And as this was evidently being done by our visitors in 1953, it must be assumed that the ability to clone from skin cells was already a settled technology for them.

Hair is used in criminal forensics to identify traits like race, sex, and age, and if there is DNA present in the follicle, more information can be gained. Also, even if there is no DNA, the hair itself doesn't decay. Thus, if a sample of this witness was being created and it was planned to store it, inclusion of hair in the package would make sense for use as an identifying marker.

Fingernails can tell a great deal about the health status of an individual. They record the presence of certain diseases, trauma, dietary deficiencies, and the presence of poisons and other impurities in the body.

What was being done here probably did involve just what the child was told. Even as an adult in 1988, it is unlikely that she would have understood how to design a package that could be used to clone "a new you" that would include identifiers and a health profile as well. This sampling is so logical and was so little understood in 1988, let alone in 1953, one is almost compelled to think that what is being described here actually happened. But let's not take the conclusions too far. If a "clone package" was being created, by whom and for what reason remain unanswered questions. We know what the witnesses remembered, but that may or may not be what was actually there.

What has happened to the material since it was removed? We cannot know, but it probably wasn't used to create a clone that lived here on Earth. As to how often this is done, or exactly why, there is also no way to tell.

Given this story and all the stories of sexual material being removed, another reason for missing time becomes evident. If too many people remembered these sorts of things happening to them, there would be little doubt that a program involving the replication of humankind was under way. Such knowledge might shake us out of the passivity that our current ignorance, reinforced by official denial and orchestrated ridicule, ensures. Somebody sampling us so intimately would likely be concerned that there might be resistance, conceivably even violent resistance, if the truth was known.

As a person who has lost sexual material to this experience, as I have said, I am haunted by the idea that I may have children unknown to me, but the thought of new people, strange mirrors of us, existing somewhere is, frankly, even more disturbing. Where are they? What sort of lives are they living? Above all, *why* are they?

Perhaps that question is answered in the letter that the correspondent reports she received from her mother toward the end of her life. "My mother sent me a letter one time before she died about a 'vision' she had of 'Earth's demise.' It was total carnage, she said, but we would survive it. In her vision, she asked if her children would survive; 'whomever' answered 'Yes.'"

Which children, though—those we have made, or those they have?

Given that our visitors' warnings about environmental peril and nuclear war must mean that they don't want us to disappear altogether, they might well be motivated to create a genetic record of humanity. But "a new you" doesn't mean something kept in a seed bank. If we take the words literally, then the plan is to replicate people. As to where those people might be, we cannot know. If a possible extinction event here on Earth is the reason for the program, then any creatures who have emerged out of it—and there is no reason to assume that the project is confined to the human species— are likely to be somewhere else.

Now that I am so very sure that this is really happening, I look up at the stars at night with a new sort of wonder. Where is that "new you"? Where are our children, and do they even know that they have parents and families and a faraway ancestral home?

As we go deeper into close encounter, we will find that family might have a very different meaning from the one we are used to, and until we understand it better, we are not going to understand contact.

If we are being replicated, then we are wanted. To understand why we might be very much wanted, let's look at what we might do if we were a star-traveling species and found a planet like ours, straining under the pressure of a teeming population that was in danger of collapse, even extinction, that had no idea how to travel in space and had never before encountered anybody from a world other than their own.

If we found them wanting—possessed of insufficient intelligence or in some other way defective—we would probably just move on. Even if we found them wonderful, we might not do anything if the effort was too great and the likelihood of success too small. But if we found them in some way valuable, we would not move on.

Under those circumstances, perhaps our expedition would become a rescue mission. But what if they were terrified of us, hurled their spears at us when we attempted to approach them, completely misunderstood our motives, and reacted with hysterical fear when we made any attempt at contact? Worse, what if the attempts they made to understand us were based on their own incorrect or incomplete ideas about reality, and they therefore completely lost the thread of possible communication by integrating us into their folklore?

We would become trapped in a maze of what they had created out of their mistaken beliefs about us, which is where I think our visitors find themselves right now.

If this happened to us, and we couldn't overcome the troubled species' confusion, we would either become frustrated and leave their planet because helping them was too difficult, or if there were overriding ethical considerations or other aims, we might stay but pursue those aims in secret.

If so, then what might those aims be?

When you look at the question from the standpoint of what we might do if we were the visitors to a planet in crisis, the extraordinary complexity of the situation becomes apparent. If there was something about the native species that we valued, even that we needed, that adds a further layer of complexity.

In general, when contact between different human cultures has happened in our world, the more powerful have taken from the weaker, generally with little regard for the rights of the victims. I am sure that the Indigenous populations of most of the world would agree with this assessment. If we needed to exploit people who didn't have even rudimentary legal rights, such as creatures living on another planet, ethical considerations might not even come up. If our own history is any indicator, we would take from them whatever we wanted, and one of the things we might very much want would be samples of the beings themselves. We would probably at least discuss whether or not to take biological material from them, but I think that the answer would be a foregone conclusion: we'd tell ourselves that if we don't do it, they might disappear and be lost forever, and so we would sample them.

Judging from what the mother wrote in her late-life letter, a motive here is likely to be the preservation of a sample of the human species, and probably others as well. There is also an indication that it's not a random sampling: "You have been chosen."

It can be concluded that—probably because they fear our extinction and, for their own reasons, do not wish to lose us—one of the things they are doing is extracting biological material necessary to preserve a sample of us.

If they are using that biological material to create human beings somewhere else in the universe, it can only be hoped that whatever sort of lives they may be living are worthwhile.

Because of the long tradition of secrecy that conceals their presence here, the public has never had the chance offer input that might lead to meaningful public policy on this. Absent knowledge, absent policy, we are completely passive, entirely open to their activities.

As I've mentioned, in recent years, abductions have become much less widespread. Contact continues but not on the same level that it did in during the abduction days. Official secrecy is also eroding, but slowly, and thus far there has been only the most halting attempt to connect the UAP phenomenon to close encounters.

Most contacts involve a single remembered incident, or just a few incidents, as was the case in all of the accounts we have so far examined. But this is not always the case, and repeat contact can be harrowing if it is unwanted. But for those witnesses who turn toward the visitors and attempt to relate to them, there is often a long-developing relationship that goes from terror to acceptance to eventual companionship, but not of a kind that fits normal human experience.

What is it like to have the visitors in your life? What does that phrase actually mean to them and, therefore, to the people who come into a state of frequent interaction with them?

Let's have a look at just such a life experience.

CHAPTER 8
ENCOUNTER: ME WITHIN THEE

At some point in our lives, all of us touch, in one way or another, the greater living presence that surrounds us. We may perceive it simply as the grandeur of the sky on some lost childhood night, barely remembered, if at all, or it can be an intimation far larger, stirring mind and heart and soul and changing everything forever.

That's what happened here.

THE LETTER: THE PRESENCE

I've only told one other person, my husband, about the uneasiness and fear I've encountered time and time again since the age seven or eight or possibly earlier. I can't be certain. I'm frightened of putting my thoughts about all of this on paper. I've always felt "monitored" in some way. The words "tagged" and "tracked" have been a vivid memory ever since I can remember. Unless someone has walked in my shoes, they can't possibly even come close to being able to understand such events.

You mentioned a smell like cheese. I've also noted this with one exception: It's more like a "yeasty" odor like rising bread dough, not overtly offensive, but certainly not pleasing. You also mentioned the "voice" coming out as a "deep bass sound."

To me, it was in spurts, like a computerized, synthesized version of language. Their mouths remained closed, and their language came from somewhere within, or on, them. It was monotone, nonexpressive, and unnatural sounding to me.

One very eerie detail you wrote about was the appearance of a wolf, and his howling. I got a gut-wrenching feeling in the pit of my stomach about that. For years on a nightly basis, I had recurring nightmares of a huge, glowing, red-eyed wolf, the size of the one in

"Little Red Riding Hood." These "dreams" were always the same, to start with, and also I knew I hadn't been asleep when they occurred. I was deathly afraid of going to sleep at night, and often I'd find myself sitting wide-eyed in bed with the bedclothes disrupted, soaking wet from sweat and with my heart leaping through my nightgown. I was too scared or too numb to scream, no matter how hard I tried.

Until the past eight years or so, I've always sensed something coming up from behind me. I'd turn quickly and gasp, as if someone had brushed my shoulder or blown air onto my neck. I can also remember many episodic occurrences, as currently as three years ago. I'd be in bed and very much aware of my surroundings: how the pillows were arranged, my robe lying in a certain way on the chair, our dog asleep on the edge of the bed. (No, he didn't react any more than your animals did, which led me to believe I must have been hallucinating since animals would certainly have been aware if they observed someone!) I'd feel uneasy, as if I needed to turn over on my other side, as if somehow that would make it go away, this same panicky feeling that I'd sensed as a child with the elf visits. I'd then hear our clock radio playing on the bedside table and logically know that no one had turned it on; my husband had left for work and it didn't just go on by itself. I'd hear music, interrupted by a mechanical type of voice, but I could never remember what it said. I'd feel the mattress depress and the springs pressing down, and I knew someone had sat down beside me. But I was paralyzed and couldn't utter a sound, swallow, or move in any way. My eyes were open, though I was always in the opposite direction from where "the presence" remained. It would be there about ten minutes, it seemed. I'd pray, from my Catholic upbringing, that God would spare me this and protect me. Like you, I often also prayed to Mary. I'd slightly relax, and then boom! I'd somehow jerk hard and be back in control. No radio would be on, the dog would be sound asleep, and it was utterly quiet. It would be much later; I lost two to three hours each time. I'd have a headache and dizziness and would feel "flu like." I felt hazy and as if I was moving in slow motion. When I did things, I'd stare blankly a lot until I'd become aware of it and tell myself to stop.

I too went through disturbing episodes of nasal bleeding. In my case, they became projectile and frightening. I associated sleep with nosebleeds.

As a very young child in the '50s, I can remember a cartoon on "Lunchtime Little Theatre," a TV show. It was called, "Love in an Airship." I'd become rigid with fear and would run out of the room when I saw it, not knowing why. There were three characters: a woman, a man, and one that horrified me whom I referred to as the "Big Beard Man," They went up into the sky in a helium balloon, and I remember nothing else about it. I'd like the chance to view this again to see if I'd react in the same way.

You mentioned being inquisitive and asking many questions in school. I shared that particular trait and would often drive my teachers crazy in a "verbal checkers" sort of exchange/match. At around six, I developed an intense curiosity about the medical field and desired to be an anesthesiologist. My parents and grandparents could never understand why I'd choose that specialty. No one had undergone any surgery. I certainly hadn't even been given Novocain at that time, and no one we'd met were doctors, except our family doctor. I remember being torn between that and the idea of becoming a nun. I was devoted to the religious part of my life and attended weekly catechism classes, made my communion and confirmation, etc. I remained devoted until my second year of high school, at age fifteen. Then my interest gradually waned. I felt sadness about that, but I'd lost my faith in the nuns and priests as examples. I had an endlessly questioning mind, filled to the brim with what they considered to be bizarre questions, and I thirsted for answers. I'd try to pry answers out of them, as if they kept secret and hidden truths from us. I was usually told to "believe and all would be well." I couldn't accept that, and I stopped wearing my scapular that year. When my daughter was born, I didn't have her baptized or take her to church because I wanted her to able to choose for herself. I have, however, remained close to God in my head and my heart. But I don't share the universal beliefs about this or about creation or about what I consider to be "symbolic" stories from the

Bible. I have yet to learn of a religion that truly shares my own beliefs.

I felt "different" from other children and had difficulty in forming relationships with them. I remember always drawing as a kind of a tension reliever; even as an adult, I occasionally do so. The pictures I seemed to focus on were of a group of people: One woman carried a small child in her arms. The child was crying and pointing at an object in the sky, a huge, illuminated roundish thing that at that time I viewed as a "planet with ringed circles rounding it." Later I grew to believe it was a large craft.

I've awakened with unexplained bruises, cuts, specks of blood, etc., many times. Recently I had a V-shaped skin removal from my inner nailbeds of my fingers on my right hand. This has occurred many times. My husband is fully aware of this. They hurt and are deep and heal slowly. I also have a specific set of symptoms at the same time: lethargic and "flu like," feverish chills, mild nausea, swollen eyes and body pain, bruises and odd rash-like areas that itch intensely, all over. This lasts several days to a week or so. I get that odor/scent, which vividly surrounds me. It's that yeasty, burnt, methane-like gas stench, and it makes me ill. It's almost mold like, in a way.

I've also had several EEGs done. One, done about eleven years ago, showed "increased uptake in the left temporal lobe, indicative of seizure." At other times, totally normal readings were given. Your "temporal lobe invasion" theory makes perfect sense to me.

I feel this may cause a short-term physical abnormality to be present, as on my EEG reading. How can all these exact similarities be utter coincidence?!

I have episodes of having had an abundance of "electricity" in my body. I've had hairdryers, clocks, watches, TVs, etc. malfunction or break during these times. My husband can detect these episodes, at times, when I'm unaware of them. There's a "humming" feeling, a "buzzing" that stems from within my body and is detectable as [a] sort of force field around me. If he puts his hand two to three inches away from my skin, the hairs on my body stand on end. I sense the humming, and he feels extreme static discharge. We've mentioned this to many doctors and have never been able to get an answer.

Some events include my grandmother, brother, and husband. I'm thirty-nine and look back on these events with the knowledge that they dealt with something outside of our world, possibly paranormal phenomenon, or hallucinatory experiences or mental abnormalities. But if that's true, why do seemingly normal people report such detailed and similar experiences? How many of us have dismissed these patterns as "daydreaming" or "imagination"? There is no doubt in my mind that I've experienced visits, as you described in your book. That was the reason my husband bought it for me because I felt disturbed and isolated about this and needed to know that someone else had experienced them too. What is happening?!

During one of these episodes, I recalled the words, "It is the me within thee." Could that mean that we are a part of them, that they are a part of us? Are we one and the same? I'm quite sincere, and I believe within my heart and soul the validity of my feelings.

ANALYSIS

I could easily have chosen a letter to illustrate repeat visits that did not also involve temporal lobe epilepsy. In fact, this is the only one that I am aware of receiving that does mention both things. The reason I chose it is both for its content and as a reminder that we must keep open the questions that these stories raise.

The correspondent's experience lies on the shadow line between seizure-related hallucinatory phenomena and—well—something else. Characteristic of temporal lobe epilepsy, she experiences strong odors during her experiences. She finds herself unable to move, and when she does, the effects disappear. But her story is too complex to be identified entirely as hallucinatory material of a kind that is understood.

Throughout her childhood, she sees elf-like figures and is menaced by a huge wolf with red eyes. She understands these as recurring dreams, but the fact that she dreamed about the wolf "for years on a nightly basis" suggests that hers was an unusual dream life. The fear was extreme. She'd find herself "sitting wide-eyed in bed with the bedclothes disrupted, soaking wet from sweat and with my heart leaping."

In her adult life, she has experienced episodes of what seem like a haunting. She would be alone in bed, her husband off at work, when she'd hear the springs creak and feel a weight come down onto the bed beside her. The bedside radio would turn itself on. She would know that somebody was there but be unable to turn over so she could look at them. When she regained body movement, she'd find that the radio wasn't on and an improbable amount of time, two to three hours, had passed. She experienced nosebleeds, often violent.

At least some of this could be symptomatic of a seizure-inducing issue in the brain. But there's more. She often awakened with unexplained bruises, cuts and blood on her sheets. She would find a V-shaped area of skin removed from beneath a fingernail on her right hand. Electrical appliances such as hairdryers, clocks, watches, televisions and so forth malfunctioned during her electric episodes, when she felt that her body had acquired an electric field. Her husband perceived this state as "a humming" and found that if he put his hand a few inches away from her body, her body hairs would stand up. He felt, at that point, "an extreme static discharge."

If what this individual is describing is a type of seizure, it has an electromagnetic component and is yet to be described and diagnosed. How it works I have no idea, but I do know that she is not alone in reporting this.

Upon hearing the words, "It is the me within thee," she asks the questions, "Could that mean that we are a part of them, that they are a part of us? Are we one and the same?"

Over the years, a general assumption has been adopted by western culture that "the alien" is separate from "the human." "The grays" are not us. And yet, when you are face to face with them, as I have been, that isn't necessarily how it feels.

I am reminded once again of Bruce Lee's story. I always assumed either that the two "aliens" were somehow preventing people from seeing them or that they were so impossible that people's brains just filtered them out. But this story suggests a third possibility: What if they did appear as people when they walked down the street? What if we are not alone within ourselves, and "the me within thee" is a statement of fact, so when we encounter our visitors, we are really encountering another version of ourselves? It's a provocative question, and although there is at present no way to take it further, I can suggest it is a much more serious and interesting one than it may first appear.

Metamorphic species are not uncommon on planet Earth. Tadpoles go through a remarkable series of changes as they grow into frogs. In effect, they are hatched from their mother's eggs while still fetuses, and mature into an entirely new form, tadpoles, while outside of her body. Then they change again, becoming frogs. The whole journey from fetus to mature individual happens in the pond. By contrast, a mammal will grow into an immature form in the womb then continue to maturity outside of it, but without completely changing form. A butterfly starts out as a caterpillar, a creature so radically different that it is almost impossible to imagine that its transformation within the cocoon doesn't have some bizarre magic in it. (It doesn't, of course, only the very real magic of nature.)

What if we, also, are like that? What if "me within thee" reflects the existence of another human form, perhaps not a physical form but one that exists in some less tangible way, yet is still very much a part of the human makeup?

When the piles of letters began to overwhelm even Anne, she hired a secretary, Lorie Barnes, whom she had found among our correspondents and who happened to live down the street from us in Greenwich Village. In the letter Lorie sent us about her experiences, which I have discussed in *A New World,* she says that she found herself, when a young woman and pregnant with her first child, staring in horror at a line of dark blue "troll-like" figures who had appeared beside her bed at eleven o'clock at night. As her husband was working, she was alone and reacted with absolute terror.

The leader of the group reassured her, saying "we aren't here for you, we're interested in the girl child you're carrying." (It was a girl, now an adult, and I have interviewed her on Dreamland. She is a lovely and successful woman, and there is no obvious indication why "aliens" would have been interested in her before she was born. But if they were, in some way, her forebears, then the interest would be explained.)

But are we dealing with aliens or "me within thee?" When Lorie recoiled at the leader's touch, he asked her, "Why do you fear us?" She replied, "Because you're so ugly." His response was to lay his gloved hand gently on her wrist and say, "One day, my dear, you will look just like us."

When our correspondent heard that voice saying, "It is the me within thee," could she have been hearing from her own inner self? The deeper we go into the enigma of the close encounter experience, the more different ways we are likely to meet ourselves. To at least some degree, we probably are the alien, insofar as it is a mystery within us and of us.

If we do exist in different forms, there is no reason to assume that our other forms would be bound by the same physical laws that we are and possess the same knowledge and technology. More likely they wouldn't. So when we regard the star-faring "alien," are we really looking at a mature form of humankind, long since master of space and possibly even inhabiting other planets? Could the reason that "a new you" was being created out of our previous correspondent not be because an alien species was bent on preserving humanity but because the mature form of us needs to make certain that we, the foundational form of the species, will continue to grow and breed?

Wild speculation? Perhaps. But if we are going to understand this extraordinary enigma, we must step beyond the borders of our assumptions whenever we can.

To gain some real insight into who "they" are, it is as necessary, I think, to blur some lines as it is to clarify others. The line between "us" and "them" needs to be blurred, but carefully. In order to do that, certain possibilities must be entertained, chief among them the most fantastic of all, which is that we and they might not be as separate as we appear and that other forms of human beings may be participants in this life and world with us.

Given the heedless way we consume, it seems appropriate to compare us to the caterpillar phase of a multiform species. Caterpillars eat so voraciously because they need tremendous energy to grow their chrysalis and transform inside while eating nothing. They will destroy plants and leave them wasted in order to achieve a goal that that they cannot imagine but that is buried deeply within them.

I have wondered if that might not be why we, also, are insatiable consumers and then, more deeply, if the entities we are encountering have something to do with a transformative process that we ourselves are pursuing, the goal of which we cannot, in our current biological state, understand.

One can only wonder what a caterpillar might think of a butterfly fluttering past on a summer afternoon. Probably not "Next summer that will be me!" The gulf is too great, the imagination too small.

And how would the caterpillar appear to the butterfly? Not, surely, as something intimately connected to itself—in fact, completely dependent upon itself for its very existence. And if a caterpillar has any awareness at all, might it not be haunted by the shadow of the butterfly dancing above? Are those great, dark eyes, then, like the shadow of the butterfly, an indicator of our own hidden truth? If so, then the cloning project, if it exists, is, like the warnings about climate and nuclear war and technological dependence, part of an effort by this other level of humankind to save not only us but also itself.

These have to remain speculations, of course. But at this stage of knowledge, writing about this subject in terms of certainties must always trigger the sharpshooter fallacy. A person draws a target on the side of a barn then fires randomly at the barn, accidentally hitting the target. He then claims to be a sharpshooter. What we cannot do is focus on single points in the huge close encounter dataset and expect that the conclusions we draw from them must be final.

I am as haunted by the idea that our visitors might have their organic history rooted in another planet as I am that they might be from here.

Could "me within thee" be the butterfly lurking within the busy

caterpillar, only sensed fleetingly during the lush days of the caterpillar's gluttonous midsummer, but more often—and more desperately
—as the bells of autumn begin to toll?

CHAPTER 9
ENCOUNTER: LET US BEGIN

This next letter also involves an entire family and an ongoing contact situation, but there is no suggestion here of a causative factor like temporal lobe epilepsy. I wouldn't claim that, therefore, seizure is not a possibility here also, but only that there is no report of a diagnosis. In addition, the experiences described don't have the characteristic signs of being seizure induced but *do* fit in with tens of thousands of reports of phenomena such as poltergeists and electronic interference.

There is something more here, as extraordinary as it is revealing, that is very different from most other experiences but is at the same time an eerie echo of the letter from the man who was nearly pulled out of his body.

It's not that, though. In fact, it's the opposite. Nobody wanted to evict this woman from her body. Instead, somebody wanted to share it.

THE LETTER: THE FUNNY MOON

I have just recently, in fact about a week ago, spoken my first words to another human being regarding these fascinating memories and experiences.

What could possibly explain what has been happening over the years—physical contact with thin, gray short beings, sometimes in my room, sometimes in dark, drab rooms foreign in appearance to anything I have seen elsewhere, sometimes in open, stone-hewn buildings where I am sent with others to learn, but almost always utterly terrifying.

I have had memories for years of several different sightings of UFOs, which I have remembered ever since they occurred. My first memory of sighting was when I was only about three years old, in the summer of 1964. I remember looking at "the funny moon" with one older sister and two older brothers, gazing out of the window in my brothers' room. I remember it dancing in the distance, a silver-gray, iridescent disk, over the woods that used to stand, at that time, behind my house. We were frightened and mesmerized at the same time. I recall seeing something that looked like a rooftop-type TV antenna sticking out of the bottom of it. We giggled as we watched it move up and down, then shoot toward the city, but then we all screamed as it darted close to the house, and then the memory ends.

My next sighting was much later, when I was thirteen, in 1974. I was going to bed one night and my mother and sister were downstairs. I saw, about a mile or so off, a silver-gray, iridescent disk, which seemed to be wobbling on its vertical axis as it stood otherwise motionless in the air. I was filled with terror and plastered myself against the bedroom wall beside the window so "they" couldn't see me. I wasn't consciously aware of just who "they" might be at the time, but I felt certain that they knew I had seen them. I finally worked up the courage to peel myself off the wall, get off the bed, and run out of my room and down the steps to my sister and mother to tell them that we needed to run and hide. My mother sent me to bed. I lay awake for some time, praying.

The next sighting was not too long afterward. My mother and sister and I were driving home in the evening in a deserted, forested part of the state. I decided to lie down on the back seat for a while and look up at the nighttime sky out of the rear window. I noticed a star that seemed to be pulsating. It started to move, slowly at first, then faster. It shot across the freeway behind us some distance away, then doubled back, and came much, much closer. It was cigar shaped and seemed almost split down the middle, color-wise. One half was a bright, intense kelly green, and the other, scarlet red. The next thing I remember, it was a little after one in the morning, and we were sitting at home at our dining room table. We still had our jackets on, sitting around the table, saying nothing. My mother asked me to check if she put the car in the garage or not. It was. Nothing else was said between us. I was extremely tired and went straight to bed and fell immediately asleep. We never spoke of the incident.

I was in my bunk bed one night thinking. I thought I was awake. I saw a small ball of light traveling across the floor and thought that it must have been a small glow-in-the-dark super ball. The light was whitish yellow. It went under the bed, and I went under the bed to retrieve it. In my dream, I could even hear my sister breathing as she slept in the bunk over me. As I crawled under the bed, I was no longer under there but instead in a dank, gray-brown cavern. Many people were being led to their fate by skeletons with large, slanted, glowing eyes. The ball of light I had followed then drifted past me and entered the eye of one of the skeletons. It turned to face me, hissed loudly, and blew a kind of smoke at me.

Our "friend in the basement" used to make things fly off the back of the kitchen table when we would walk past, make the bread loaf fly off the top of the oven at us, terrify pets, and unnerve us kids. My mother insisted that it was nothing to be afraid of, that it was completely harmless. Activity regarding "the friend" had settled down over the years, as my sibs moved out and our daily schedules picked up. But during this time of meditation and development, I changed. I started having nightmares of the thing and could only see large, black, slanted eyes in the basement of my dreams. I find this interesting since at this point in time, there were no pictures of visitors as we see them today. One time in particular was exceptionally frightening. I was lying down in my bed, writing in my journal. I felt the presence of the thing in the room with me, and I was terrified. I tried to run, to get to the garage to my bike. Upon reaching my bike, the thing came up on my back, and I took off into flight—riding my bike through the air, struggling in vain to escape but instead being overtaken. The last thing I remember is its voice coming over my vocal cords, from within me, and I was totally not in control. It said, "Let us begin."

Something extraordinary happened to my son Kevin (not his real name) a few months ago. The boys had said they'd seen the little people in their room. One morning, after one such night, Kevin woke up with a triangular-shaped mark on his left temple, similar to a scrape or brush burn mark, except that it was a perfect little isosceles triangle. When I asked him how he had gotten the mark, he said he had no idea and didn't know it was there.

My memories of actual events upon visitation are very fragmented. I have glimpses of a dark room, with a very strange smell, almost like moist dirt. The lights are very dim. I remember lying on a metal table, but it was warm instead of cold. I remember the visitors,

I remember me screaming. I remember one being, in particular, whom I perceived as a male, who was always there. I knew him, and he was the one who could always calm me. I remember being reassured by his presence. The eyes were crazy—almost black, shiny, but they didn't seem moist to me. They had almost a fine texture to their surface, like the surface of a fly's eyes might appear under a microscope. The face reminded me of a praying mantis. Their bodies reminded me of a child's but thinner, around four to five feet in height. I don't remember what the clothes were like. The touch of their skin reminded me of soft glove leather, but again, it didn't seem as moist as ours. Some had little potbellies, with really thin arms and legs.

Every time this happens, I wake up with a migraine and a nasty allergy attack that lasts for several days. I have one clear memory of lying back on a table, naked but warm. There were three grays around me, but I had the impression there were many more in the background. There was one of them, very tall and mean looking, and I thought at the time he was the leader, but he impressed me as being almost mechanical. They had two rods shaped like long drumsticks, which appeared made of some copper alloy, which they held in their hands. They were pressing the ends of' the rods at various places on my body, and sound was emitted of varying pitch, like a tone, when they pressed them. The tone changed as they moved them to different points on my body. Each time the sound was emitted they looked over at what I perceived to be a screen of some type. I remember a metal object, shaped roughly like a microphone, being inserted up my rectum. I remember the male telling me that it would be okay, that they wouldn't hurt me. But they did. I feel at times they were surprised by the presence of pain. I told them I wanted to go home, and why were they doing this to me? They told me I was one of the chosen ones. At the time, it made sense to me.

ANALYSIS

A careful reading of this letter suggests either that this correspondent is having a lifetime of contact with some very otherworldly beings or that what is driving her experiences is even stranger than that. Let's see if we can open some doors into more than one vision of what is being described here.

She writes, "My first memory of sighting was when I was only about three years old." She and her siblings saw what she says they thought of as a "funny moon." It was an iridescent disk with a structure protruding from its base that looked "like a rooftop-type TV antenna." At first, it seemed to back away from the wooded area behind their family home. Then, as it swept closer to them, she remembers that "we all screamed"—and there the memory ends.

Such blackouts are a commonplace side effect of stress and trauma. The moment of an automobile accident or a plane crash is often not remembered. Stressful events such as rape may also be blocked out. This condition is known as dissociative amnesia. The stress involved causes the victim to detach and block out the memory. This is commonly reported by abduction victims. When it is accompanied by a sense that time itself has disappeared, it becomes a missing time experience.

She does not say specifically whether her siblings also remembered this event, and as we have been unable to determine her whereabouts or status after these twenty-five years, I cannot ask her. Even so, a substantial number of the anomalous events described appear to have been witnessed by the whole family group.

Five types of events are described: the approach of unexplainable flying objects, interactions with small "grays," events that can be classified as visionary experiences, poltergeist activity, some kind of internal voice that seems to want to share the body.

The common thread is that they all elicit intense reactions from the witnesses. The first UAP sighting causes the children to run screaming. When it happens to this correspondent again at age thirteen—as she is going to bed, she sees, "about a mile or so off, a silver-gray, iridescent disk" out her bedroom window—she is absolutely terrified, and reacts much like the woman confronted by the visitors in the trees: she hides from what she perceives as a threat, shrinking back against the bedroom wall to avoid being seen. When she goes downstairs to tell her mother and sisters, she's sent back up to bed, where she lies awake and praying.

A few nights later, she and her mother and sister are driving home through a "deserted, forested part of the state" when she sees through the rear window of the car what appears to be a pulsating star. It came closer and now appeared to be a cigar-shaped, pulsating object, half green, half red. Then it is "a little after one in the morning"—a significant chunk of missing time!—"and we were sitting at home at our dining table," still wearing jackets, in confused silence. They went to bed and never spoke of the incident.

On a later night, she observes a "small ball of light" moving across the floor. When she looks under the bed to see where it has gone, she is confronted by a vision of a cavern. People are "being led to their fate by skeletons with large, slanted, glowing eyes." The vision ends when some sort of smoke is blown in her face.

She next mentions what her mother called "our friend in the basement," who "used to make things fly off the back of the kitchen table" when members of the family would walk past, "make the bread loaf fly off the top of the oven at us, terrify pets, and unnerve us kids." Incredibly, their mother said that it was all "completely harmless." But why? Something very extraordinary was happening, something that came from outside of normal life. So why was she so sure that it was harmless?

Poltergeist activity is a commonplace phenomenon that has been extensively studied but never really explained. It was once thought to involve restless ghosts, demons, and so forth, but now it is more commonly attributed to psychokinetic activity that seems to be connected to an individual. If this interpretation is correct, then the correspondent herself and/or one or more of her siblings might be responsible for making "things fly." As our correspondent's sisters moved out, the poltergeist activity subsided.

Psychokinetic phenomena have been studied under controlled conditions, and while the subject still lies well outside the scientific mainstream, there has been enough competent observation to conclude that it is an unexplained phenomenon, not something imaginary. Michael Persinger studied a friend of mine for years, and I have witnessed both her psychokinetic abilities and my own much more modest ones, but no scientific study has ever identified a mechanism we can presently understand that would explain the phenomenon.

After her sisters move out, the letter writer reports that "I changed." At this point, there are no more UAP sightings, but she began having nightmares in which she could see "large, black, slanted eyes." She says that this now surprises her because at that time, in the early '60s, "there were no pictures of visitors as we see them today." (There probably were, but certainly not in any mainstream media. That would not happen until *Close Encounters of the Third Kind* was released in 1977. *Communion* in 1988 would make the image iconic.) And yet, there they were in her dreams.

Finally, a climactic moment is reached. She is in bed writing in her journal when she feels "the presence of the thing in the room with me" and is "terrified." Having lived with such presences now for a good part of my life, I cannot say that they terrify me, but when the manifestations are strong, they can still be unsettling. I can certainly see how a young woman, alone in a bedroom, would feel terror when one of these bizarre manifestations appeared. When it happens, there is no sense of dream or hallucination, but I would not conclude that, therefore, the presences are not being generated by the mind of the witness. In fact, I wouldn't conclude anything because there is nothing to conclude. What can be done is to describe experience and try to interpret it as best we can.

She is so frightened that she abandons her journaling and runs to the garage, hoping to escape on her bike. At this point, it can be assumed that she is awake and not in any sort of presleep trance.

Her perceptions now leave the realm of the known entirely. She finds herself riding her bicycle through the air—a witch on her broomstick, perhaps, having been rubbed with the balm of the impossible. (Later, of course, ET enjoyed a similar journey across the night sky. She wrote us in 1989; ET was released in 1982. It cannot be known whether or not her mind reconstructed her memory around the famous image from the film. But if what actually happened to her was sufficiently strange, there is certainly a possibility that she reached for a familiar image to make sense of it.) She was unable to retake control of her bicycle. The next thing she knew, she heard a voice coming out of her own throat, literally from *inside* herself, over which she had no control. The voice said, "Let us begin."

Interestingly, this suggests a phenomenon akin to mediumistic trance or even demonic possession. I have witnessed some accomplished mediums at work, and they appear to release control of their body to another entity, either—as they generally believe—a spirit who is not part of their own inner life or perhaps another aspect of personality that they have unwittingly self-generated. But if this is so, then there is something about ourselves that we don't fully understand, relating to how multiple personalities form and function.

So "me within thee" may mean some other aspect of self as easily as something with an external origin.

"Let us begin" was from one viewpoint as deeply personal a statement as can be imagined. It was *her* statement, after all; it came from inside her. But it felt as if her voice was being used, not that she was generating the words in her mind and then constructing them with her lungs and vocal cords.

This complex tangle of dream and physical experience, of intrusion from the outside and emergence from within, speaks of broken borders and suggests that nothing less than that a new way of experiencing existence may be emerging from the close encounter experiences— a journey into a part of life that has been hidden very deeply. Is it the proverbial unconscious, if such a thing exists, calling to us from an inner land of different meanings, rules, and aspirations? Or is this what it is like when aliens, who experience reality through the meshes of a very different mind, seek to share consciousness with us? Does somebody indeed want to share as profoundly as my wife thought when she named our book *Communion*? Could such sharing even be possible, us linked to these others so deeply that they can speak through our lips? And if so, is it a one-way street, or do we get to share their being, too?

Is entering and using a body one was not born with even possible? If so, why want this?

I have thought that our visitors might live outside of time, or be in possession of all knowledge, and thus have a motive to share in our innocent sense of novelty. I wonder now, though, if those thoughts are not really an expression of a deep fear of being absorbed into a more powerful culture. Communion might be a deeper business than merely peering through human eyes. A sharing of stories, morals, culture, history, and memories would be a far greater challenge for both sides, especially if different brains, wired in different ways, are involved. They might not just see the world differently but actually construct those perceptions into meanings fundamentally different from ours. The world might literally look and even function differently for them than it does for us. When we observe how far we are from communicating with brilliant animals like dolphins and killer whales, who have evolved right here on Earth, we can see the problem.

This sort of communion would, of course, also be an invasion. It would have to be, for they would have to enter our most intimate spaces before they had any hope of understanding us. It is not a matter of our land and houses being taken, though, but rather of a place being made for them within our being itself. With it would conceivably come an offer of a place in theirs.

This has already been the theme of popular entertainments. *Invasion of the Body Snatchers*, *Village of the Damned* and *The Thing* all come to mind. They bring with them a question: are we fearful of this because we sense that it might overwhelm us? Do we fear being smothered beneath the sheer weight of their attention?

If this experience is being conveyed accurately, then it would seem that they want to share our bounding, unstuck lives—not with the dispassion of observers but rather with the intensity of participants, collaborators, lovers, perhaps thieves, caring for and tasting of the vibrant sweetness of human experience. They are here for the only reason anyone does anything: they are here to get something that they want.

It would seem that "me within thee" began at the beginning—not the day they arrived but the day they first became aware of us and started us both on this journey.

CHAPTER 10

ENCOUNTER: I HATE YOU, MOMMY!

W hat does "me within thee" mean? Is it a matter of possession, as in what demons are purported to do? Is it not that but rather the deep form of sharing of experience that is implied by the word "communion"?

This next letter takes matters to a new level. The story relates close encounter to contact with, as Anne put it, "what we call the dead." So now we reach the deepest level of the encounter experience and, by so doing, dig down to the very the core of our own meaning.

THE LETTER: A FAMILY AFFAIR

I was born in Texas in 1945. I've had OBEs since I was a small child and never thought it unusual, rather that they were private and no one talked about it much. They became very intense during my freshman year in college, leading up to a period where I went completely blind for three days. My ESP seemed to become more and more prevalent, so since I was a "very rational" honor student, I began psychotherapy, thinking something was severely wrong with me and I wanted to get back to "normal" as soon as possible. I got married while still in college and would stay during summer sessions as well. We had a child in 1966. In the early summer of '68, my daughter and I drove to New Mexico to visit some friends who had a small ranch there before going west to meet my husband. Leaving Taos, we drove to Flagstaff and waited there until the early evening, to cross the Mojave Desert at night.

About two hours outside of Flagstaff, my daughter began to shout that she saw a spaceship in the sky. How did she know what it was? The sky was unusually cloudy, and I looked to where she was pointing and saw first two and then three lights moving rapidly in the sky, turning at ninety-degree angles, pulsating and disappearing, etc. I decided to pull off the road onto a dirt trail I saw to the right, leading into the desert. We were away from the road lights, but I thought I could still see them at a distance. We watched the sky together, she in the back seat and I in front, when suddenly in front of the car there appeared a huge, dark and glowing object with a partial row of lights in the middle.

The next thing I remember is my breath being knocked out of me as I somehow went through the windshield of the car. I remember looking back for an instant and the car was completely empty of myself or my daughter, and I was stepping into an opening in a vehicle. I couldn't see my daughter, and I asked in terror about her. "She's going to be all right" was what I heard in the center of my mind, and I was strangely soothed and unusually happy.

These beings were tall, about six and a half feet, and seemed to be robed in a fabric that emitted a type of light periodically, during movement. Their skin was silvery and their eyes were round, and a violet blue that sometimes streamed out on me with a feeling of love or long-lost family; it was almost like a homecoming. Their eyes were closer to the surface of their faces than humans', and the nose wasn't well defined. Their mouths were fascinating. Sometimes it seemed that they weren't dressed at all, and the body definition wasn't sexually differentiated. I was standing with two of them and noticing that they had no hair, but there was something like fabric that was crumpled and folded behind their backs.

They seemed to be smiling, without moving their mouths. As soon as I thought "hair," one of them seemed to produce beautiful reddish gold hair all over its head, smiling. This frightened me. The room I was looking into was about twenty-five feet wide and semicircular. It was rather dark and filled with TV screens running the full wall area, stacked upon one another three and sometimes four rows high. All sorts of pictures appeared on the screens, and strange symbols, and terrains I'd never seen. Under the screens was a type of built-in desk, curving all along the wall. In the middle of the room was a long table with three or four chairs that were moveable. There were three beings in the chairs, two of them facing the screens and moving around, while another one at the desk area stood from time to time, moving things around. They did not look up. They seemed to be of the same slender body type as the two that stood with me but were not quite so tall. Those two seemed to be laughing all the time, and sometimes there was a sound like wind. They kept saying "Welcome, welcome!" in my mind and laughing. They then told me some strange things about human origins and alien intervention on the planet Earth at various times in the past and future. Then they started speaking to me about my individual history. This will sound outrageous, Whitley, but I'll say it anyway:

There was a whole generation of beings that came to Earth in the far past and took up Earth life. They were from the family of Ranm. That root family name was their name root also, but either that planet wasn't in existence anymore or it was now inaccessible. They said that was why the old god names were as they were on Earth: Rama, Brahma, Ra in Egypt, and Abraham, etc., in order that humans might remember. But so much confusion set in that the names became designations for gods or heroes, and that wasn't the point at all. Rather it indicated the name form of the origin of them, and some of us, being from other star systems. Then they began telling me my name in their tongue, "Shalisha Li Ekimu Ranm," and kept saying it in my head until I got it right. They said those words meant much more and could be found in Earth literature. There was such love flowing through them as they helped me with the name and the Earth lineages that went back to the stars. Understand, this wasn't exactly like words, but were rather images or sound pictures that moved between us.

Then they took me through a gray curved corridor to the right of the entrance where I'd come in. I can remember not being able to walk and then walking with ease. We came to a room at the end and to the left of the corridor. This room contained the ship's driving mechanism. This happened in 1968. I was twenty-two and had no idea what I was looking at. In front of me was a huge crystal, perhaps three feet across in the middle. It looked like two pyramids placed base to base, although at times it seemed multifaceted and totally brilliant and jewellike. The crystal seemed suspended in the air, and around it was a matrix of wires or tubes connected into a solid type of material concealing the ends of the tubes in a dark smooth mass, so that the entire thing rose about four feet from the floor. They told me to put my mind into the crystal, and as I did I'd be able to learn how to fly the ship! One of them telepathized how to do it. I tried and failed, but they kept coaxing me and I could hear them smiling: "Go on, you can do it!" Finally, I got it right and we began to move out, first above the Earth and then through the angular pattern of space that was also time. I asked why I had to do this and they only said, "So that you can remember flying and piloting when necessary," and then there was laughter. After the initial information was placed in the crystal and wire matrix, nothing more was necessary, but we stood there anyway until they said, "Time to return to Earth."

Frantically, I panicked and asked about my daughter and was soothed again by them saying she was okay. Then they said they were sorry but didn't say why, and then there was great love. As we moved to the exit place, they said my name again several times and some-thing about "soul lineage." I was reluctant to go, but the next thing I knew I had gone through the car windshield again and found myself hanging out of the window gasping for air; I had been crying and was covered with sweat. My daughter was in the back seat crying. She told me never to touch her again and that she knew who I was and she hated me. I tried to calm her and ask what had happened to her and she shouted, "I'll never tell you! Leave me alone!" I had a notebook in the car, and before we left I forced myself to write these things down as I remembered them. I looked at the stars in a daze. It was almost midnight, and we had lost about two and a half hours. At that moment the scene seemed uncanny, yet so perfectly normal. I felt then that this was the first time I'd been able to remember, but that it had happened before and I was blocked in remembering. I drove on to California as if nothing had happened.

I couldn't tell anyone ever and swore to myself to never discuss it. I then began getting afraid of going to sleep at night and became really ill and nauseous. My hair began to fall out and my mouth started bleeding, and I was exhausted. I took more vitamins.

One night my daughter woke up screaming, and I went to her bed and she said very factually, "Mommy, I'm going to die. The spaceship people told me so. They said little bugs had gotten into my body and they were sorry, but there was nothing they could do since I'm a little girl." Then she went back to sleep. This frightened me beyond belief. That morning, she woke up with a high fever and had severe joint swelling. I took her to the hospital, and she was diagnosed as having rheumatoid arthritis, yet they weren't too sure. They wondered if she'd been exposed to radiation. She was in great pain. I took her out of the hospital and drove back to Texas and put her in the hospital, only to find out that she had a very rare cancer of the nervous system, neuroblastoma, and it had metastasized, and she had just a few months to live. She lived until September of 1969. Before her death, she began to draw extraordinary pictures that were more advanced than a ten-year-old's, even though she was only three and a half. She began to write poetry, which I sometimes wrote out for her. The doctors were amazed and thought it might be the chemotherapy but were not sure.

The day after her funeral, a friend of mine who was a graduate honor student at UT called me from Austin hysterically, saying that she had to drive to Houston immediately and tell me something that had happened. Without glasses, she was legally blind, but she drove anyway. I didn't think I could handle another emotional crisis since I was in such grief, however, she came that day. We went for pizza, and she told me what had happened. She said that two nights before at about 2:20 AM, she was awakened by a noise and then saw her roof begin to dissolve. In the air above, she saw a type of spaceship. Two tall beings appeared, and in between them was my daughter. They told her they hadn't been able to get through to me because of something but to let me know that my daughter was okay and was with them! She thought at that point that she'd gone completely insane. At that point in her story, I broke my promise to myself and told her what had happened that night in the desert, and we both cried and cried.

ANALYSIS

Like the other stories examined here, elements of this one suggest the involvement of a powerful and, frankly, eerie mind that does not work as our minds do. It is a very good mind, deep and knowledgeable. But is it an alien mind, or is this really a book about the fact that we do not yet have a complete understanding of the true nature of humanity? Or are the human and the alien so deeply entwined that they are essentially one—darkness and light wound together? The intimate story of a family spread across the vastness of time and space suggests just this.

It begins with an episode of hysterical blindness. Such experiences are caused by stress, and our correspondent describes a period in her first year of college when out-of-body experiences that she'd been having since childhood became more intense, and incidents of extrasensory perception started to trouble her enough that she sought psychiatric help.

It is clear that this "very rational honor student," as she describes herself, viewed these phenomena, not as unexplained but real events, but as an indication that she was troubled.

Hysterical blindness is one of a group of functional neurological disorders that cause patients to experience symptoms that mimic physical illness. They are not particularly common. When they do appear, the context is usually high stress.

She then reports that she and her two-year-old daughter "drove to New Mexico" in the summer of 1968. How long after the episode of hysterical blindness they did this is unclear. After seeing friends in Taos, they proceeded to Flagstaff, Arizona, about a seven-hour drive. There, they waited for evening to fall before continuing across the Mojave Desert.

That storied desert is not only the source of the menacing giant ants of *Them* but also the location of the Trinity site where the first atomic bomb was exploded in 1945, which, in the movie, was used to explain why the ants had become monsters. It is also the site, as Jacques Vallée and Paola Harris claim in their 2021 book *Trinity,* of the first UAP crash that involved living beings—in this case, creatures who were seen by two boys.

Once the mother and daughter enter the Mojave, the story that unfolds is filled with implications, many disturbing in the extreme, and ultimately tragic. Its most telling aspect involves a "name" in which, as we shall see, extraordinarily subtle meaning is hidden. In fact, it is the existence of this group of words that elevate this story to the same level as the others in this group: the author of the letter is extremely unlikely to have devised the phrase on her own. The words in it are drawn from very ancient sources, all but one of them quite obscure. The letter writer would have had to have been a philologist, conversant in historical linguistics and capable of stringing together a list of ancient names to conceal a coded message that could be interpreted only by somebody steeped in ancient esoteric knowledge.

First, the little girl reports seeing a "spaceship" in the sky. But she's two, so her mother is naturally confused. How can she know?

It looks as if she's correct because the mother soon sees lights darting around overhead, too. She "saw first two and then three lights moving rapidly in the sky." Her reaction to seeing them is so much at variance with what might be expected that it is hard not to consider the possibility either that she, like her daughter, was anticipating this event, or that she was compelled by unknown means to do what she did next. "I decided to pull off the road onto a dirt trail ... leading into the desert."

One might conceivably stop to get a better look or, if the strange lights inspired fear, speed up instead. But surely not take off into the desert, unless, of course, one was heading for a prearranged meeting or was under some sort of hidden compulsion. (The close encounter narrative contains many cases, such as this one and the Corina Saebels case mentioned previously, of people finding themselves compelled to travel to a certain spot where they then meet the visitors.)

An object next appears right in front of the car, close enough to reveal details such as a row of glowing lights. There then occurs an event so incredible that the only choice we can really make is to simply say that this is what the witness reports: "The next thing I remember is my breath being knocked out of me as I somehow went through the windshield of the car." (Our visitors have been seen to move through walls, and there are occasional witness descriptions of movements similar to the one reported here, one even involving being pulled up out of a moving subway train.) She then looks back and sees that the car is empty, meaning that both she and her daughter are no longer physically in it.

She then finds herself "stepping into an opening in a vehicle." She is, naturally, terrified for her child. She then hears a voice "in the center of my mind" that reassures her, leaving her feeling "unusually happy." This type of completely inappropriate mood swing may occur in cases of extreme stress, and this was obviously a very stressful situation. It could also be induced, of course, using drugs or other means. Either could be the case here. What is clear is that there seems to have been little reason to be happy about anything that was unfolding. Along with her little daughter, she had been spirited into the unknown, and the child was now nowhere to be seen. Reassurances or not, she had no reason for the happiness she reports.

She is now inside what she describes as the "vehicle" and begins to interact with beings who seem to her to be well over six feet tall. She describes them wearing clothes of some sort of reflective material; then, as she observes her surroundings, she makes another unexpected comment, but one that will be familiar to many close encounter witnesses. She experiences a "feeling of love or long-lost family" and describes the event as "almost like a homecoming."

After looking around a room filled with mostly familiar technology such as television screens, she notices that the beings are bald. As soon as she thinks about hair, one of them, to her discomfiture, produces "beautiful reddish gold hair" on its head.

Her brain is struggling to form a coherent picture by comparing the visual input it is receiving to past experience. Normally, this process is relatively smooth, but not this time. There isn't any past experience to compare. Therefore, a certain amount of chaos may now be getting delivered to her cerebral cortex. Whether she saw hair emerge out of this being's scalp or if it emerged out of a rapidly blurring line between dream and reality cannot be known. As she looks around the room, she sees all sorts of images on the TV screens, unfamiliar symbols, what appear to be scenes from other worlds—a richness of imagery unknown to her.

The story then morphs into an ancient aliens narrative, but it must be noted that this letter was written before such stories were much in the public discourse.

From earliest times, there has been a belief that human beings came from the stars. The oldest religious text in existence, which is inscribed on the walls of the pyramid of Unas and dated to 2400 BCE, contains a set of instructions intended to enable the pharaoh to return to the stars, specifically to Orion. This theme of return to the heavens is repeated so extensively in world myth that it can be said to be one of the oldest of human aspirations. Our correspondent tells what is essentially a version of a fundamental creation myth: "a whole generation of beings that came to Earth in the far past and took up Earth life." They are described as being "from the family of Ranm." It is then mentioned that the home planet is either no longer in existence or has become in some way inaccessible. (Could it be that others before us have used up their planets?)

These entities, presumably, are wanderers among the stars. She goes on to say that she was told that "old god names" such as Rama, Ra, Brahma, and Abraham are derivations of the name of the home planet, so "humans might remember," presumably, where we came from. Are we a lost colony, then, unable to return to a planet somewhere that is "now inaccessible"?

Then occurs the phrase I discussed earlier. She is told that she is a member of the family of the people who have kidnapped her and her daughter and that her name is "Shalisha Li Ekimu Ranm." I thought when I saw it in her letter that, even if it is a name, it is also a phrase, maybe a sentence. The entities take great care to make certain that she remembers the words clearly. They also offer her the clue that they are old words and can be found in ancient world literature.

Let's follow the clue and do a brief survey of that literature to see what we can find.

The first word, "shalisha," appears to be Hebrew, and a search in the bible reveals that Shalisha was the name of the district mentioned in 1 Samuel 9 as the region Saul passed through looking for the lost donkeys of his father Kish. It also appears as part of the name Baal Shalisha ("Baal of the three parts") in 2 Kings 4, where it is described as the place from which a man came and gave Elisha twenty loaves of bread, with which he was able to feed a much larger number of people than seemed possible—as in the story of Jesus and the loaves and the fishes in the gospel. In fact, any place in the Hebrew bible where *three* is mentioned, a version of this word is used. An example is in 4 Ecclesiastes 12: "Two are better than one, and a cord of three (shalash) strands is not quickly snapped."

According to some authorities, most notably the Armenian mystic and philosopher G. I. Gurdjieff, what he terms "the law of three" has ancient significance. Indeed, it may well be expressed in the Sphinx, which would date it at least to the Egyptian Old Kingdom (2700–2200 BCE) and, as authorities such as geologist Robert Schoch assert, possibly closer to 10,000 BCE, or the time that the Göbekli Tepe structures were being created in Turkey.

The idea of the law is that there are three basic forces in the universe: active, passive, and balancing. The Sphinx has the haunches of a bull, the claws of a lion, and the head of a man. In it, the passive force would be the bull, the active force the lion, and the balancing force the intelligence of the man. In the Christian and many other trinities, the father is the passive force, silent and waiting for his will to be done; the son is the active force, enacting that will in the world; and the holy spirit is what connects, or balances, the two.

Does this principle, then, somehow fit logically into the phrase? If so, then it has to make sense in connection to the other words and, to some extent, their sequence. (We must bear in mind that sequence is different from language to language. For example, Latin languages do not share the same word order rules with English, and Chinese is different from both.)

The next word in the name is "Li." Once again, as we were told, it is very ancient. It is also an expression of balance. In Confucianism, it is associated with balanced living and social propriety. The word also refers to human participation in the ordering of the universe by means of symbolic actions. These actions, if performed correctly, make visible the underlying order of reality. In other words, li refers to the relationship between the human mind and reality and sees the mind as a maintaining and balancing presence upon which the structure of the world as we perceive it depends. In this sense, it also reflects the modern Western hypothesis that the observer's presence is what draws reality out of an indeterminate state and into the structures that we see around us.

We will return to modern concepts of the connection between mind and reality in a later chapter. At this point, though, I would like to comment that li, reflecting as it does the presence of this fundamental indeterminacy and the need for the observer to bring it into balance, is certainly a sophisticated philosophical concept.

The first word expresses the three forces that must be balanced, and the second the human state that can balance them. The lion and the bull are the two parts of shalisha that must be balanced by the third, which is li, or human knowledge and understanding.

Shalisha is an expression of the three parts of being: the force of emotions and the strength of the physical body as balanced and mediated by intellect. To understand how that works, we have to look at them more deeply, and that is what the next two words do, referring to a being of dark and one of light. Ekimu, more usually spelled ekimmu, is an ancient Sumerian vampire, mentioned in Mesopotamian texts that date as far back as 2000 BCE. The ekimmu were believed to be the souls of the dead who had been improperly buried. They are primarily associated, in the old texts, with sucking the life out of children—an ominous foreshadowing, in this case, and one which adds another level of density to the "name" given our correspondent.

At the same time that ekimmu were stalking the lands of the Sumerians, Ra was emerging as the preeminent solar deity in the Egyptian pantheon. Ekimmu can thus be seen as the dark opposite of Ra. One creeps through the night sucking the essence of life out of children; the other fills the world with light and life.

Taken as a sentence, the words make sense, and it is sublime.

"Shalisha li" can be said to mean "three in balance." The next two words describe what is to be balanced, that is to say, the dangerous darkness of the child-eating vampire is balanced by the light of the sun god. Ekimmu wanders the night. Ra spreads light. Ekimmu is thus the active force in this triad, a once-human creature who was not properly put to rest. In other words, ekimmu is the part of us that is angry over being unjustly treated and wanders the world seeking vengeance. Ra is a passive force, rising each morning to spread his light, revealing the vampire for what he is, a helpless shadow who can do no more than retreat into his own wounds.

What brings balance between them is li, whose wise understanding of the inner nature of human life and man's relationship to the world enables us to accept our own darkness while taking full advantage of our light.

It would seem that this random list of words is not so random after all. Here's how it translates: "There are three forces within us. The force of light enables us to grow and prosper, even as our own inner darkness seeks our destruction. A third force, called li, balances the two."

Whoever devised this phrase could think very well about human life (in fact, they seemed a lot more familiar with us than some of the entities described in the other witness letters). But they were not using human thought processes. We don't encode meaning in the way it is encoded in this phrase, and we think of names as identifiers of personalities and things, not as philosophical signposts.

Yet this name belongs to us all. It should: it describes the human journey in all its splendor and peril, exquisitely compressed into just a few exceedingly well-chosen words.

"They said those words meant much more and could be found in Earth literature." They certainly do and, as we can see, are indeed found in our literature. Also present in them is a warning that proved to be all too true, for ekimmu was abroad on this terrible night, and a child's life was in play.

This is far from the only way names are used in contact experiences. Another example was posted by Raven Dana in her blog on September 5, 2022, just as I was finishing this chapter. She had no idea what I was writing about.

Raven has had a lifetime of encounter experiences, including one at our cabin that is mentioned in my book *Transformation* and elsewhere. She writes that she "learned through myth and fairy tales that knowing one's true name is very powerful." She goes on to say, "I was about seven years old when I asked for a name" (the name of one of the entities that she was seeing). She was told, "F.A.R.B.," and it was explained that "this was what he was not."

At age thirteen, she was "a freshman in high school and taking my first biology class" when the teacher wrote four fundamental animal categories on the blackboard: "fish, amphibians, reptiles, birds." At once, she thought F.A.R.B.: what he is not. She concludes, "Through the years, my encounters with the visitors often held clues that, when I least expected it, would come back around. My ongoing experience, though sometimes frightening, has given me wonder and understanding, and the immense intimacy of direct contact."

She is not alone with this trajectory of sentiments, from fear to wonder and understanding.

But understanding what? Obviously, he did not answer her question about his name. What he *did* do was illustrate for her a method of information transfer that is very different from our own but, in its own way, richly effective. At age seven she was given a question that she could not forget. Then five years later, she found an answer that at once laid the question to rest and deepened it on many different levels. Not the least of these was whether or not the entity knew, when she was seven, not just what she would see when she was thirteen, but also that she would remember. And I have to ask myself the question, also, "Did it know that she would happen to send me this blog just as I was writing about the visitors' different way of thinking about and using names?" Is each moment of life actually new, or is it that we see life in such a way that it seems new, thus giving us the chance to experience it to the fullest even though it is, in fact, more like an unfolding drama than a random walk into the future?

Visitor communication is not only subtle, it is rich with meaning and a powerful generator of questions. It is designed to challenge the mind at every possible level. It is also structured differently from the way we communicate. I think it's probable that this is because it comes from a mind that, while excellent, is embedded in a brain biology different from ours, which therefore sees the world differently.

Our correspondent is then moved on to a new sort of experience entirely. She is shown a crystal that "looked like two pyramids placed base to base" that appeared to be suspended in the air. Another close encounter witness, Paul Lander, described seeing something similar during an experience aboard a UAP. He spent years trying to understand what he had seen and published a book about his experiments called *Tapping into the Total Power of the Universe.*

She was told to put her mind into the crystal, which would then enable her to fly the ship. She eventually manages this task and is further told that she is being taught how to do it so that "you can remember flying and piloting when necessary." With this, the "onboard" part of the experience ends.

As in a dream (usually a nightmare), she suddenly recalls that her daughter is somewhere else on the ship and panics. She is told that the child is all right but notices that there is now a sense of sadness. The next thing she knows, she's back in the car. She finds herself hanging out the window gasping for air. She doesn't remember crying, but she knows that she has been. She then sees that her daughter is with her and asks her what happened to her. The answer is a fierce and completely improbable "I'll never tell you! Leave me alone!"

What?

Coming from a little child, what could this mean? The question goes unanswered ... for the present.

They then drive on to California, and a few days later, the mother experiences symptoms similar to those that afflicted the woman who had seen the visitors in the trees: she "became really ill and nauseous. My hair began to fall out and my mouth started bleeding, and I was exhausted." These are symptoms of many diseases, one of which is radiation poisoning.

Her daughter then woke up screaming and said to her mother that she had been told by the "spaceship people" that she was going to die. She soon exhibited swollen joints. A visit to a hospital resulted in a diagnosis of rheumatoid arthritis. The doctors theorized radiation poisoning.

She then took her daughter back to Texas, where she was diagnosed with neuroblastoma, a childhood cancer of the nervous system that often has a genetic origin. It remains an extremely dangerous illness today, but when this child was diagnosed it was generally fatal, and, in fact, the little girl died in September of 1969.

Her mother reports that her daughter drew "extraordinary pictures" before she died at three and a half. She did not provide any of the pictures, and a letter requesting them went unanswered. In those days, it was not so easy as snapping a photo on a phone and shooting off an email, which may be one reason there was no response.

The mother was then living in Houston where her little girl was under care. The day after her death, a friend telephoned from Austin and announced that, though legally blind, she was going to drive to Houston to tell her of "something that had happened."

She had been awakened by a noise and had seen her roof dissolve. She then saw "two tall beings" appear with the deceased child between them. They told the friend that she was to tell the mother that her daughter was fine and was with them. "At that point in her story, I broke my promise to myself and told her what had happened that night in the desert, and we both cried and cried."

It was after reading this letter that Anne came out of her office and said what may well be one of the most important things ever said about the entire close encounter experience: "This has something to do with what we call the dead."

As I have reported in my previous books, there is significant evidence that the dead, who are not, according to conventional wisdom, even supposed to exist, not only continue to do so but also have some sort of connection with our visitors—or perhaps *are* our visitors ... It is even possible that the whole enormous arc of phenomena from ghosts to demons and angels to aliens is interconnected, and that we, also, are somewhere on that arc. If any of this is true, and I believe that at least some of it must be, then it must be concluded that we don't know as much about our world as we imagine. While the Enlightenment and the scientific revolution have provided us with profound insights into the way things work, these stories suggest that there is more for us to learn, and that, if we are willing to embrace the challenge, we can.

For example, as we have seen, the name this witness was given can be interpreted, just as her kidnappers said, through an examination of world literature. But there can be no certainty here. My interpretation may be wrong. It may be that I'm reading something into the words that is not there. Still, though, there is a logic to the interpretation and an uncanny and, frankly, frightening connection between one of the words—the name of a vampire whose myth says it targets children—and the death of the little girl from a true modern vampire, cancer.

No matter in which direction our exploration of this material takes us, it is shadowed by the profound intensity of the contact experience, the mystery of how our brains organize the perceptual input, and the shadow of a greater human meaning that has to do with the dead, who are not, perhaps, dead at all.

And therein lies, perhaps, the greatest enigma presented by the close encounter experience. What is it an encounter *with*? Why would we see our own dead? Why would our visitors so often be accompanied by the souls of the human dead, who seem entirely solid and normal during these encounters and usually reassure the witness that they are all right?

Is it, simply, true? If so, then the dead continue to exist as conscious, coherent entities. Or is it a deception? If that is the case, it would mean that our visitors might have a predatory motive that they wish to conceal behind the illusion that our dead still exist.

In either case, one thing is clear: this is not only about the living. It is about something more than this life as we understand it, something that is perhaps of more fundamental importance than the physical level.

If our visitors are in control of a soul that is real, but which we don't even know exists, and if they possess technology that can affect it and motives for doing so, it is absolutely urgent that we understand this.

But how? Where do we even start?

Perhaps they have already told us.

CHAPTER 11
ENCOUNTER: THE STORY OF THE GREEN-EYED MONSTER

These stories are an eloquent reminder not only that we live in a world that we do not fully understand, but that, despite living inside our familiar brains and bodies, know ourselves only to a limited degree.

Seen one way, the human brain is a few pounds of tissue. Seen another, it is truly immense, containing 86 billion neurons that are connected by 100 trillion synapses. It is also quite new, having entered its present form just 200,000 years ago. It would not therefore be surprising if we found that it has capabilities that are rarely used, and therefore that we have not yet identified

For example, there exist a few seemingly credible stories of human levitation, two of which I will be discussing in later chapters. But "Me Within Thee" hints at something else which is—incredibly—even stranger than an ability that can sometimes cause a hundred plus pound bag of water to become weightless. But there is more, much more, and reports of this other ability are far more common than stories of levitation, and are found in virtually all world cultures, including even that of the rational west.

What is it? Welcome to my world, for it has happened to me. This correspondent was not a direct participant, though.

Rather, he saw it happen before his eyes.

The Letter: A One Night Stand to Remember

One day, there was a knock on the door and when I answered it, there
was a very attractive young woman standing there. She told me that
she was my down stairs neighbor. She just wanted to introduce
herself, and invited me down for coffee. She was in her 20s, about 5
feet tall, very thin stature, weighed maybe 110 pounds, she had dish-
water blond hair, and the most intriguing green eyes I had ever seen.
I think I remember wondering at the time, "Why me" I was nothing
special. I think it was just a day later in the morning, and she showed
up again at my door with a full breakfast plate and coffee. Very
strange for someone I just met.

As time went on, we started spending a lot of time together but
never actually went anywhere. One day she told me she was from
Texas, and that she liked to play backgammon, and as luck would
have it I owned a computer that had a backgammon game on it. After
teaching me how to play, we spent hours on end playing the game.
The first thing that happened that was somewhat strange, was one
night we were playing backgammon, and she wanted to wrestle with
me, she claimed that she could pin me with no problem.

As I mentioned before was weighed 110 lbs, I was in top shape
being in the military. So I took the challenge, without going in to
blow by blow detail, she did what she said she would do. She pinned
me to the floor with hardly any effort at all. I am not sure just how
long we had known each other, and without getting into details, one
evening we got intimate after playing backgammon all night. Need-
less to say, I was only 24, and I had fallen head over heels for her.

One other thing that I remember very well, one night, she was at
my place, and we were just playing around and I really do not
remember how we got into the conversation, but I brought up just
how intriguing I thought her eyes were, it was almost hypnotic
looking at them. She then proceeded to tell me something to the

effect that if she wanted to, she could look at me with her eyes in a way that would scare me to death. I believed her instantly.

This is where things start to get weird. As I said we got intimate, which turned out to be only once, and from that time on, things got rocky. I was in love with this girl and I thought she felt the same at first, but later she didn't want much to do with me after that.

After an emotional roller coaster, over the next couple of weeks, and not seeing her, out of the blue, she called and invited me down to her place. I assumed that it was just to finalize the end of a short relationship.

It was in the late evening, and I was expecting the worst, something like OK, we're done; don't want to see you again, etc. Up to this point, nothing too out of the ordinary, boy meets girl, boy looses girl, it happens every day. But what happened next is the whole reason that I am writing this. This is something that I have tried to deal with ever since it happened, and I still often wonder to this day what really happen that evening.

When I got to her apartment, she greeted me at the door, and was very pleasant to me. She was dressed in a long skirt and blouse, and looked very nice. Mind you, I had not seen her for a couple of weeks, which it was hard not to, since I had to pass by her place every day to get home. So when I saw her, all the emotion started coming back, but for some reason I knew there was no argument, it was over.

Anyway, she went over and sat down on a couch and I sat down in a chair across from her. We were probably 5 to 6 feet apart. We talked for a while and she said that she was moving and would not be around much longer. Then everything went silent, and we just sat there looking at each other.

There was a lamp next to her by the couch, and although slightly dimmed, I could see every detail of her. What happened next took me completely by surprise, and this is the part I am having such a problem trying to rationalize in my mind, I was trying to figure out if what I was seeing was really happening.

The first thing I noticed was that her clothing was slowly fading out, like disappearing and her body completely changed from a Thin

but normal looking female human body, to a very frail and feature-
less frame. Next her hair slowly disappeared, her face grew extremely
thin, her mouth all but disappeared, as well as her nose; her eyes
turned pure black, very large and slanted. I didn't know it at the time,
but what I was looking at, was what is known today, as a grey.

During this time, I was as awake and alert as I am right now.
What I did next was what I would assume most people would do in
this situation; I closed my eyes, shook my head from side to side, and
opened my eyes again, I could not believe what I was seeing and I
had never seen anything like this before. I figured that when I opened
my eyes again, it would be gone and I would know that it was just a
trick of the light, or I just imagined something out of the ordinary, or
that it was not really there, but the Image was still there. The only
emotion I remember was total disbelief.

Then, as I was still looking at her, as slowly as it happened, the
reverse started. Her facial features slowly faded back into the face
that I knew, and then her hair came back as slowly as it left, then her
body and clothing went back to normal. The whole thing from the
time she started the transformation to the time she came back took' I
would say 45 to 60 seconds, but it seemed like a lifetime. The
strangest thing was, after all this transpired, I did not have the
slightest inkling to say anything to her, like, did I just see what I
thought I saw, or are you alright. I really don't even remember leaving
her place that night, although I must have. Within just one or two
days after that, I came home from work, and her apartment was
empty. To this day, I often wonder if she was just letting me know that
a long-term relationship was just not possible.

As the years went by, I moved on with my life, got out of the military, went to college and had all but forgotten about that experience,
until a few years later when Whitley Strieber published his book
"Communion". When I first saw the picture of the creature depicted
on the cover of that book, I got the chill of my life, and the first
thought that came into my mind was "That's her." There were some
differences, like color and texture of the skin, but overall pretty much
the same.

The memories came flooding in as vivid as they were that night, and I have never forgotten them since.

Up until the time I saw that picture, to my recall, I had never seen or even heard of a Grey, let alone, one that looked almost exactly like what I saw that night. Someday I want to maybe have someone do a regression and maybe find out what really happen that night so many years ago.

I would like to know, if am I the only one who has ever witnessed anything like this. In all the cases that have ever heard of researched regarding abductions, I wonder if anyone ever reported anything similar to this?

Since that time, I have had some other strange things happen, like waking up in the middle of the night, unable to move, and feeling like someone was standing next to my bed, but I think that was really the sleep paralysis, I have heard about, very weird feeling though, It has only happened once.

When I was about six years old I remember one day I was in my bedroom playing, and heard the strangest sounds coming from outside my windows, I got up on my bed and opened the curtains, and to my surprise I saw the strangest thing, there was a large ball outside hovering about 2 feet off the ground. It was maybe 6 or 7 feet in diameter, and had what seemed like clouds around it, and what looked like lightning bolts coming out of it, and it was making a very strange hissing sound. It went by my window on the west side of the house, then turned the corner and proceeded to go by the window on the north side of the house. I followed it with my eyes until it went out of sight. As young as I was, I still remember this vividly.

In 1984, while still in the Army and stationed in West Germany, I was married at the time and my family had just gotten in country. We were assigned temporary housing in a building that was 5 stories high. We were living on the very top floor which was more like an attic, with 8 rooms. It had skylights in every room. I vaguely remember it but apparently late one night my wife was trying to wake me up, saying that there was something strange hovering above the house, something round with lights going around it, and she was trying to get me up to see it from the skylight, but I could not wake up. I could hear and feel her yelling and pulling on me to get up, but I just couldn't get up. I don't remember anything after that, and the next day, not a word was mentioned about it by either of us. It was not until a few years later that I even recalled the incident. After talking to someone in MUFON about it, I was told that I experienced what was known as being switched off.

Well, that is my story, I know what I saw, and it is as vivid in my memory today as it was the night it happened.

ANALYSIS

As with all of these stories, I have no way to tell how accurate the witness's description of events may be. As far as the stories being, simply, fiction, of course this is possible. And yet, there is, uniformly, a desire not to be identified, as was the case with this correspondent. His original email (received in January of 2023) is very specific that his name must not be used and locations must be disguised. This makes it seem more likely that he perceives this as a real memory. But I don't care to be too credulous. What if he made a bet with a friend that he could fool me—or any of them, for that matter, set out to have me on?

Why choose this, then? Surely he would invent a roaring abduction, featuring a lovingly described rectal probe. But no, here we have an intimately personal story of a strange event that has remained vivid in his mind for forty and more years.

But of what? The close encounter literature is full of stories of alien-human hybrids and shape-shifters. The idea that Queen Elizabeth II was a giant alien reptile shape-shifted into the body of that rather slight woman was a popular urban myth for years. I suppose, if I looked, I could find people wanting to disinter the coffin to find whether or not there's a dead reptile inside, or perhaps just a few bricks.

Leaving that aside, let's discuss what might have actually happened. And no, I'm not going to try either to advocate for it as a straightforward description of a real event, or to explain it away. I would like to address it through what amounts to a filter of the unknown, which is the human mind.

All of those neurons! "What rough beast" might be slouching along those hundred trillion byways that connect them?

I would suggest that my correspondent saw something, but where was it? Could it have been in his mind? Of course. Could she have actually shape-shifted? You might expect that I would say 'no, certainly not, that's impossible,' but I have no intention of doing that. One of the cabin witnesses, Peter Frohe, experienced a shift like this happening to him.

Peter was a massage therapist in a practice that often involved his providing therapy to fragile or medically compromised clients. One day, he was treating an elderly woman who had a serious heart condition. The room contained a chair, the massage table and some cabinets. Across from where Peter stood was a wall-length mirror. As he worked, he felt a strange vibration in his body and glanced up at the mirror.

To his horror, he did not see himself doing the massage, but rather the same sort of creature that our correspondent's girlfriend became: a thin figure with huge black eyes. He was extremely concerned, because he feared that, if this was actually how he now looked and his client opened her eyes the shock might well kill her.

The only thing he could do was to continue the massage and hope for the best, and after a few minutes, he saw that he was once again his normal self. He did not observe any moments of transition. The client was not disturbed. As of the time he told me the story, it had not happened to him again.

As I reported in *Super Natural,* I had an experience of this as well. I was lying on a couch. Anne was sitting nearby reading. Like Peter, I felt a strange vibration in my body. On some level I must have known what was about to happen because I thought to myself that Anne was at last going to see an alien. Then one of our cats jumped onto my chest, yowled because he received an electric shock (there were sparks.) He jumped off and I didn't change. But later that night the vibrations came back, and this time there was no cat to interrupt the process.

I rose up off the bed a transformed being. I was extremely light and could glide rather than walk. It was as if I was at once a physical being and a flutter of dream-stuff.

Unable to wake my wife, I set off upstairs to my son's bedroom. When I glided in, he saw me and smiled. Soon after, I resumed my normal form. The next day he was furious and said that I was not to allow any of "your people" into his room again. (At the present time, he remembers nothing of this or any of the other strange incidents that he witnessed as a child. As discussed in "Visitors in the Trees," memory is a major issue when it comes to high strangeness experiences. Maybe he doesn't remember actual events that were so strange or frightening that he has blocked them out, or maybe they simply didn't happen. As is true of this entire are of experience, it is not time to close such questions.)

Rather than speculate about whether or not there are aliens hiding in our bodies, I would like to discuss the long tradition of shape-shifting that is so prevalent in human culture that it could be said to be almost universal. Even the rational west has a long tradition of werewolves, one that I myself have explored in my novels *The Wolfen* and *The Wild*.

In the Americas, the Hopi and the Navajo have traditions of shape-shifting. In Navajo myth, there is a creature called "ye'iitsoh" that can shift into various animal forms. Shapeshifters are ubiquitous in Aboriginal Australian tribes, and there are also such stories in Africa and Siberia.

Does this, therefore, mean that human beings are something other than we in the west have come to believe, which is, essentially, physical bodies and nothing more? Obviously, it depends on experience and on definitions. A shaman, wearing the skin of a buffalo, quite certainly enters the spirit of the beast, and given my own life experience, this letter and Peter's story, I wouldn't be at all surprised if he doesn't literally become the beast, his heart beating with the great buffalo heart, and by so doing drawing his fellows toward the waiting bows of the hunters.

What happened to me happened. What happened to Peter did, too. What our correspondent witnessed happened to the young woman. And Lorie Barnes was given that haunting promise: one day you will look just like us...

Who are we, then, creatures hidden within ourselves? But if so, people die all the time and I would be surprised if there was anyone other than an old queen inside Elizabeth's coffin.

But what was it? He tells me that he was (understandably) not in touch with her after the incident. So did she get into a flying saucer and go off into outer space? There's no reason not to entertain that possibility, but if so, then I'm jealous. What about my saucer?

I wonder what really happened in that apartment all those years ago. Are some of us—or maybe all of us—also something else? Do aliens walk among us wearing the human form, and if so, then are some of them, like me and Peter, trapped in the human shape—prisoners, perhaps, or unfortunates whose shape-shifting machinery has gone on the fritz?

I wonder how she lived, afterward. Did she simply go on with her life, and, looking back, think fondly or ruefully from time to time about the brief fling she'd had with a soldier she never really knew? And did she have any idea of what he had seen when she sat him down to tell him goodbye?

Or was she an alien, come here to get pregnant by him and then return home with booty that consisted of a baby in her belly?

Many years ago, a witness was given a possibly crucial piece of information: "we rearrange atoms." If that is true, then it would mean that they understand the "strong force," which is what binds atoms together. But not only understand it, the use of the word "rearrange" means that they can manipulate it. They would presumably therefore be able to change anything into anything. To do so, though, some sort of energy would need to be applied. What would that feel like in a nervous system? Vibrations, perhaps, some subtle electricity?

What are we, indeed, and what lies within?

CHAPTER 12
GLIMPSES OF AN UNKNOWN MIND

These stories are all about one thing: somebody with a mind that is not like ours is trying to engage with us. Three of them —"The Critics Speak Out"; "Visitors in the Trees"; and "I Hate You, Mommy"—are attempts to communicate and inform. "Call of the Morlocks," is an example of the actions of a mind that we don't understand, with needs that are not our needs. Why would the visitors have to call a meeting with people who are connected with them beside a busy road? And why choose two passers-by to notice the whole thing then threaten them when they stopped to look? What the meeting was about I cannot speculate. What's more, the people who attended may or may not have any memories of it. As to the two witnesses, I might note that curiosity and fear are constantly at war in the human mind, and curiosity is generally stronger; it usually wins out. If you wanted to experiment and observe this in action, you might put on a strange, foreboding display; then, when the witnesses' curiosity overcame their fear and they approached, scare them away. If you had the ability to look inside their brains or read their minds as they acted, you'd learn a great deal about us very economically. But after being here for at least seventy years and probably longer, would you even need to do this? Surely you would already know. Unless, of course, our visitors are not a monolithic presence. The sheer variety of actions on display just in these few letters suggest that this is the case. From the two thousand or so such letters that I've read, it does seem as if there are many different approaches to us and, therefore, many different personalities, or even species, involved.

"Through the Night Window," and "Where Did That Time Go," are both abductions. In each case, the witness remembers nothing of what happened. From personal experience and many other reports, we can infer that the removal of sexual material may have been involved, and yet neither witness reports the discomfort usually associated with this type of assault. As well, there are many examples of sexual attack that *are* remembered, so why choose to keep some secret?

This is one of the reasons that I chose these two letters. They are not unique, and they do serve as a reminder that there may be parts of close encounter that have been kept entirely hidden from us.

In many of these cases, the witness came back with a fragment of information.

Let's unpack this a bit, and see what we can find.

"An Entity of Total Evil" leaves us with the question: what would have happened if this man's soul had been pulled out of his body? Also, can this be done? (I will not return to a discussion of whether or not there is a soul, as my reasons for believing there is are fully explored in *Afterlife Revolution* and touched on in this book.) Both questions combine to create a third: Can one soul be removed from a body and replaced with another?

If this is the case, then humankind, living as we do in a state of soul blindness, would be very vulnerable to such an assault. Or is it that? Perhaps there are more souls than bodies, and periodically one may get changed out so that another can harvest the riches of temporal experience. Because we have no science of the soul, we are unable to address issues like this. Our science, grounded in observation of detectable phenomena, can't find anything to detect. We need to find novel ways to solve this problem, or we are going to remain open to what may be a type of manipulation of almost incalculable importance to us.

"A New You," is about the creation of a clone of the witness, or perhaps the gathering of genetic material to put into a gene bank for later use. Adults might be carefully shielded from knowledge that this is being done, but an innocent child, being cloned long before we had any inkling that it *could* be done, or how, might be treated more openly. If this is part of what the visitors want with us, it becomes obvious, now that we understand something of cloning and genetics, why memories of abductions might be erased.

"Me Within Thee," and "Let Us Begin," both hint at symbiosis, in which another entity shares the witness's body but does not possess it in the same sense that may have been the object of the "Entity of Total Evil" attack.

If we assume that our visitors are indeed from somewhere else, then what these letters reveal is a multifaceted, highly complex relationship that is unfolding between us and quite probably a number of different types of entities with differently configured brains and therefore different minds and even different ways of being part of the real world.

And yet, for all the complexity, the overall situation can be summed up as follows:

1. Efforts are being made in different ways to sample us, even possibly to recreate us. Artificial and managed birthing through the use of sexual material and re-creation through cloning would appear to be methods being employed.

2. Large-scale activities are taking place involving people— ordinary humans—who may or may not be consciously connected with our visitors. Their purpose is unknown, but a careful analysis of the letters in the archive at Rice and of the close encounter narrative in general may provide more insights.

3. At least some of our visitors understand and want to help us overcome the inability of our minds to remember our encounters. Given that so much of what is being done is invasive, the motive for their desire to do this is unclear. It may be that factions are involved, and if so, then some of them do not think we should be kept in what amounts to a state of mass hypnosis generating denial that flies in the face of the facts. (In part 2, we will discuss exactly how this denial has been orchestrated by at least some of our visitors, using our own military and political authorities as unwitting surrogates.)

There are activities that appear directed toward exploiting our souls, or using our bodies in some sort of soul exchange, that, because of our soul blindness, we passively ignore. In this sense, we are like pigs wallowing in a sty, completely oblivious to the reason that they are fed. In the context of the relationship between us and our visitors, the soul, not the body, is what is being fattened, and the experiences of life are the food it is being fed.

A huge undertaking is going on here, and to me it is fantastic that, on so many levels, it is being methodically denied and ignored. But before we lay blame for this on any part of the human side of the relationship, I will shortly demonstrate that, from the beginning, it has been our visitors who have orchestrated the secrecy. They brilliantly ensured that governments would drop a cloak over their presence. And while they are certainly very clever, their motives for doing this, and therefore the policies and actions they have taken, can most assuredly be understood.

If we discover that a tiger seeks meat, we know that's what it eats. We don't need to understand how tigers communicate with each other to understand how we need to respond to them. Similarly, if we see a swift in the evening light, we know that it flies. Careful observation can reveal to us the details of its reasons for doing so, but we don't need to be ornithologists to understand that it is darting around because it's feeding on insects.

A man, though, might have an array of needs, not all of which he will reveal. And somebody from another realm of intelligent life, with needs that we don't share, might not even be hiding them, but we will be as ignorant of them as the wild pig is of the tiger, whose stripes—visible to us—render him invisible to the pig's differently structured eyes.

Given this, wouldn't understanding the needs of our visitors be even more difficult than understanding those of another human being? Won't they be both hidden *and*, even when in plain sight, still as invisible to us as the tiger is to the pig?

Well, actually, no—not if we apply our analytical abilities objectively and with dispassion, instead of looking at the situation as we do now, through emotions of denial and fear and the resulting screen of confusion. Instead, we need to do exactly what we did with the simpler creatures: simply observe the actions of the man or the visitor. In both cases, though, another level must be recognized and never forgotten: creatures with developed intellects can deceive and may want things from us that give them reason to do just that.

I dimly recall asking the old lady of *Communion* what I could give her. She responded, "Child, what could I possibly want from you?" That is to say, she lied. Now that we know that our visitors are engaged in creating human bodies, or gathering biological material from us that gives them the ability to do so, and also that they seem to be able to move souls in and out of bodies, it is necessary to consider that they may want to create bodies that work like ours but that belong to their race and contain their souls.

That may sound far-fetched, but in the last chapter of this book, I will make a case from personal experience that this may already be happening. And I'm sorry if I offend people who cling to the belief that we are in control of our world. As long as we refuse to face the truth, we are not in control of anything.

In *The Book of the Damned,* Charles Fort famously said, "The Earth is a farm. We are someone else's property."

In some ways, I wish that this was true, but it cannot be, not quite. A farmer's first job is to make sure his farm doesn't fail. He culls his herds, keeps them healthy, makes sure that there's enough fodder for them and water for his animals and his crops. If not, the farm falls apart, and because Earth's ecosystem is falling apart, our planet is not a farm and our visitors are not farmers. Instead, when we look at how they are exploiting us, it must be concluded that they are something much more like hunters, here to take advantage of the human herd as long as it lasts.

Contact is mysterious and dangerous, like a great, dark wave rising in the night. It is a wave of discovery—that we are a prey species. But it also hints at productive change so deep that we can only guess at its ultimate meaning. Even as we discover this humbling and, frankly, frightening truth about ourselves, we also gain a new and more accurate understanding of our human meaning. The pig that doesn't understand the farmer or the tiger is helpless. But if the pig ever *does* understand, then he becomes a different sort of beast.

We are at once reaching toward just such understanding—and being guided toward it ... by the very hunters who are preying on us.

But why would they do this?

Is it that they are a house divided against itself and have two contradictory needs—one to use us and the other, perhaps, to relieve their own loneliness?

Real contact, objectively understood, will sweep our current history away and start a new history, one that includes in it an understanding of our role as nourishment or replenishment and, paradoxically, also our status as students in a school that teaches companionship. In this new history, we come face to face with the tiger who has been hidden in the tall grass of ignorance and denial, the swift whose flight we have only just begun to admit we have been recording in the form of Tic Tac, Gimbal, and Aguadilla objects, and the woman who claims that she could not possibly want anything from the child she nevertheless embraces.

Can we ever come to terms with all this? Right now, we, also, are a house divided against itself when it comes to our visitors, with our best minds still in a state of almost total denial and the community of experiencers forced to keep a low profile if they value their places in society and the economy, and sometimes even in their own homes. Our governmental leadership is caught in the bear trap of secrecy sprung on it by the visitors, and our intellectuals—frightened to their core to face the fact that they are not the most knowledgeable species on planet Earth—willingly embrace official denial as truth.

Prior to 2015, it was believed by most people engaged in the mind sciences that intelligence could not be changed. In that year, though, a breakthrough study was published that argued that the conventional wisdom of the day was wrong. "Improving Fluid Intelligence with Training on Working Memory," by Jacky Au and colleagues, showed that challenging the mind to interpret new information caused significant and lasting increases in intelligence.

My wife called the UAP mystery "a theater in the sky," and thought from the first that it was about forcing us to ask questions that we couldn't ignore and also couldn't answer. "That's how the mind grows," she said. One aspect of contact, she concluded, is that our visitors are looking for companionship.

She died the year the fluid intelligence paper was published, but it would not have surprised her. Not only the mystery of the UAPs, but also the burning questions raised by persistent official secrecy and the enigmatic and threatening quality of the close encounter experience, may be challenging us in exactly the way described in the paper, and therefore having the effect of increasing intelligence on a mass scale.

If so, then this would be another reason that the visitors continue to hide. Revealing themselves would close the primary question that they are using to increase our intelligence.

If this is really happening, can we measure it?

Probably so.

Given that a study of more than 78,000 people published in *Nature Genetics* in 2017 identified a broad range of genes that influence intelligence, would it be possible to detect changes in these genes that would be a signature of increasing intelligence? To my knowledge, this has never been explored.

Right now, there is no sign that this is going to happen, and certainly, if it does, the way it is now, the UAP/close encounter mystery will be carefully denied as a possible catalyst. Conventionally, close encounter experiences are dismissed as false memories generated when suggestible people are hypnotized. This is despite the fact that few witnesses are ever hypnotized. They are not describing false memories, at least not as defined by memory experts such as Elizabeth Loftus.

Instead of dismissing the experience, it might be worthwhile to explore it in another context. Specifically, what might *we* do if we could travel among the stars and found a planet populated by a species that had never left it and had only vague and confused ideas about extraplanetary life? If we also saw that the planet was involved in an extinction event that might happen faster than we could learn to communicate with this species, we might well take steps to preserve its genes even though we couldn't explain our actions to them. Would we also engage in the exotic forms of predation suggested by some of the letters? As we are now, we would not. We couldn't. But if we eventually identify an aspect of energy that is conscious, and learn to relate to it, we might find all sorts of new avenues, including some that involve attempts to communicate with us that look like predation but actually are much more symbiotic than they appear. I refer here to the stories of attempts to enter the bodies of witnesses and possibly to seemingly exchange souls with them.

If communication with our visitors does go forward, we would be well advised to understand why they have chosen to communicate with us using a language woven out of ancient myths and relying on demonstration and example rather than, say, conventional speech. Why make it so much harder than would seem necessary?

I can advance some possible reasons. The first is that, like everyone, they act from what they know, and this is the closest they can come to our communications methods. Additionally, if they really are from another planet and traveling in a conventional way over vast distances, say reaching a percentage of the speed of light, then time dilation might be affecting their contacts with us. To them, having departed and later returned at, say, 40 percent of the speed of light, perhaps only fifty years would have passed in their experience while thousands of years would have passed on Earth. Thus they would be explaining themselves in the context of long-lost family connections and philosophical ideas that have, among us, disappeared into the mists of time.

Given all these unanswered questions and all this mystery, what is the way forward? Or is there one?

If we cannot reverse climate change, we are, over the next few years, going to become increasingly desperate. If some of us have indeed been taught to fly the amazing craft we see around us, will we be given the means of escape, should it come to that? Or will our visitors, perceiving that our world is doomed, simply move on?

My life's work is not about preparing to face the abyss of an extinction event but rather about preventing that abyss from ever opening up. *Warday, Nature's End, Communion, Superstorm, A New World,* and this book all revolve around the central theme of human survival. My books about contact are an effort to provide tools that will facilitate useful contact, enable it to unfold on a wide scale as soon as possible, and for it to provide us with new knowledge that we can use to our benefit. For this to happen, we need to understand not only our own needs and limitations but also how revealing themselves and their needs to us might help our visitors get more of what they want out of the relationship, and communicate to them that we know this. Unless we have their help, even if it is indirect, I think that we are going to have an increasingly difficult time here. If, God forbid, we die out, this would mean that an almost limitless number of novel expressions of the total universe of human genes will never get to unfold. I am talking about billions more unique people simply not happening—all those lives, loves, ideas, successes, mistakes, hatreds, and creations just never coming into being.

If you look at the richness of any single human being, you cannot but think that this magnificent expression of nature that is us must not be allowed to disappear, a candle in the void snuffed out, or a song silenced.

Even though the belief that an alien presence is here is now bolstered by official video confirming that unknown objects are in our skies, the presence controlling them, alien or otherwise, has not yet come into focus. As yet, we don't even know if there is a definite link between close encounters and the unknown objects flying around in our skies.

I am not saying that there is no link, though, any more than the UAPs are proof of anything except what we can see about them: that they are here and that they perform in ways that could not happen using methods of propulsion that we understand. As we have recorded them doing so, we can be sure of this.

These are the only certainties: the UAPs are in some way real and of unknown origin, and the close encounter accounts are a social reality. But are the encounter narratives accurate—that is to say, do the accounts reflect memories that can be relied upon?

In all but one of the cases discussed here, there is a corroborating witness. Still, though, my purpose is not to advocate for the literal accuracy of these memories. Rather, I would assert that they are a testament of unusual experiences of some kind, and that—especially in the multiple-witness cases—the overall structure of the reports probably reflects actual events.

To those who are swept away in an extinction event, evolution is a catastrophe. The dinosaurs, the mammoths, the Neanderthals, and the other 99 percent of all species who have lived on Earth and gone extinct would certainly not support the idea that there is anything good about evolution—which leads to interesting questions about life itself: Are life forms essentially experimental by their very nature; is nature in itself an experiment devised by some elusive wizard; or is it simply what it appears to be, a system characterized by long eons of quiet development punctuated by brief periods of violent upheaval and mass extinction? It may be that our visitors are here not to prevent an extinction event from taking place but to help us manage it. I say this because their secrecy seems to contradict their warnings about our survival. They certainly want us to survive, but perhaps only a select group of us, and they will decide who that is going to be. Their presence, at once obtrusive and passive, could mean that we are not facing total extinction like the dinosaurs but evolutionary change that will leave us in some ways intact, even thriving.

Look at the greatest known extinction event, the end of the Permian. Two hundred fifty million years ago, something happened to change the balance of nature, and more than 95 percent of all creatures died out. Like four of the five great extinction events that we know of, according to Peter Brannen in *The Ends of the World,* this one appears to have been caused by a dramatic rise in carbon dioxide in the atmosphere. The exact mechanism has not been identified. It was followed by ten million years of an almost lifeless Earth.

What happened afterward is characteristic of extinction events and is arguably the single most important mechanism of evolution. Permian animals and plants were replaced by the middle of the next epoch—the Triassic—by more modern, robust ones, primarily the reptile family and later the dinosaurs. In other words, instead of starting anew, the catastrophe resulted in the appearance of new, more efficient, and more physically advanced creatures. In fact, this happens, to a greater or lesser extent, after all mass extinction events. It's part of the process, and if we go extinct, or nearly so, it will happen again, and it might be that this is exactly what our visitors want, and what they are here to manage.

But we will try to save ourselves, too. The human mind will try to manage things, of course. With our attempts to wean ourselves from fossil fuels and so much else, we're trying now. Part of our effort may be unconscious. Our survival threatened, we are looking harder at the world around us, and perhaps one result is that we have begun to see our visitors more as what they are. During past existential crises, we looked to our gods. As we have moved away from faith in supernatural entities, the shadows that used to swim in the mysterious ocean of belief have faded.

When we cease to see gods, angels, fairy folk, and the rest, is this what is left—these strangely aggressive, elusive, and rather horrible

entities? If so, could our growing awareness of them be not only
something they are orchestrating but also the human mind awakening to the reality that our world includes them—or, just as likely,
that this is their world and we are part of it? Their reason for wanting
us to survive and yet concealing themselves, even though that makes
our survival more problematic, may be that we aren't valuable to
them unless our life journey is protected from their own vast
knowledge.

As D. B. H. Kuiper and Mark Morris point out in Vol. 196 of *Science*
(April 1977), an advanced civilization would want nothing from us
except what they do not have. It is sometimes theorized that they
might come here for resources like gold or uranium, but that simply
cannot be true. All elements are plentiful in the universe. In fact,
everything is plentiful, minerals, metals, gasses, water—all of it. But
what about novelty? Is newness common and discovery endless?
Kuiper and Morris think of "what they do not have" as *innovation*—
not so much its products but its process. Their interest would be not
in our technology, our artistic works, or anything else we have made
in the physical world. Rather, they would be seeking a wellspring of
new experience or knowledge, and the unique ways of sensing and
solving life that we discover might be their best hope of finding this.

Frankly, the universe looks like a vast desert, rich in physical
resources but almost empty of life, and therefore also of discovery,
joy, excitement, and love. I think that Kuiper and Morris are probably
right—and it is not our cellphones and electric cars they are after but
our hearts and souls.

Letters like "Me Within Thee" and "Let Us Begin" suggest that
they are not here only to observe but to actually participate with us in
our lives. Never to touch our life journey in any way but to be there as
a silent witness, absorbing with us the continuous excitement of
the new.

Interestingly, we may already sense that our visitors are doing
this.

As I have mentioned, this belief has evolved in the modern
UAP/alien folklore into stories of walk-ins, or soul exchanges. Could

Ruth Montgomery's seemingly fanciful tale have caught on because we sense that such sharing is happening to us now?

In her book, she offers no corroboration beyond saying the information she received about the walk-in idea came from an anonymous fan letter. This fan, after noticing that she hadn't published anything in two years, wrote, "Are you looking for ideas for future books?" Her correspondent goes on to explain that a walk-in is a "highly evolved entity" who always enters the body with "permission" and chooses people who want to leave life before their bodies have died.

Examples offered in the book include Benjamin Franklin, but it's not clear why she believes that he was a replacement soul.

Sheila Seppi's 2020 book, *Walk-Ins: The Cosmology of the Soul*, is a good example of the genre that has evolved from the original Montgomery story. Ms. Seppi explains that walk-ins come from groups of star beings, all from different star systems and dimensions. She mentions Sirians, Arcturians, Mantis-beings, Lyrans, Vegans, Andromedans, and entities from what she describes as the seventh and thirteenth dimensions.

I wouldn't expect that these claims are accurate in detail, but as most folklore starts with observations that cannot be explained, and there are reports of seeming soul exchange in the contact narrative, they might reflect a phenomenon of which we have little awareness or understanding.

There is, of course, another sort of walk-in—one that might be heralded by a sense of the presence of "ultimate evil" and who might have drastic reasons to take over a human body.

The walk-in idea is new, but stories of demonic possession go back a very long way. The idea that mental illness involves psychological issues and brain function did not begin to be accepted until just the late nineteenth century.

Exorcism is still an accepted practice in many religions. The Roman Catholic Church, for example, has an established procedure called "Major Exorcism," which is included in the official Roman *Ritualis*. Regarding its meaning and efficacy, Paul Eno, in his book *Dancing Past the Graveyard*, chronicles (among many other experiences) some events from his early years as a novice priest assisting a prominent exorcist. At one point, a disturbed patient who was believed to be possessed levitated out of her wheelchair right in front of Paul, the exorcist, a psychiatrist, and others. The exorcist calmly asked Paul to push her back down into the chair, which he did. He told me that it "felt like she was floating. There was a little resistance when I pushed her, not much." He added that he didn't think her levitation necessarily meant that she was possessed by a demon. In fact, he eventually left the priesthood, largely because he thought that there must be rational, if presently unknown, explanations for phenomena like this.

Given what I have seen and lived with, I wouldn't rule out the existence of beings who, because of their powers and how they exercise them, might as well be called demons. Whether they are fallen angels is another question, and addressing it is not within the scope of this book.

From the time of the Enlightenment until the arrival of the film *The Exorcist* in 1973, exorcisms were in decline in the Western world. In the 1970s their numbers rose significantly but have dwindled again in recent years.

The stories of soul attack I have related here are hardly the only ones in the close encounter literature. They are not as common as stories of physical abduction, but they are reported with steady persistence. What if there is indeed something "wandering the world" and preying on us in ways that we don't understand?

If souls can exist outside of bodies, then there could be a whole incorporeal "biology," containing who knows how many different sorts of entity. In fact, if consciousness is nonlocal and there is somebody here who understands this, I think that we can expect to have what for us are going to be some very strange experiences.

Judging from the stories I have discussed, there is an exploitative side to the close encounter experience, but also a possibility that this can be changed into something more desirable to us. As long as we can provide our visitors with the experience of the new that they seem to want, once we have accepted the idea that they are a presence in some way separate from us, we might be able to develop and evolve our understanding in all sorts of innovative ways. But right now, that's not our direction. We don't believe in the soul, so even the slightest effort to quantify it in some way is not going to be made. Our scientists and most other intellectuals continue to follow the lead of the military and deny that our visitors even exist.

But what of the military? After all, its first public involvement with the phenomenon came in Roswell, New Mexico, just a few weeks after Kenneth Arnold reported his Mt. Rainier sighting. To explore further, we'll have to leave behind, for now, the common man —us—and our struggles to endure and understand contact. Let's step into the shadows and meet some of the keepers of the secrets—our leaders and our guardian soldiers.

PART II

Solders, Strangeness, Secrets and the Dead

"Everything we call real is made of things that cannot be regarded as real."
 —Niels Bohr

"You've got to be careful if you don't know where you're going, because you might not get there."
 —Yogi Berra

CHAPTER 13
SHOOT THEM DOWN

I n *A New World,* I discussed a number of early UAP incidents, from the Roswell Incident through the great UAP flap of 1952. Since writing that book, I have learned a great deal more about what may have happened then. Despite the recent impression being spread by the general media—which has no awareness of the history and only repeats the official story—that the official world is just now noticing the UAP mystery, it is on the record that the Department of Defense knew that UAPs were not of this world as early as 1947. Fortunately, Congress is aware of this, and the 2023 National Defense Authorization Act requires a joint Defense Department/Office of the Director of National Intelligence program to begin investigating all reports dating back to January 1, 1945. What is required is "a report detailing the historical record of the United States government relating to" UFOs and related phenomena.

As we shall see, this is likely to be an incomplete history and, insofar as it is complete, unlikely to reach the public very extensively.

On September 20 of 1947, General Nathan Twining, then Commanding General of the Air Materiel Command at Wright Field, Ohio, sent his now famous memorandum to Brigadier General George Schulgen, Chief of Air Intelligence in Washington, saying that "the phenomenon reported is something real and not visionary or fictitious." He continued, "the reported operating characteristics such as extreme rates of climb, maneuverability (particularly in roll), and action which must be considered <u>evasive</u> when sighted ... lend belief to the possibility that some of the objects are controlled either manually, automatically, or remotely." He enumerated six characteristics, including metallic or reflective surfaces, formation flying, lack of any exhaust trail except when moving very fast, a circular shape with a flat bottom and sometimes a dome, level flight above 300 knots, and no sound except in a few instances. Now, seventy years later, all of these characteristics can be observed in the Gimbal, Tic Tac, and Aguadilla videos. The Gimbal video was taken off the carrier USS *Theodore Roosevelt* in 2015, and the Tic Tac video off the USS *Nimitz* in 2004. The Aguadilla video was unexpectedly released by an individual who had access to it in 2013. The Tic Tac and Gimbal videos were originally released by Luis "Lue" Elizondo, former director of the now-canceled Advanced Aerospace Threat Identification Program. In 2020, they were confirmed in a Navy Department press release that read, "The Department of Defense has authorized the release of three unclassified Navy videos, one taken in November 2004 and the other two in January 2015, which have been circulating in the public domain after unauthorized releases. ... The U.S. Navy previously acknowledged that these ... were indeed Navy videos. After a thorough review, the department has determined that the authorized release of these unclassified videos does not reveal any sensitive capabilities or systems and does not impinge on any subsequent investigations of military air space incursions by unidentified aerial phenomena. DoD is releasing the videos in order to clear up any misconceptions by the public on whether or not the footage that has been circulating was real or whether or not there is more to the videos. The aerial phenomena observed in the videos remain characterized as 'unidentified.'"

Senator Harry Reid said that the footage that has been released "only scratches the surface" of what is available, and called on the Department of Defense to fully inform the public.

As we shall see, however, he might not have been right about their ability to do that.

Given that Senator Reid knew many of the secrets, it can be inferred that, unlike the defense establishment, he did not think that a release would harm national security. But did he know them all? Or, for that matter, at this point does anybody? Every president, from Dwight Eisenhower to the current officeholder, Joe Biden, has supposedly had access to the most critical secrets, and none of them have released anything. Senior Barack Obama advisor John Podesta tweeted on February 13, 2015, "My biggest failure of 2014: once again not securing the disclosure of the UFO files."

So when, in 2022, Ron Moultrie said, when asked if we had evidence of "space aliens" that "we have nothing," one has to wonder what Mr. Podesta was referring to? Or perhaps there was a bit of hair-splitting going on. Evidence of objects of unknown origin is not specific evidence of their origin or the nature of their designers.

Like Reid, Podesta would have known a lot, but not necessarily everything, and not, perhaps, what has prevented all those presidents and defense officials from telling the public the truth about this subject, if that truth does indeed involve an identifiable intelligent presence of unknown origin on Earth.

As mentioned previously, the Navy has now refused to release more video, saying that doing so would "harm national security." One must ask what it is about the unreleased videos that makes them different from the ones already released. The statement also said that release of the videos "may provide adversaries valuable information regarding Department of Defense/Navy operations, vulnerabilities, and/or capabilities."

Passive engagement, such as what we see in the Gimbal and Tic Tac videos, reveals operational tactics and some information about systems. It does not reveal either vulnerabilities or capabilities, but videos of combat engagements reveal both. Can it be, then, that at least some of the videos being withheld contain combat footage, and the fear is that, if any more footage is released, then that is liable to end up in congressional or public hands as well?

Is there now, or has there ever been, combat between military forces and unknown objects?

As we are about to see, there is evidence that the U.S. military shot at UAPs during the summer of 1952, which leads to the chilling thought that this may still be happening. That would certainly be a reason for keeping more than a few secrets, especially given some evidence that there have been pilot injuries, and worse, which I will be discussing in the next chapter.

If there is a conflict situation, why it started must be the first question asked. The military would have had to have a motive to attack unknown objects. In other words, the objects or their behavior would need to have fulfilled the definition of a threat.

At 10:58 p.m. on June 20, 1952, a U.S. Air Force F-86 attempted to intercept an unknown light that had entered the protected airspace of the Oak Ridge National Laboratory in Tennessee. The plane was on "combat air patrol," which requires confrontation with any unidentified or hostile aircraft that is located. As soon as the light was discovered in prohibited airspace, the F-86 pilot was alerted and did locate the object. When the pilot confronted it, the object responded by making what are described in Captain Edward Ruppelt's book *The Report on Unidentified Flying Objects*, originally published in 1956, as "ramming attacks." To the pilot, it appeared to be quite small, just a little less than a foot in diameter, but it was obviously aggressive. Whether or not the pilot shot at it is not recorded.

This was not the first confrontation at Oak Ridge. In the declassified FBI UFO files is an account of a series of events that had taken place at Oak Ridge in October of 1950. On October 12, "USAF radar installation at Knoxville ... picked up indications of eleven objects and perhaps more traveling across controlled area of Atomic Energy installation at Oak Ridge." Over the next few months and into 1951, there were dozens of incursions into Oak Ridge restricted airspace. "The opinions of the Security Division, AEC Oak Ridge; Security Branch, NEPA Division, Oak Ridge; AEC Security Patrol, Oak Ridge; FBI Knoxville; and the OSI, Knoxville, Tennessee, fail to evolve an adequate explanation for objects sighted over Oak Ridge, Tennessee."

There is no record of any of these incursions resulting in the scrambling of fighters. However, it is possible that this information is classified and, if there are still such confrontations, would probably still be.

The FBI report from 1951 offers numerous possible explanations but specifically rules out "the fantastic," which, given the tenor of the times, was intended to mean UAPs. What else the FBI might have thought was involved they don't say. They were trying to avoid ridicule while still communicating the facts as reported to them.

By the next year, an apparent nonconfrontational policy had obviously changed, or there would never have been a dogfight with, of all things, a tiny light. What had happened between October of 1950 and June of 1952 to cause that change is unknown. Given the unstable record-keeping that has been associated with extreme secrecy, that may never be known.

Even a close read reveals no indication of how the pilot responded to the aggression that the light displayed. But I do see, from 1950 until June of 1952, a number of what look like escalating provocations on the part of our visitors.

Were they looking for a fight?

As an aside, I want to mention that this is only what it looks like from reading publicly available information. If there was an engagement, a classified record might still be preserved, but possibly not. The reason is that, then as now, a substantial part of this story is not officially recorded. Brigadier General Arthur Exon, who had been a lieutenant colonel at the Air Materiel Command at Wright Field when the debris and bodies were brought from Roswell (but said publicly that he did not personally see the bodies), said that so much was not written down that, as late as 1988, he was still being called on to go to Wright-Patterson to fill in the scientific team working on the UAP question on incidents that had been discussed in the 1950s and 1960s. A friend who has told me that he has exposure to the classified side has said to me that "pencils up" is routine in meetings. Because of this, and because documents have been illegally destroyed, it may never be possible to write a full history of the official response to the phenomenon, with the result that the legal mandate now in place will not produce results that fully reflect what has actually happened.

In fact, it is probable that much of this history will have to be reconstructed from peripheral materials like press reports. Initially, this seems like a fraught endeavor, but it is a pattern in reportage that initially accurate stories are replaced by official lies, as happened with the Roswell Incident. By going back to original stories and discarding the later official pronouncements, it is possible that some sort of coherent history could be recovered.

It is also essential to attempt to analyze the material more deeply, rather than being stopped on the first "Did this happen?" step. It is worth asking, for example, why Oak Ridge, specifically, was receiving this unwanted attention. Why not Lawrence Livermore, for example, or Hanford, or one of the other atomic weapons facilities? They have all recorded UAP incursions, but none so extensive as what took place at Oak Ridge.

Perhaps the answer lies in the work of the lab. Could what they were doing have drawn the extraordinary attention?

The lab was built in 1942 to create plutonium out of uranium for the Manhattan Project. But by 1946, it had met that and other military objectives, and its future was in question. In *Oak Ridge National Laboratory, the First Fifty Years* by Leland Johnson and Daniel Schaffer, it is reported that there was discussion about shutting the lab down, but then it was decided to use it to produce medical isotopes. In 1950, the lab's primary mission was to design and produce reactors for energy generation. In other words, by the time of the 1950 flyovers, it was not engaged in military activities. Unless there was classified work of a military nature going on, this would seem to be the first major atomic facility in the world that had been repurposed to nonmilitary uses. So, whatever the motive behind the overflights, it was not to gather intelligence on a military nuclear facility.

Why, then, the concentration on the one nuclear facility that was *not* oriented toward weapons design and production?

There is no evidence that this question, or any of this material, was ever presented to an anthropologist or behavioral scientist of any kind for analysis. On the contrary, the public continued to be bombarded with cultural signals that these events, secretly being taken seriously by the military, were so absurd that even speculating about them would brand someone a fool. In academic and scientific circles, exquisitely sensitive to any sign of intellectual failure, UAP interest could and did ruin careers. The people who might have been able to understand were thus locked in an invisible prison of lies by others who had no more idea than anybody else of how contact should proceed. Their only response was to shoot at unknown craft that violated their rules, with no way to know whether whoever was controlling the craft was even aware of those rules, or able to understand them, or even if they could receive the radio warnings that were routinely transmitted.

That is where our modern relationship with our visitors started. I am not placing blame. I believe that it was all inevitable, and, as the evidence of conflict is so spotty, we are left to trust the judgement of defense officials about what the public should know. If the abductions happened, though, then it would seem that the right of those who have suffered these assaults to know all that is understood about them is very compelling. If such a secret is being kept, then the reason for doing so must be of more consequence than the rights of these people to understand the assaults they have endured, and to be treated, insofar as that is possible, for the injuries that they have sustained, not to mention the pain and suffering that has resulted from the social opprobrium caused by official denial and ridicule.

This cannot be done by a few vague disclosures and halting admissions. There must be a deeper level of social engagement based on fundamental cultural change.

If we are ever to progress toward useful understanding and accurate and efficient interaction with our visitors, we are going to have to enlist a broad range of the intellectual community and the general public. The whole of humanity needs to be able to think about this and be given information and tools that will enable it to do so without prejudice. The defense establishment is likely to resist real change, probably more because it is hiding its own mistakes than to protect us from some danger that might result from the release of information.

As we saw in part 1, there is danger. But the public is hardly being protected by being kept ignorant of it. All this does is enforce passivity—that is to say, official denial causes public vulnerability, and this is so obviously true that it raises the question I referred to earlier: Who is actually responsible for the secrecy? Since it imperils the public, the policy must originate with the visitors. The primary effect of official denial, ridicule, and silence regarding the truth is to make it easier for the visitors to approach members of the public at will. Therefore, it is not our policy but theirs. By protecting its secrets, the official world is exposing the public to harm. Therefore, it is not acting in support of our policy, which would be to protect the public, but in support of the visitors' policies, which are to exploit the public, albeit in ways we don't fully understand. So apparently without realizing it, our government is working for the visitors.

The summer of 1952 continued to be extremely active. The provocation that had gradually heated up starting in 1950 now came to full boil. From July 12 through July 29, UAP swarms overflew Washington, D.C., causing an international uproar and a great deal of trouble for the U.S. Air Force.

The Air Force was called upon publicly by the media, and no doubt also in the secret halls of government, to explain and manage what was assumed then, as it is now, to be a more-or-less conventional threat of intrusion into airspace we consider our own.

It could not explain but it could and did attempt to manage.

On July 28, 1952, the United Press news service reported that "the Air Defense Command alerted jet interceptor pilots Monday to take off instantly in pursuit of any 'flying saucers' sighted in the country." It was further reported in the *San Francisco Examiner* on July 29 that orders had been issued to "shoot down" the flying saucers if they refused to land.

Under the circumstances—with the Cold War just starting and the origin of the disks unknown—this response was, sadly, inevitable. From the standpoint of the occupants of the unknown craft (and there were occupants, as we shall see), their incursions could have had a number of purposes. Among them might have been a reconnaissance of our military capabilities, but their overall stance did not indicate or result in any sort of conventional attack from their side. Despite Air Force denials at the time, it seems probable that we did attack them. One reason would be that some unexplained events and UAP incursions did take place over sensitive facilities.

One example unfolded at the DuPont Savannah River Site on August 2. Nuclear materials for hydrogen bombs were being created at the site, making it a highly sensitive area. At 7:30 a.m., what was described as "a shapeless, incandescent flash of light" was seen overhead. It was never explained, but we can be sure that it was investigated as thoroughly as possible, and its strangeness would have added to the atmosphere of concern that the unknown lights and objects in U.S. skies were causing the Department of Defense and the Air Force. UAPs had been observed over the site on May 10.

Over the course of the summer, more UAP sightings and, worryingly, what seemed to the official world to be more and stranger provocations, continued to take place around the country. The strangest and most famous of these was the Flatwoods Monster case, which unfolded 206 miles west of Washington in West Virginia.

On the night of September 12, three flaming objects flew in from the Atlantic and over the East Coast. One of them was seen to drop down in the area of Wallow Gap, Virginia, another near Charleston, West Virginia, with reports from Morgantown, WV, and Zanesville, Ohio. In Cabin Creek, WV, "it looked like it stopped right in midair just before it came down." As they flew, all were moving at between 300 and 500 miles an hour and were all seen to be dropping flaming debris. At 8:00 p.m., one of them violated the Washington Air Defense Identification Zone, crossing over the city while engulfed in flames. By failing to give warning of its presence or identify itself, it triggered standing USAF rules of engagement. Even so, no planes were scrambled, and the object continued moving westward. Why they were not scrambled will become evident shortly, and the answer is both surprising and disturbing.

Twenty-five minutes after the Washington overflight, some boys playing football in the town of Flatwoods, West Virginia, observed a flaming object pass overhead and apparently drop down into a nearby field. As Flatwoods is 206 miles from Washington, D.C., the object was traveling around 490–500 miles per hour. Meteors travel in the atmosphere at an average speed of 30,000 miles an hour. In September of 2022, one observed over Ireland and parts of England was moving at about 6,000 miles per hour and was considered unusually slow. Clearly, this was almost certainly not a meteor. In addition, the object was on a much flatter trajectory than would be expected from a meteor, and like the others, it was seen to be dropping bits of debris as it descended across the skies of the eastern U.S. Nevertheless, this and the other two objects that came in from the Atlantic at the same time were dismissed as meteors. Even state troopers who saw these objects assumed that they were aircraft in distress.

If the West Virginia witnesses are to be believed, what landed in Flatwoods was a craft of unknown origin. At the time, of course, the witnesses were ridiculed, but the exhaustive testimony that researcher Frank Feschino amassed in his 2007 book *Shoot Them Down!: The Flying Saucer Air Wars of 1952,* suggests that something did happen there, and specifically that an object that appeared to be some sort of escape capsule was what the boys saw.

All three objects would have entered the Atlantic coastal air defense zone prior to passing over the coastline. Were they attacked with rockets fired from jets, and was that why they were in flames and why they crashed?

Feschino collected a total of forty-two witness accounts of the overflights, most of them describing flaming objects. The Flatwoods object was seen by six witnesses to disintegrate or disappear in the minutes before the Flatwoods Monster was discovered by the local children. Given that we now know for certain that unknown objects are real, it seems clear that Feschino's work should not have been ignored. As a "UFO researcher" he, along with hundreds of others over three generations, has been isolated in a ghetto that is, to put it simply, considered irrelevant. UFO-related books are generally ignored by reviewing media that is not itself inside the ghetto.

Feschino was unable, like most other authors working in this field, to find a publisher for his book. Another important effort, *Peculiar Phenomenon: Early United States Efforts to Collect and Analyze Flying Discs*, by New Mexico State Representative J. Andrew Kissner, exists in the public space only on Linda Moulton Howe's Earthfiles website.

The thorough research and competent historicity of both authors are evident throughout their books.

The difficulty of publishing books in this field is not only because of prejudice in the publishing industry. It is also because the books don't sell widely to a public that has been led to believe the subject isn't worth thinking about. The public, in turn, has been led there by official elements compelled by their need conceal their inability to control the situation to deny that there even *is* one. And as I have said, the visitors, by what they have done in our skies and in our bedrooms, have forced the official world to resort to denial. How can they do otherwise? They cannot admit that somebody is entering peoples' homes and taking sexual material right out of their bodies, and that the law enforcement and defense establishments can't do anything about it.

Mr. Kissner was one of the advisers to New Mexico Congressman Steven Schiff, to whom I and others also provided advice. Responding to requests from his constituents, Congressman Schiff, after being stonewalled by the Department of Defense for some time, in 1993 got the General Accounting Office (now the Government Accountability Office) to conduct an investigation. In the end, it was found that all records from the Roswell air base between 1947 and 1952 had disappeared. They had, in other words, been illegally destroyed.

Mr. Kissner, like Frank Feschino, set about researching original news sources and ignored and overlooked testimony, and also built a powerful case that, from 1947 on, conflict had occurred between elements of the U.S. military and the visitors.

While the U.S. Air Force claimed in 1994 that none of its aircraft were involved in accidents in the Roswell area in July of 1947, Mr. Kissner determined that a P-80A jet had crashed near Carrizozo, New Mexico. For unknown reasons, the FBI became involved in the investigation. The Atomic Energy Commission told the public to stay away from the area due to "continuing radiation studies."

The P-80A had a payload capacity of approximately 5,000 pounds, but the lightest atomic bombs in the U.S. inventory at the time weighed in excess of 9,000 pounds, so the jet was unlikely to have been carrying an atomic bomb. Why, then, was the AEC involved, and why was there a radiation warning?

At the same time, the Air Materiel Command deployed the first surface-to-air missile system to New Mexico and West Texas. The missiles were moved from Wendover Field in Utah. Previously, on May 15, a German V-2 rocket that had been test-fired from White Sands went astray due to what Lieutenant Colonel Harold R. Turner, the White Sands Proving Ground commanding officer, described to the *Las Cruces Sun-News* as "peculiar circumstances." According to *United States Civilian Space Programs* (p. 166), as the rocket ascended, radar operators reported that an unknown object had appeared near it when it reached an altitude of forty miles. The rocket immediately changed course and was destroyed by ground control officers two minutes later.

"Peculiar circumstances" indeed.

According to a story published in the paper on May 20, the proving ground was locked down and access was cut off after the incident.

Another launch failed on May 29, and the rocket crashed in Mexico near Juarez. A July 3 launch also failed, but the rocket remained on the White Sands facility.

None of these are mentioned in the published history of the White Sands V-2 launches.

There was further activity on May 29 that suggests that something strange was happening in the area. At 5:30 p.m., according to the *Las Cruces Sun-News,* and again at 6:00, Navy Helldivers met with accidents. The first crash was reported as a landing gear failure. The second was said to involve a student pilot, whose landing attempt caused the plane to turn over.

According to the *El Paso Times* of May 30, 1947, at 7:15 p.m. a Wasserfall surface-to-air missile was fired at unidentified radar targets that had appeared in the area. The missile's proximity warhead detonated at an altitude of 60,000 feet.

Over the next two months, more than sixty military aircraft were lost, most of them over the continental United States. One hundred twenty airmen were killed and seventy-four injured. The Roswell Incident took place in July.

A quiet period seems to have begun in 1948, with few incidents reported until 1952, when another and very different wave of sightings and events unfolded.

One thing is clear about what happened in the summer of 1952: it was not the sort of invasion the Defense Department might have been expecting. Nobody landed, overwhelmed our defenses, and enslaved or annihilated the population. But that's what invasion meant to the soldiers of that era. Most of them had served in World War II, which had been caused, in large part, by Adolf Hitler's ambition to do just that to the rest of Europe.

What, then, might have been intended? The Washington overflights in July involved no threatening maneuvers and so cannot be called a show of force. If the media reports mentioned above are correct, the United States government reacted by generating new rules of engagement that would result in unknown objects being fired on if they did not respond to demands.

Analysis of the ten close encounter witness letters made it clear that we are dealing with something that, while logical, thinks very differently than we do—so differently that it is fair to speculate we may be dealing with a brain that processes input differently from the way ours do.

Based on this, I think that what happened in 1952 may well have been an attempt at communication. Public overflights without any hostile or intimidating behavior don't convey an aggressive message. In fact, if we wanted to show ourselves to an intelligent species we had discovered on another planet, we might well do the same.

Any means the occupants of the craft may have used to communicate directly with us did not work, or they didn't attempt anything more than the overflights themselves. From this we can conclude that either they didn't expect our reaction or they wanted to draw fire.

Given how UAP sightings and close encounter experiences have evolved since the decades after 1947, it would appear that they have used the time and all the overflights and contacts to gain knowledge of us. Two things can be determined: the first is that the theater in the sky has become part of life. Anomalous lights moving through the night skies are no longer rare. In fact, some observers who have learned to distinguish them from satellites report that they see them nightly. There are even camera tours in some places.

We now can see, over the past seventy years, three general phases of contact. The first involved overflights and military provocations. These tested our level of aggression and our weapons. Starting in the 1960s, the abduction phenomenon followed. Now, it's mostly overflights.

Three phases of contact can be observed. In the first, our defensive capabilities were assessed and an effort may have been made to ensure that our military would keep the reality of the situation secret. In the second, an extensive program of physical contact that involved abduction and the extraction of sexual material from human beings and possibly other species took place. The human abductions peaked in the 1970s then gradually declined until they are no longer reported. The third phase involves extensive day and night overflights, which, as this is being written, are increasing steadily. At the same time, the official stance of denial is changing, and the U.S. Congress is pressuring the defense establishment for more openness.

If I am correct about the way this pattern is evolving, what we are seeing is a slow approach that first tested our defenses and level of aggression, then took a deep dive into our physical and psychological makeup, and now is engaged in a gradual emergence into the public eye.

I wouldn't assume that this is going to be a particularly pleasant event, should it come to pass. If what has happened so far is any indication of what we can expect, we are more likely to find ourselves confronting a presence that is not very flexible in its approach to us and uncompromising in its treatment. I don't see any evidence of hostility, but also little evidence that it will be respecting the rights and cultural space that we afford one another. Depending on the motive that brought it here, this could become a very difficult situation for us. To know that motive, we have to understand the reason for the abductions. It may be possible for us to get a reasonable idea of this, but the people who were abducted are getting older, so every day that passes means that less evidence can be gathered from them. As I have said before, we need physical and psychological studies and the evolution of a stable narrative in order to even begin to theorize. As we shall see, the development of such a narrative may well be possible.

To understand what sort of response we might evolve if we want contact to become something valuable for us, let's look at a situation right here in human society similar to the one the visitors face with us.

After the tsunami that devastated coastal communities around the Indian Ocean in 2004, the Indian government became concerned about a tribe on an isolated island in the middle of that ocean. These were the inhabitants of Sentinel Island, whose isolation is carefully protected. (This is out of altruism on the part of the Indian government because the islanders have indicated that they want it badly enough to have killed intruders from the outside world in the past.) As their remote island was directly in the path of the tsunami, it was feared that the entire tribe might have perished. (As was found, they had anticipated the tsunami and moved to higher ground with the animals and so survived.)

They are among the first settlers of the Andaman Islands, coming from Africa around 55,000 years ago. Their language is virtually unique. They know little of the outside world and want nothing to do with it. When a helicopter was sent to investigate and see if they needed help, their reaction was strikingly similar to that of the USAF to the flying saucers of the late 1940s and 1950s: One of the islanders ran out onto the beach and shot arrows at it. Obviously, the tribe had survived. The government left them alone.

We have reacted to our visitors in exactly the same way as the islanders did to the helicopter. This wasn't stupid. It was inevitable. Not only that, I think the evidence is strong that it was induced by the visitors. From the first, they made sure that our official world would keep them a deep, dark secret. Similarly, when they deem that the time is right, they will control their own revelation. It must never be forgotten that no human entity is in control of the situation. They are.

As our planet continues to wear out and our peril increases, if they conclude that they can help us, I think they will get closer to us.

This does not necessarily mean that they are entirely altruistic and benevolent. As we have seen, their overall stance toward us so far is much more that of a military organization on a mission than a scientific group undertaking a study. They induced conflict then shot back. They kidnapped thousands of people and extracted sexual material from them without explaining themselves. Now, they are acclimatizing us to the fact that they are here, but not to themselves as creatures (if that is even what they are) or to their intent.

The reaction of the Sentinelese islanders resulted in the helicopter leaving the area. Perhaps there were people on the island who could have used help. That will never be known. The helicopter pilot had his orders, and he followed them. Had he been a Portuguese seafarer in the sixteenth century, his reaction would have been different. He might have come ashore, rounded up the islanders and taken them off to sell as slaves. If any resisted, they would have been killed.

From the way our visitors have approached us so far, I think that it's reasonable to expect that they will be prepared to enforce any demands they may make of us, but at the same time, there will be payback in the form of a vast increase in human knowledge, indeed, one so profound that it will entirely change not only how we understand ourselves and the world around us but, in many ways, even what we are. If there is a soul, and the barrier between us as physical beings and us as conscious energy falls, then we will become an entirely different presence in reality. Even if that is not the case, merely integrating our visitors into our lives as a cultural reality is going to change us more profoundly than any other event in human history.

If whoever is out there started out with an intention to make immediate contact, they must have seen that we would not be able to respond usefully—especially if part of their purpose here is at least in part exploitative, which does seem to be the case.

Whatever happened in 1952 seems to have caused damage to their craft and may have even required the rescue of a downed pilot, so they cannot have been prepared to defend against it. This means that our visitors' early policy toward us did not include the possibility that we might be hostile.

If Frank Feschino's lonely and determined effort is correct, then what happened on that day was that we attacked somebody who did not understand that this was going to happen but who did possess breathtakingly advanced technology and a very different mind. Where that has led is not to a fight but to a carefully orchestrated effort, first to understand us and now to make what appears to be a more direct and open approach to us.

Does this mean that they were different from those who were reacting to our missile tests in the New Mexico desert five years earlier? Without more insight into the minds of the visitors, there is no way to know.

One thing does seem clear: there is a great deal more to the story of the military's relationship with our visitors than even the best researchers have uncovered. It involves strange weapons, bizarre injuries, and the consequences of aggression toward them in the lives of those who have ended up on the front lines. To explore further, we move from the troubled skies of the early 1950s to medical labs of the present time and, sadly, also, to morgues. In doing so, though, we enter deep into the heart and mind of man, into our very soul, which is where, from the day they arrived, our visitors have gone in search of us, trying to bring into a focus that they can understand the enigma that is mankind—and perhaps not fully realizing, if at all, that we are a mystery also to ourselves.

What of the other mystery here, the visitors? Theirs is, after all, half the story of this conflict.

I think that it begins during World War II and intensifies dramatically after the first atomic bomb test at the Trinity site in New Mexico on July 16, 1945. According to *Trinity* by renowned researcher Jacques Vallée and his co-author Paola Harris, the first crash ever to be witnessed took place at the site in August, just a few weeks later. Two boys happened on the object, which was intact but damaged. They saw occupants inside who were about four feet tall and humanoid. They didn't have helmets. They stayed inside the vehicle, and when the military arrived to collect it some days later, they were gone.

The visitors next appeared during the White Sands V-2 tests, then again in close proximity to the Roswell Army Air Field and its atomic bomber wing.

They crashed at the Trinity site, disrupted the V-2 launches and possibly crashed doing that as well, then crashed again at Roswell.

This is not a picture of somebody engaging in hostilities, at least, not yet. It looks more like a poorly planned effort to investigate and disrupt military activities related to atomic weapons. Then, between 1950 and 1952, comes more interest in atomic facilities and what may have been an attempt both to create a show of force with the Washington flyovers and possibly to communicate.

As I have mentioned, in later years there have been well-documented incursions into sensitive areas involved with either nuclear missiles or nuclear reactors and manufacturing.

Their early attempts to warn about nuclear danger—if that was indeed the purpose—were a mix of intimidation and failed communication. This is probably because they were trying to do two contradictory things at the same time: warn us and assess our military capabilities using provocation. The reason I think that warning might have been part of it is that they later visited U.S. and Russian nuclear installations and sabotaged them in such a way that, to the Russians, it looked as if the visitors could override the military's control of the missiles and, in the case of the U.S., that they could alter targets.

This may reflect an awareness of the different fears of the two military cultures. The Russians, with their rigidly hierarchical system, would most fear somebody injecting themselves into the command structure. Robert Hastings, in his book *UFOs and Nukes: Extraordinary Encounters at Nuclear Weapons Sites*, offers accounts based on witness testimony that illustrate the two different types of disruption.

On October 4, 1982, according to Hastings's book, a disk hovered over a Soviet IRBM base in Ukraine for some time, whereupon the missiles activated and began their launch sequence, an event that should have been impossible without direct action at the highest command levels. Only at the last minute was the launch sequence stopped. The Russians elected to completely dismantle the command center where the event had taken place.

An event that apparently took place at Malmstrom AFB in Montana in 1967 is currently steeped in controversy, but Senator Harry Reid, who had access to classified information and initiated the Advanced Aerospace Threat Identification Program in 2007, expressed an awareness of interference with missiles in the James Fox documentary *The Phenomenon*, and Captain David Schindele goes into detail in his 2017 book *It Never Happened* about how a UAP took all ten of his missiles offline at Minot AFB in North Dakota in 1966. Neither the senator's statement nor Captain Schindele's claims are in dispute.

The conclusion seems obvious: the visitors are making choices in this situation that are very different from the ones we would make. When they have attempted to indicate a concern about nuclear weapons, their method has only led to confusion.

Why not simply contact presidents and generals, prime ministers and religious leaders? The impact would be enormous. But instead, we see this strange, chaotic attempt to point out the dangers without directly communicating with anybody—an attempt that, it seems blatantly obvious, was and is certain to fail. In the end, it left a number of our visitors killed, initiated a hostile relationship with the U.S. military that continues to this day, and, given the continuing level of nuclear danger, didn't come anywhere close to achieving its apparent objective.

The whole period from 1947 through 1952 is an exercise in confusion and miscommunication. The problem erupts again in 1973 and continues into the present.

The military may well be dealing with the following situation: It seems possible that it is engaged in a hidden conflict and has been for years and is concealing it behind a shield of denial. Whether it has tried to do so or not, it has not prevented uncontrolled close encounters and abductions. The only time the true extent of the encounter phenomenon emerged, however briefly, was when Anne and I received hundreds of thousands of letters after *Communion* was published. I'm sure that the military possesses advanced weapons that we in the public know nothing about, but it seems pretty clear that can't dominate this strange, shadow-haunted battlefield, if it is even trying.

Thus, we continue on, the public neutralized by the denials, the media generally supporting the position they have taken from the beginning, that there is no evidence of a nonhuman presence on Earth, and a smattering of soldiers and scientific and medical support personnel apparently keeping the truth a closely guarded secret.

What will our visitors do next? Have they learned enough to finally communicate with us in a way we can understand? Or will they, as the oceans close over our cities and the dark winds rise, quietly steal away, back into the mystery from which they emerged?

But what about changing our approach? Do we need to keep shooting? Do we need to keep lying?

We come now to a hidden world of powerful religious zealots, scientists frustrated by a system that puts secrecy before knowledge, and courageous soldiers, some with destroyed minds, some in their graves.

CHAPTER 14
THE TRAGEDY OF SECRECY

T he shooting war that defense officials claim never happened at all may not only have actually happened in the '40s and '50s, it may still be going on. In 2022 a soldier who had been deployed to Afghanistan in 2008 posted a video on YouTube that was taken on May 3, 2011. It shows what happens to be a group of four stationary lights hanging over a U.S. Army forward firebase. It is not the usual simple fake that abounds on YouTube, blurred to conceal computer graphics effects. Initially and judging from the material that can be seen dripping from them, it might be possible to identify them as flares. However, they are absolutely stationary in the sky. Flares drift slowly downward and may be affected by wind. These objects are as still as stones.

The images were captured by a target acquisition camera, and all the characteristic identifiers included by such cameras are present on the video. At first, the four lights are seen hanging motionless in the sky.

A few seconds into the video, the camera locks onto two of the objects. An instant later, they are struck by missiles. There are dramatic explosions that completely engulf both objects. When the smoke clears, the objects are still present in the sky. They have not moved in any way whatsoever. They were impervious to the missile strikes.

Not flares, then, or drones, or, in fact, anything we can understand. The detonations of the missiles coincided with their arrival at the targets, meaning that the missile targeting systems interpreted them as solid objects. There was a tremendous release of kinetic energy in the form of two simultaneous explosions. And yet the objects didn't even shudder. Not only that, the material dripping out of their lower surfaces remained undisturbed.

Were the objects, then, some distance *behind* the missiles? If so, then why did the warheads detonate?

This is all impossible. And yet, there it is on video from a targeting camera. It can be found on YouTube in a video entitled "US Fighter Jets Battle UFOs over Afghanistan."

It is understandable that the soldiers involved, operating on an isolated forward base in hostile territory and confronted with objects that they could not identify as friendly, called in a missile strike. What is wrong here is not what the soldiers did, but rather that they had no orders telling them not to. What happened after the failure we have no way to know, and so far the witness who sent the video to the YouTube channel has not come forward.

What this video shows is a significant change from what was happening in the 1950s. In those days, if the damage to the craft that fell near Flatwoods was due to fighter action over the Atlantic, our weapons seem to have had an effect. Now, much more powerful and sophisticated missiles have none. It can be inferred, then, that our visitors can now react to our attacks using passive countermeasures. One might suppose, then, that they are treating us like frightened and dangerous animals, doing nothing to explain themselves while at the same time protecting themselves like divers do when they film from the safety of a shark cage.

Probably the most important question to ask about the incident is why, at this late date, are we still shooting. In this case, the answer may be that nobody in the chain of command involved knew anything about the visitors. Given how extreme the secrecy around the subject is, it seems possible that low- and middle-ranking soldiers in an ordinary military unit would have no information about them or any orders governing what to do if they appeared.

All they probably knew was that unknown objects were engaging in the surveillance of a sensitive location. Their response was inevitable, and given the complete lack of effect the missile strikes had, the operators of the objects had prepared for the attack; after all these years of entering restricted and sensitive airspace, they must have expected the reaction they got.

One of the greatest tragedies of the modern world of information sharing, and a great impediment to the advance of knowledge, is something called "need to know." It is the most basic protocol of the classification system. Classified information cannot be shared, even among people with identical levels of clearance, unless they have a specific and carefully defined need to know, and the more secret the information, the more narrow the definition becomes.

This is a good way of keeping secrets, but it is also an institution-alization of human fallibility. Somebody must decide who has need to know and who does not. Enter politics, prejudice, confusion, and fear, the four horsemen of this particular apocalypse. Add to it the devastation of pencils up and liberal funding, and you have a hidden official culture popularly known as the secret government or, more grandly, the breakaway civilization. (I might add here that the Pentagon's bookkeeping is notoriously haphazard and a great deal of money is routinely unaccounted for. In fact, in its 2022 audit, only 39 percent of its assets could be accounted for.) However the inner circle is constituted, from a small group of "read-in" specialists to a huge operation, it controls a repository of knowledge vital to the welfare of mankind and human progress. This knowledge is not only not allowed to enter the commonweal, as I have suggested, it probably can't even be the subject of a secret history. It is kept in such tiny, isolated information compartments that, as they shift and change, it is, in all probability, routinely lost.

This next story illustrates this problem.

After his death, some unusual documents were found among the effects of astronaut Dr. Edgar Mitchell. In 1973, Mitchell had created the Institute of Noetic Sciences after a profound personal experience of the boundless nature of consciousness and the preciousness of life that occurred while he was gazing back toward Earth from the moon. This experience inspired him to seek a way of applying scientific techniques to the study of numinous reality, which remains a basic objective of the institute.

These particular papers, however, have nothing to do with noetic sciences. Instead, they are about attempts to organize, or simply to find, information about UAPs and other such matters within the secret government. There are two different sets of documents. The first, from 1985, is a group of nine slides outlining a plan to set up an organization within the Department of Defense that would gather UAP information and arrange for it to be organized and analyzed. The second is a set of notes of a meeting between astrophysicist Eric W. Davis and former director of the Defense Intelligence Agency, Admiral Thomas Wilson. Admiral Wilson has denied their authenticity, but the fact that they mention a meeting between Edgar Mitchell and UFO investigator Dr. Steven Greer in 1997 that Dr. Mitchell discussed personally with me suggests that they do have some credibility. In our conversation, Dr. Mitchell went over a number of things that he had discussed with Dr. Greer and asked my opinion about them, which I gave him.

Among the people referenced in these documents whom I know or knew are Dr. Mitchell, Dr. Hal Puthoff, Colonel John Alexander, reporter and author Leslie Kean, Colonel Philip Corso, and Dr. Christopher "Kit" Green. I have met Dr. Greer but do not know him well. Given that I have discussed the precise issues referenced in the documents with all of these people over the years, I would say I believe that the documents are authentic. They are not, however, some kind of smoking gun, and I am not discussing them here in an attempt to determine whether they may contain or suggest the contents of official secrets. My purpose is to illustrate the difficulty interested parties, even those with specialized access paths, encounter in trying to untangle the knots that classification procedures produce. I am sure that this particular tranche of documents is a record of one of many such meetings held over the years by these particular individuals and many others.

Let's take a brief journey through the documents to see what this group of intelligence professionals was seeking to learn and what they wanted to do.

The overall set of documents begins with a Department of Defense Request for Visit or Access Approval for an Advanced Theoretical Physics Conference dated on May 8, 1985. There follows an outline of a meeting convened to set up a central facility that would gather UAP information both from inside the Department of Defense and from companies working with it and coordinate research. But why, in 1985, didn't such a facility already exist? Or did it, and these particular individuals were not read-in on it? The fact that they couldn't answer those two questions then, and we can't answer them now, is the core of the problem and the critical weakness of the entire classification system. By the way it is constructed, while it keeps secrets fairly effectively, it is also virtually certain to lose some in the process.

Before I discuss the 1985 notes in detail, I would like to address something that UFO researcher Richard Dolan said in his blog post of June 15, 2019, on his Richard Dolan Members website. He commented, "As more and more people realize these notes are genuine, another, more powerful realization will settle in: that our official government has lost control over the black budget program to reverse engineer extraterrestrial technology."

This is a disturbing reminder both of Ron Moultrie's confident assertion that the Department of Defense had no information indicating a nonhuman presence and was not in possession of any materials of unknown origin and a warning about what the outcome of the 2023 Defense Authorization Act's mandate that the Defense Department look back through its records all the way to 1945 to see if it has any such information. I think that it is probable that it does have some information, but likely that it doesn't have everything, and probably not anything of real importance.

In the 1980s, these officials had obviously realized that organization was lacking. Their notes display an effort to determine what records different agencies may possess in order to create a sort of central clearing house. They suspected or perhaps knew that there were active programs and that somebody had knowledge of what was going on. They were trying to find them.

I have known of one program since 1986 and another since 1988, but neither involved intelligence gathering. Rather, they concerned the study of materials—the very sort of materials that Mr. Moultrie now believes that the DoD does not possess and never has possessed. Admittedly, these studies might be carried out not by the department itself but within the defense industry, but there should still be records of them in the department.

Understand, as I have said before, I don't think that Mr. Moultrie was lying or attempting to cover anything up. I think that he was speaking based on the information that is available to him.

I came to knowledge of the first program in the following way. I'd had my series of close encounters in the fourth quarter of 1985. By March of 1986, I had determined that they were of unknown origin. In that same month, I'd met Budd Hopkins, who had a good knowledge of the UAP research community. In May of that year, I had begun working on *Communion*. By July, I was in search of any physical evidence of the existence of an advanced, possibly nonhuman, presence on Earth. I knew that my book needed corroboration, but I was also trying to understand the extent of what UFO researchers knew about the subject.

Budd introduced me to Stanton Friedman, telling me that he was one of the leading researchers. He had a rather strange background, with a master's in nuclear physics rather than a PhD. But when I checked his research, it proved to be more than extensive. It was absolutely exhaustive. This man was obsessed with UFOs. I asked him if he knew anybody who might have access to direct knowledge of physical extraterrestrial objects in the possession of U.S. authorities or private industry and might be willing to talk to me. He offered the name of Dr. Robert Sarbacher, telling me that there was a published letter written by Dr. Sarbacher stating that he had worked with debris from recovered flying saucers and did not understand why there was so much secrecy surrounding the subject. On July 23, 1986, or very close to that date, I telephoned Dr. Sarbacher. Because of the disturbing event that happened immediately after our conversation, I reported in *Communion* only the publicly available information. I was beginning to realize that I was entangled in something that was fraught with secrecy and I was uneasy about the matter—made more so by what happened to Dr. Sarbacher.

He told me that "fabric we obtained at Roswell had molecular welds so small you couldn't even identify what they were until the '60s, when the microscopes to do it became available."

He then asked me to write down my experiences and send them to him via overnight express, which I did, dispatching them via UPS overnight from my Upstate New York cabin on July 25.

A few days later, a UPS agent called me and told me that the package couldn't be delivered because Dr. Sarbacher had died, having fallen off his boat. Members of his family later stated that he died of natural causes. The agent told me that my package would be returned, but it never was.

Perhaps I should have seen this as a coincidence, but the timing of his death frightened me, and then when my document was not returned, I was even more distressed. Was some sort of malign intervention, official or unofficial, involved? I never found out.

My point here is that there was clearly work going on in 1986 involving strange materials that, in Dr. Sarbacher's mind, were associated with UFOs. Dr. Sarbacher was not shy about his interest. He spoke to UFO researchers William Steinman, Jerome Clark, Stanton Friedman, and William Moore, saying that he had been officially informed of the crash of an extraterrestrial craft in the Southwest in the early 1950s. It has never been clear if this was the Roswell Incident or another crash. In a letter to William Steinman dated November 29, 1983, he said that "John Von Neumann" (among others) was definitely involved in the study of the materials from crashes. I mention this specifically because General Arthur Exon, a family friend and later commandant of Wright-Patterson Air Force Base, told me personally that Dr. Von Neumann, a physicist called by the media at the time "the smartest man in the world" was involved in study of the material obtained.

He also stated in the letter, "I got the impression these 'aliens' were constructed like certain insects we have observed on Earth," which correlates to many other descriptions, including that of General Exon, who said to me that he had seen the biological remains.

As I have mentioned, General Exon told me in 1988 that at that time he was still involved on a regular basis with a scientific committee at Wright-Patterson who were working on the materials and biological remains obtained at Roswell.

So why is it that, in 1985, this group of highly cleared individuals are seen to be struggling to locate information within the defense establishment and coordinate its study? Nothing is mentioned about General Exon, and it's as if Robert Sarbacher didn't exist. There is even speculation in the documents about whether or not the defense establishment possesses any intact disks or other technology.

If this state of affairs existed in 1985, it is not surprising that, in 2022, the Deputy Secretary of Defense for Intelligence might say and believe that DoD has no materials and no information about any crashes.

It seems to me that need to know, pencils up, and probably inter-service rivalries have conspired to turn what should be the most vital and important line of study in all of science and the academy into a morass of confusion that is impeding research even behind the wall of secrecy. To make matters worse, a vast social engineering project dedicated to denial has been operating since the beginning, and one must come to the dismaying realization that Dolan is exactly right and we are face to face with a human disaster of the first order. It is made worse, in my mind, by the knowledge that there has been extensive work on the Roswell materials and many other things, but it is so compartmentalized that many people who could be very helpful are not even aware that such projects exist.

When I think of what Steven Hawking might have discovered about gravitic propulsion, or what insights Carl Jung might have had into the relationship between our own myths and the way we experience contact with these unknown entities, or how our great academics, scientists, and philosophers might react right now to the knowledge that this mystery exists behind the closed doors of secrecy, I find myself frustrated and deeply saddened. (Note that I do not use the phrase "antigravity" here. That is thought of as the process of creating a space in which there is no gravity. I am using "gravitic" to refer to research into systems that generate their own gravity. Such systems would function in a state of physics-independency, outside of universal gravity, and would have functionality similar to what we see in the official videos that have been released.)

What has happened is that humanity, because of a fundamentally flawed classification system that causes information to be lost, has been denied the chance to ask the most important questions ever asked. So far, at any rate.

But why? I can easily understand why some of our visitors might want to keep their activities secret, but why do we want to hide their presence?

My best guess is that there is no policy. So much has been lost in the system that we can no longer tell what we're hiding, and possibly not even why.

Our secret-keeping process was developed when the Cold War was just starting. The United States was not an experienced secret keeper but found itself plunged into a situation where there was an absolutely urgent need to do just that. Early mistakes, such as the way need to know is structured, became institutionalized before it was realized how much they could hamper the sharing of information and impede the ability to declassify. In addition, when mistakes were made, the temptation to hide them behind classification was and is, I would think, irresistible. We now have a black budget so huge that it supports what amounts to a hidden country that is all around us. Its borders are not legal boundaries but the enforced silence of its citizens. I am not at all sure that it is an intentional creation. It seems to me that it is more likely to reflect deeper, more organic dysfunction, a side effect of a flawed system.

The Directorate of National Intelligence that was formed after 9/11 has the mission of facilitating communication between different intelligence organizations, including the military, but its oversight does not extend to the external defense industry, where company secrecy combines with official secrecy to turn many companies into what amounts to impregnable safes.

Given what I was told by Dr. Sarbacher and General Exon, programs were underway in the 1980s that involved engineering issues and metallurgy. But what of the abductions? As a victim, I'm more than a little interested in whether or not anything was known of them in the official world.

I did have a hint from Dr. David Webb, a member of the National Commission on Space, whose distinguished career included the creation of the International Space Studies Program at the University of North Dakota and many other achievements. Among his consulting clients were the Department of Defense, DARPA, the U.S. Air Force, NASA, McDonnell Douglas, Rockwell International, Rock-etdyne, and numerous universities. He became a good friend and spent a number of nights at our cabin, where he was frank that there were concerns within the intelligence community about the abductions. He did not indicate that he knew that they were happening as reported, but he and I and Anne spent many hours discussing the reasons why, if they were, why somebody from elsewhere might wish to do this. Theories that I still explore today came out of those conversations, most prominently the idea that somebody might be creating human beings in their own cultural milieu in order to use a sort of "organic modeling" to attempt to understand us.

The sophistication of his thinking reflected a deep interest, and while he did suggest that there was a level of official awareness and concern, he never identified any specific programs that might be related or agencies that might be involved.

I remembered him in the acknowledgements included in *Communion*.

Any suggestion that abductions might really be happening would have to have been as incendiary in the 1980s as it would be now, but in the Mitchell documents there is only one brief handwritten note that states "defer UFO/abduction review." This may mean that, while the abductions were at their peak between 1970 and 1980, the intelligence community was not aware of their extent, or perhaps that the individuals in the meeting only had public hearsay to go on and were unaware of any official concern.

As has been shown in part 1 of this book, careful analysis of the close encounter narrative laid down by members of the public is almost certainly the first place to go to start to understand what the contact issue is actually all about. I don't mean simply reading the narrative and doing, say, statistical analysis—how many people described what type of entity, and so forth—but rather analyzing the descriptive material as deeply as possible. It might even be useful to explore the genetic makeup of the witnesses and, when possible, to ask them to repeat their stories while being observed in a functional MRI scanner, to see which parts of the brain are contributing to the construction of the narrative. Given a large enough sample, this would enable researchers to tell if there were any memories across the whole class that were being generated by experiences the brain perceived as factual, as opposed to imaginary memories it was constructing or had been deceived into believing. (I will discuss the issue of distorted and altered perceptions more fully in chapter 14.)

Within months of *Communion* being published, the whole world knew of the possibility that people were being abducted under strange circumstances. However, Dr. Webb engaged with us well prior to its publication. So he was certainly interested as early as 1985–86, and it's not clear to me that it was entirely personal curiosity.

Even before *Communion*, there were numerous disquieting stories, starting with the Betty and Barney Hill case of 1961, which received substantial publicity. There were also even more disturbing cases, which must have been explored within the intelligence community. As one example, on the evening of December 29, 1980, Betty Cash, Vicki Landrum, and her grandson Colby Landrum observed a flaming diamond-shaped object cross the sky near Houston. It was soon surrounded by, at Betty Cash's count, twenty-three helicopters, some of them Chinooks with their distinctive double rotor systems. Immediately afterward, the women became ill in ways strikingly similar to what happened to the mothers in the "Visitors in the Trees" and "I Hate You, Mommy" events discussed previously.

Both women experienced nausea, vomiting, diarrhea, eye pain, and sunburn. Betty was the most severely affected, and her health problems continued long after the incident. In 1982, the women sued the U.S. government for damages. The case was dismissed in 1986 because NASA and other officials testified that nothing like the object described by the witnesses could be found in the U.S. arsenal, and the base where the helicopters were stationed could not be located. The public was thus led to believe that nothing had really happened, but that cannot be true, and more careful observers in the intelligence community would have known that. So I feel sure that there were investigations that did not reach the judge and that there may still be records of that and other cases where there were physical outcomes that could be identified and investigated.

There is also some evidence that research has been conducted into radiance technologies focused on energetic beam weapons and that this has some connection with conflict with UAP. It is possible that just such a weapon was fired from the secretive U.S.-Australian Pine Gap satellite surveillance base in Australia as NASA Shuttle Mission STS-48 passed overhead on September 15, 1991, at an altitude of 355 miles. Shuttle video shows a number of objects near the orbiter, one of which darts away less than a second after a flash of light comes up from below. NASA claimed that the objects were debris generated by the orbiter and illuminated by the sun, the flash of light was a thruster firing, and the change in motion of the particle that moved was caused by the jet from the thruster. According to a paper by researcher Lan Fleming published in *New Frontiers in Science*, telemetry data does not indicate a thruster firing at the time claimed.

Dr. Jack Kasher analyzed the event and showed persuasively that the object could not have been an ice particle and that it was reacting to the rapidly ascending flash. His paper, published in 1994, provides mathematical evidence that is difficult to dispute, and as I said in the introduction, I think that it's time to get past the fallacious denials and face some facts, one of which is that somebody appears to be deploying radiance technologies and firing them. The STS-48 analysis is the most exhaustive, but there have been a number of other cases involving shuttle missions and strange objects.

In particular, Dr. Mark Carlotto published a commentary in *New Frontiers in Science* on a somewhat similar situation that can be viewed on STS-80 video. There are numerous unidentified objects in the video, including a quite large one that seems to rise from below, emitting an exhaust trail and maneuvering strangely, and some streaks of light that could be energetic beams. According to Dr. Carlotto's analysis, they are not meteors. The way the cameras are operated during the incident suggests that somebody either aboard the shuttle or on the ground was interested in the display, but astronaut Dr. Story Musgrave, who was onboard as a mission specialist, has said that he noticed nothing unusual.

Given that the so-called black budget is in the hundreds of billions of dollars, and on September 10, 2001, Secretary of Defense Donald Rumsfeld announced that the Pentagon had lost track of 2.3 trillion dollars, it's not hard to imagine that it might possess craft and weapons that are not known beyond a small circle of project participants and might be funding not only those technologies but that much more, conceivably even entire intelligence and other organizations might be off the books and not known outside of small, tightly compartmentalized groups.

This failure to keep track of its assets has continued into the present. As of December 2022, the Defense Department has failed, in its last five audits, to account for over half of its assets. It is one thing to fail in this way once or twice for such a large organization, but for that deficiency to continue for five years running suggests the possibility that it may be institutionalized, that is to say, they are not trying to identify the assets at all because they are not lost to the record but concealed from it.

Perhaps the efforts now underway will at last bring the sort of order to the situation that the individuals in the meeting memorialized in the Mitchell Papers were trying to achieve. But it's not clear that the public will be informed.

The Airborne Object Identification and Management Synchronization Group, mandated in the 2022 National Defense Authorization Act, is supposed to coordinate all reports of unknown aircraft, but it doesn't require hidden organizations that might be feeding it information to reveal themselves. There is also nothing in the act that requires that the source of the reports be revealed to the public. So while a plan of sorts may now exist, public reports are not mandated, meaning that the Department of Defense will be free to say whatever it pleases publicly, no matter what the group's actual conclusions may be.

Whether or not they will even address the issue of the abductions is unclear. But so far the entire thrust of the project has been about UAP and their functionality, what we know about them now, and what we have known in the past but lost in the system. I find it concerning that the abductions are so little mentioned. My fear is that the official world might be well aware of them but also in an emotional state of denial that is preventing it from facing them.

This brings me to the issue of threat—specifically, is there one? Clearly, in 1985 this was an open question. Given that the "Preliminary Assessment" declassified and released on June 25, 2021, by the Office of the Director of National Intelligence isn't exactly clear on this point. The document contains this remarkable and, frankly, disturbing statement: "The limited amount of high-quality reporting on unidentified aerial phenomena (UAP) hampers our ability to draw firm conclusions about the nature or intent of UAPs." This can mean only one thing: pencils up and need to know have caused the past to be lost in the classified maze. And given the Pentagon's apparent inability to oversee and presumably therefore manage its assets, there may be an element of intention here.

Is there any way to see beyond pencils up, to what amounts to a level of lost knowledge? Not directly, at least not from where we sit outside of the classified world, but there is an indirect approach that may bear some fruit.

Judging from their presence in the 1985 meeting and their current publicly known activities, there is reason to believe that scientists like Dr. Eric W. Davis and Hal Puthoff, who were both associated with EarthTech International, might possess knowledge of classified technologies related to UAP. Therefore, it's worth taking a look at what their nonclassified publications may tell us about their interests. (I might mention here that their Wikipedia entries, especially that of Dr. Puthoff, are apparently edited by people who are part of the external scientific world and hold them and their work in low esteem. This is another example of how secrecy and denial have damaged the scientific community and strangled the ability of its mainstream to innovate.)

The main thrust of Dr. Puthoff's publicly visible work involves what is known as zero-point energy. Dr. Puthoff and Dr. Eric Davis have authored many papers together, exploring various methods of extracting energy from the vacuum. One would assume that they have done this, at least in part, to find an explanation for whatever powers UAP. Physicist Richard Feynman created calculations that showed that an absolutely astonishing amount of energy would be released if the vacuum could be "opened." Drs. Puthoff and Davis have collaborated on five papers listed on ResearchGate, most of them concerning zero-point energy.

If their work has been inspired by UAP propulsion, it is easy to understand why they would concentrate in this area. When you watch any of the officially released UAP videos now available, you see small objects that can remain stationary, accelerate to high speed, and, in the case of the Tic Tac object, enter the water and function there as well. While the Gimbal object has some characteristics that are similar to what would appear on the ATFLIR Gimbal camera system that was in use if it was recording jet engine emission, it is hard to understand why the object would have been designated as unknown if that was the case. The radar operators would certainly have known the position of all aircraft in the area.

In any case, even if the Gimbal object is eventually identified as aircraft exhaust, the Tic Tac objects were also visually sighted, and radar showed one of them descending from 80,000 feet in less than a second. They were no larger than a fighter jet.

This means that they contain a truly robust energy source, and as objects with similar capabilities are described in the 1947 Twining memorandum, it's not too surprising that Drs. Puthoff and Davis would work on zero-point energy. It is hard to conceive of any other energy source that could account for such movement on the part of something as small as a medium-sized aircraft—or of any size, for that matter. And as scientists with clearances would have had access for years to what the general public is just now learning about the flight characteristics of UAP, it is logical to suggest that their interest in zero-point energy might arise from their knowledge of UAP flight characteristics.

Dr. Puthoff's first paper listed on ResearchGate is from 1959 and is entitled "A Theoretical of Ion Plasma Oscillations" and concerns the modulation of electron beams. This fits with his work on tunable lasers and indicates an early interest in electron beams, which causes me to wonder if something he may have explored during his career had anything to do with what Dr. Kasher analyzed in regard to Shuttle mission STS-48. Of course, I'm only speculating here.

The most recent paper that Dr. Davis has made available on ResearchGate is an effort to clarify something called the Levi-Civita spacetimes. Without getting into a physics lesson here, these equations are important in the study of gravity because the equation is used to model gravitational fields. In the paper, Dr. Davis and his colleagues seek to bring clarity to their application. This would be essential to any successful use of them in modeling the gravitational fields of different spacetimes, from black holes to, conceivably, UAP that are generating their own gravity and thus are essentially their own self-contained spacetime. I have no idea if the work of either man is being applied behind the wall of secrecy to such issues as weaponized energy beams, UAP propulsion, and control of gravity. Obviously, though, these are the three key areas that are essential to our successfully creating our own UAP and defending any hostile or unwanted intrusions by others. Combined with the metallurgical work that Dr. Sarbacher told me was under way nearly forty years ago—and assuming that there has been progress since then—I have to wonder if the rumors that we already have at least functional prototypes of such devices may be true.

The *Preliminary Assessment on Unidentified Aerial Phenomena* released by the Office of the Director of National Intelligence in June of 2021 lists, among the possible explanations for UAP, "USG or U.S. industry developmental programs and foreign adversary systems" as well as "other."

Obviously, when General Twining wrote his memo, the only possible answer was "other," but given Jack Kasher's analysis of the STS-48 video and the other evidence I have assembled here, I think that it is reasonable to speculate that we have developed weapons that might affect UAP and devices that possess similar functionality and therefore that the Russians and the Chinese may well have done or be doing the same. Russian and probably Chinese UAP are not likely to be weaponized against conventional war-fighting equipment, though, or the Russians would be using them to dominate in the Ukraine conflict. They may be in use, though.

On September 15, 2022, *Live Science* said that Ukrainian observers were reporting UAP "all over the country." U.S. intelligence gathering devices? Russian? Or "other"? They did not engage in hostile actions, but if they were Russian, then they were possibly mapping Ukrainian infrastructure prior to the missile and drone attacks that followed. If they were "other," then perhaps they were just trying to figure out what our latest conflict was about and, quite likely, whether or not nuclear weapons were liable to be used.

A letter from 2002 written by Navy Commander Willard Miller to Dr. Davis suggests that he engage with a Dr. Robert Beckwith (1919–2009), the founder of Beckwith Electric and the author of *Hypotheses: Superatoms, Neutrinos & Extraterrestrials* (1998), "A Force Model of the

Universe" (2002), and "Levitation, Teleportation & Time Travel" (2002).

Is there any reason—any at all—to even look into the work of somebody who would write papers about subjects as far off the grid of accepted reality as things like that? Time travel? Levitation? Surely not. As to teleportation, it has been demonstrated at the level of the extremely small—the quantum level—but the idea that anything of classical size could be converted into energy, "moved" via quantum entanglement, and then reconstituted seems very far from present or even future capabilities. It seems impossible. Of course, in 1850, radio did, too, and as late as 1895, physics pioneer Lord Kelvin stated that heavier than air flight was impossible.

Beyond UAP functionality, our visitors have demonstrated that they can communicate from mind to mind, and if the observations of some close encounter witnesses are accurate reflections of real events, they can move instantaneously from one place to another.

In our level of reality, not much is known about things like levitation, except that, if you take at face value the stories of people like the sixteenth century Catholic levitator Joseph of Cupertino, who made his bishop so nervous by floating toward the candles during mass that he was banished to the church steps (generally ending up after mass entangled in the trees that surrounded the church) then you must consider that it is possible. But is it, really? What experiments did Dr. Beckwith conduct? Were there levitations, movements through time, teleportations? Just how much of science fiction is fiction?

Dr. Beckwith begins his "Levitation, Teleportation & Time Travel" paper by discussing the mystery of how ancient structures such as the great pyramid were built. "Perhaps ancient civilizations understood laws of levitation, teleportation, and time travel ..." He then moves on into a discussion of Nicola Tesla's legendary 1899 experiments that resulted in odd lightning effects in the vicinity of his Colorado lab and frightened locals so much that the power company threatened to cut him off if he didn't stop causing people's fenceposts to discharge lightning, and so forth. (What, exactly, he did to cause these effects is still not known, and his notes have been lost, stolen, or confiscated.)

It is generally assumed that structures like the pyramids and some others can actually be explained by conventional means, and little remains from the ancient world suggesting that they knew much about what we think of in our era as scientific technology. There is little more than the famous Baghdad Battery and a suggestion from some bas-reliefs in the Temple of Hathor at Dendera that large tubes containing glowing filaments may have been in use. There is only a single suggestion in ancient literature that gravity was even understood as a force. There appears in the *Vaiśeṣika Sūtra* of Kanada, dating from 600 BCE, a credible description of it, so the concept was known, at least in India, as long as 2,600 years ago. The temple that houses the Dendera Light, as the bas-relief is known, was constructed around 54 BCE, but the relief itself may date from an earlier time. The Baghdad Battery dates from some time between 150 BCE and 600 AD. But these isolated fragments do not suggest the presence of significant technological capabilities.

As to time travel, an odd frieze carved on one of the rafters in the temple of Seti I at Abydos appears to portray a tank, a helicopter, and other modern devices. It's hardly an airtight case for the existence of ancient time travel, but it is an interesting anomaly, all the more so because there is no other site in Egypt where similar objects are pictured.

One of the problems that Albert Einstein had with his relativity equations was that they allowed for time travel. More recently, after going so far as to claim he had empirical evidence that time travel was impossible (no tourists), Stephen Hawking came to the conclusion that it was indeed possible but would require an enormous amount of energy, thus explaining why nobody has ever accomplished it—at least, nobody who has announced themselves. Interestingly, if there are tourists, in order to function here they would have to essentially deceive something called the principle of least action, which holds that nothing in nature will ever expend more than the minimum amount of energy necessary to do what it must.

Water running down a hill will always seek the lowest point. It will never take a detour to enjoy the view. If a time traveler didn't somehow trick this principle into not reacting to them, even if they were able to penetrate into their past, they would be essentially frozen, unable to do more than observe—*unless they tricked all who they encountered into believing that they were something that did not exist and had never existed.* Aliens, for example. Only then might they influence their past, and even then it would be difficult, nearly impossible, to change what has already happened. Shifting the dark tide of entropy, the crushing wave that forever trails the present and fixes it instant by instant in the amber of the past, could only be done by agonizing bits, maybe by causing a vast number of changes so tiny that they individually never trigger the grandfather paradox, which states that the future cannot alter its own past.

By raising the eyes of the millions to UAP sighting after UAP sighting, they might eventually inspire us to find out what makes the saucers dance. Would this then change the timeline?

In physics, a theory called retrocausality suggests that, on the quantum level—the level of the very, very small—what happens in the present can change the past. If this is true, and somebody in the present understands how to control it and make it affect larger reality, then the whole array of phenomena could result from an effort on their part of change their own past.

As to the ancients' control of gravity, there are a number of structures on Earth that cannot now be built, or which would take extraordinary effort. We could construct the great pyramid that Beckwith refers to, but it would take many years and involve complex engineering and a very high level of labor intensity. Were the ancient Egyptians able to commit a huge section of their labor force to such a project over generations in order to complete it? As too little is known about their productivity levels, we cannot be sure, but it seems possible. Still, there are other problems with the structure, such as its ultraprecise alignment and the amazing amount of information about distances that is packed into its measurements that raise questions about how it might have been planned in the first place, let alone executed with such precision.

The great stones that form the platform at Baalbek in Lebanon weigh up to 800 tons. At present, we would not be able to move a stone weighing much more than fifty tons without constructing some very elaborate equipment, and whether or not we could move a stone as large as those at Baalbek at all is an open question. So how did they do it?

Other structures around the world also resist explanation. Among them are the great fortress at Sacsayhuamán in Peru, the stones for which were quarried at the base of the plateau on which it stands. But how were they moved to where they are now? There seems to have been no way to do this.

Another is the group of artificial islands called Nan Madol in Micronesia in the South Pacific. The islands are made of huge basalt "timbers" stacked one on another to form platforms. The remains of a fire found on one of them was carbon-dated to around 1200 CE, so presumably they must have been brought by Polynesians in seagoing canoes.

I won't get further into the details of the various conventional explanations for these anomalies, beyond saying that if any of them actually worked, it would be surprising.

I think that there is at least a smattering of evidence that we conscious beings are ourselves the technology needed to accomplish these seemingly impossible feats, and because our visitors know and understand this, when they do things like disappear before our eyes, rise up into the air, or communicate with thought, it's not because they possess extraordinary technology but because they are still in contact with the extraordinary technology that is part of them—and, judging from our past engineering accomplishments, possibly also part of us.

I know of one story that may describe a ritual that causes—or used to cause—objects to levitate.

A book by Malidoma Patrice Somé called *Of Water and the Spirit* that chronicles his journey from a youth growing up in a Jesuit school in his home country of Burkina Faso to his adult return to his tribe, the Dagara, and his assumption of the role, traditional in his family, of tribal shaman, includes a detailed account of something he witnessed as a boy when he attended the funeral of his grandfather, who was a great and legendary magic maker in the tribal hierarchy.

Before I continue, I would like to briefly address the Western assumption that anything that doesn't emerge out of Western thought, especially anything that is not supposed to be "real," that is, that doesn't fit our established beliefs about the way the world works, must be false. I don't share that assumption. There are many ways of approaching reality, including physical reality, that are highly functional but very different from what has come to be called Western rationality. They are not irrational. They are not imaginary. They are simply different, and it could be that they do cause the physical world to behave differently than it does when it is addressed by the Western mind.

In the West, a choice is generally made when confronted by results generated using non-Western techniques that those results are imaginary and have no material significance. Thus it is assumed by scientists attempting to understand the powers of the visitors that they derive from technology that has been designed based on scientific principles we don't understand.

That might not be entirely true, or it might not be true at all. For example, the cosmology of the Dagara people divides reality into three realms, an upper one of the gods, a lower one of the spirits of the Earth and the ancestors, and a middle one that is not, as one might expect, the realm of the living but rather of the living and the dead *both*. In the Dagara reality, the dead do not leave the world of the living at once but remain active in material life for a long period of time. While they are here, they are capable of causing events in the physical world.

In *Of Water and the Spirit*, Dr. Somé describes such an event that involved control over gravity—or more precisely stated, an ability to reduce the mass of objects—that suggests that what we see darting through the skies might not contain a gravitic propulsion system at all ... at least, not one that is related to the existing Western idea of technology.

Of course, Dr. Somé's is not the only description of levitation, but it is important in that it shows how preceding actions led to it. After his grandfather's death, the old man lay in state in his bedroom. An elaborate ritual was then enacted that involved calling the dead to the funeral. The first sign of what would happen took place when the hairdresser who had shaved the old man's head finished and "pronounced some lugubrious words," which resulted in the "gourds and cans in the room ... knocking against one another." To the Dagara, this meant that the dead had arrived and were signaling their presence. There then followed a recitation of the names of those very dead and ritual singing. Something caused the room to be enveloped in darkness, punctuated by "a mild lightning." A humming sound came out of the gourds and cans, which were knocking against one another again. (These were attached overhead in an intricate pattern and had been there during his grandfather's life.) Then came a sound "of marching feet, pounding the ground everywhere in the tiny room." Dr. Somé then experienced a profound disorientation, and when the lights came back, he saw "a clay pot full of water boiling on the ceiling, its bottom sitting against the roof." There was also a triangular fireplace surrounded by rocks weighing more than twenty pounds each, all suspended in midair.

The world had quite literally been turned upside down.

We in the West would dismiss all of this as fantasy. The idea that it might have actually happened in the physical world would be scoffed at.

What if it did happen, though, and the ritual did result in the levitation of the objects and was a remnant of a now entirely forgotten way of connecting with a very real level of human consciousness that we have denied and forgotten, but which still does exist? (I should say here that I have published a book called *Afterlife Revolution* that describes the astonishing ways that my wife methodically proved her continued existence after she died in 2015. That, in addition to all the indications in the close encounter experience that the dead are real and are involved, makes me very wary of the idea that we are only physical bodies, and willing to entertain stories like Dr. Somé's.

When I look at the inexplicable structures of the past, and then around me at all the mysteries we are now trying to confront, I have to ask myself how flying saucers slip through the skies, and who knows what else, perhaps even journeys across the depths of space using powers that our visitors still control but that we long ago lost track of in the maze of the mind.

When we think about our visitors and their ways and abilities, it is vitally important to do what too many of us do not wish to do or, because of our lifelong conditioning, cannot do, which is to keep a genuinely open mind. By this I don't mean simply accepting the mystery but realizing that it may also involve something about us that has become dormant.

When Dr. Somé himself died in December of 2021, the same rituals were performed that were carried out for his grandfather. There was one difference: no levitations took place.

Is this because the ones he saw when he was a boy only happened in his imagination, or was it that the last of that knowledge died with his grandfather's generation?

Maybe the presence of the visitors—the theater in the sky, the abductions, the close encounters, all of it—is intended to create such intense curiosity in us that we reach a sort of internal critical mass and finally wake up to unrealized potentials we possess.

If so, then they are saying, "Look at us, freer than birds, dancing through your skies for all to see."

That statement, I would think, is meant to lead to a question: Why aren't you?

CHAPTER 15

BRAINS DAMAGED AND
BRAINS ENHANCED

Judging from the record, limited and contradictory though it is, it would appear that getting too close to UAP can be more than a little dangerous. Being aggressive toward one seems to be even more so.

The Condign Report states in chapter 5, paragraph 13, in reference to matters such as close contact, that "such events only happen (such as can cause physical injury or equipment interference on occasion) when a human being is quite close to the phenomenon." Therefore, according to the U.K. Defense Intelligence Staff, injuries do happen, and as the U.S. and U.K. intelligence operations work closely together, it is difficult to believe that the American side has not been informed of these findings. As I was injured in a close encounter, and there are numerous other documented cases, they certainly happen to members of the public, but have they happened to military personnel? The events discussed in chapter 12 would suggest that this did take place in the past, and it is to be hoped that the new mandate to attempt to recover past Defense Department records regarding the phenomenon will bring some of the incidents to light. But given the state of the record, this may not be possible, and even if something is found, the extreme sensitivity of such information would almost certainly preclude its being declassified.

The U.S. Office of National Intelligence Report on Unidentified Aerial Phenomena (unclassified version) released in January of 2023 states, "Regarding health concerns, there have also been no encounters with UAP confirmed to contribute direction to adverse health-related effects to the observer(s)." But what does that mean? Recent years, or all years? It cannot mean all years because if it does, then why is there a mandate to recover past files? And how successful can it be, given that we already know, as one example, that all the records from the 509th Bomb Wing at Roswell Army Air Field were illegally destroyed. How much more has been destroyed, and perhaps is being destroyed right now?

Nevertheless, just as there are suggestions that injuries were known to the creators of the Condign Report, there are similar suggestions in some recent literature.

I will refer here to some published comments of Stanford professor Dr. Garry Nolan and Dr. Christopher Green.

I met Dr. Nolan at a conference at the Esalen Institute in February of 2019. He holds the Rachford and Carlota A. Harris Endowed Chair in the Department of Pathology at Stanford University. He is the founder of seven biotech companies. Among his many honors and awards, he was named a National Science Foundation Fellow in 1988 and was a National Institutes of Health Fellow from 1990 until 1992. He was given an Outstanding Research Achievement award by the Nature Group in 2011 and was the first recipient of the Department of Defense's Teal Innovator award in 2012 and was given a Top Innovator award by DoD in 2017.

When we met, he was fifty-four years old. Within five minutes of meeting Garry, I knew that he is a genius. He is an honest and compassionate man, too, and, most importantly, unafraid of inquiry. His forthright attitude, as a matter of fact, reminded me of Dr. Sarbacher.

Drs Green and Dr. Nolan may or may not be bound by security clearances and confidentiality agreements. I don't know and I haven't asked. I will base what I explore in this chapter only on statements that they have made that are already a part of the public record and on statements made to me about my personal case that it is my right to reveal if I so wish.

Dr. Green served in the CIA from 1969 to 1985. After his retirement from the service, he pursued a medical career as Assistant Dean of Clinical Research for the Wayne State School of Medicine in Detroit, Michigan. He is now in private practice. He is known for manning the CIA's "weird desk" and has been involved in government research into such things as ESP and psychic abilities. The criticisms of him that involve these aspects of his work are part of the cultural dysfunction that surrounds so-called edge topics. His credentials and record speak for themselves.

He has been and is an important part of the effort to give support to people who present physical symptoms after involvement in unusual situations. What his views are on the causes of the stress and injuries involved, I cannot say.

There are many stories of injuries caused by close encounters with UAPs and other similar phenomena involving personnel and close encounter witnesses. For the most part, the close encounter witnesses receive injuries ranging from burns, needle marks, and cuts to the physical trauma of rape and disappearing or unexplainable pregnancies.

The military cases are different, most of them involving burns of various kinds and brain damage.

In 2022, Dr. Green made public the unclassified version of a paper entitled "Clinical Medical Acute and Subacute Field Effects on Human Dermal and Neurological Tissues," from which the Defense Intelligence report "Acute and Subacute Field Effects on Human Biological Tissues" was derived. Despite recent claims to the contrary, it does say that "humans have been found to have been injured from exposures to anomalous vehicles, especially airborne" and goes on to explain that these injuries are related to various types of energetic emissions and fields. Among the injuries reported are heating and burning caused by both ionizing and nonionizing radiation and also conventional thermal injuries.

Neurological effects are reported as well, including cognitive, neuromuscular, sensory, and neuropsychiatric effects involving disruption of the endocrine system. This can result in many different disorders that manifest as fatigue, cognitive issues, and other neurological problems, including auditory distortions, such as the generation of intracranial sounds. Possible communication attempts through the use of microwaves (as has been discussed previously), CO_2 lasers, or radiofrequency emissions can even lead to the production of intracranial voices "through thermoelastic expansion of intracranial spaces at 5 kHz." This would result in the hearing of voices somewhat like a person with schizophrenia might report. In someone who has no history of this, it can be extremely frightening and disorienting, as was reported by Dr. Richard Sauder and experienced by me.

Thermal effects are also discussed, including directed pain, sunburn-like skin reddening associated with first-degree burns, and second-degree burns resulting in blistering.

When the visitors told the man approaching them by the roadside in Queens to leave or "we will hurt you," in all probability he would have experienced painful heating and been left with a severe sunburn, or worse.

The report also states that muscle spasms, seizures, and loss of consciousness can be induced with high-voltage (100 kV/m) nanosecond pulsed extra-low frequency (15 hertz) stimulation of the hippocampus and the pyriform cortex sustained over one to five minutes. Abnormal skin sensations (paresthesias) have been reported, as well as dangerous increases in core body temperature up to 105.8°F. Pulsed microwaves can cause spatial disorientation, and nausea and vomiting can be induced with audible frequencies.

But how do all of these effects figure in exposure to UAPs, and are any of them weaponized? Here, the answers become more difficult to find, possibly of course, because there is no recorded connection, but also possibly because they are classified. At the same time, a significant amount of information has been made available by Dr. Nolan, and one image captured from the EarthTech life sciences page by a Twitter user showed a brain section displaying extensive demyelination, or nerve destruction, and captioned, "Patient one month following near-field exposure to unidentified aerial craft at 500 meters. Patient died two weeks later."

The brain image displays damage of a kind that would be caused by microwaves or other forms of high-energy radiation directed at the head. It could result either from getting too close to an operational UAP or being the target of some sort of energy-projecting weapon, either electromagnetic or sonic.

Despite recent claims that Havana Syndrome is a result of environmental factors, as was stated in a report issued by the Office of the Director of National Intelligence on March 1, 2023, it may also be what causes that issue. Whether the causative mechanism is something developed or possibly back-engineered by an earthly player or has another origin is not known publicly. Regarding Havana Syndrome, the March 1 report states, albeit with "varying levels of confidence," that "deliberate causal mechanisms are very unlikely to have caused the sensory phenomena and adverse symptoms." It continues that "deliberate causal mechanisms are unlikely," in the opinion of two agencies "because they judge that radiofrequency energy (RF) is a plausible cause for AHIs ..." (Havana Syndrome)

What, one might ask, makes a "deliberate causal mechanism" unlikely if radiofrequency energies are a "plausible cause?" Where might the radiofrequency energies have come from? Cellphones? Signals being generated by embassy equipment? If so, then that should have been stated instead of leaving the public and the victims with this impossibly contradictory conclusion.

But the cases we are addressing here do not involve embassies or diplomats. Dr. Nolan, who worked with Dr. Green on some of them, commented in an interview with Thobey Campion for *Vice*'s Motherboard tech column that "of the hundred or so patients that we looked at, about a quarter of them died from their injuries." He adds that the injuries were identical to what is seen in Havana syndrome—something that is decidedly not mentioned in the March report.

The injury shown in the image obtained from the EarthTech Twitter feed is in appearance similar to the injuries seen in Havana syndrome.

Given that the existence of a conflict situation with UAP is such extraordinarily important information, I do not believe that it isn't known to the defense leadership. I would conjecture that the denials currently being made, and the recent obfuscating report, are in protection of sensitive information and are unlikely to be true.

As it does appear that conflict is happening, it's fair to ask why. The Sentinelese warrior's tribe was likely watching from cover and agreed with him on what has been a fundamental policy of theirs for a long time. People who have tried to meet with the islanders in the past have been killed. But UAP/alien policy is not public policy. In fact, the only public policy now in place denies that any conflict exists and just barely admits that UAPs are of unknown origin.

Worse, an article that appeared in the *New York Times* on October 28, 2022, headlined "Many Military UFO Reports are Just Foreign Spying or Airborne Trash," stated that "government officials believe that surveillance operations by foreign powers and weather balloons or other airborne clutter explain most incidents of unidentified aerial phenomena." In other words, the same sort of denial that was published in the introduction to the Project Blue Book report is once again being recycled.

On November 1 the *Wall Street Journal* published an opinion piece by a pilot in which he states, "The public persists in pushing the UAP phenomenon through these imagined sightings, so I'm reversing that by declaring they don't exist simply because my pilot friends and I haven't seen them. Are we aviation professionals all wrong, while a few quirky nonaviators who mostly enjoy recreational marijuana are all right? I don't think so." This statement ignores the testimony of thousands of pilots over more than seventy years who have reported UAP sightings. Absurdly, it even ignores the fact that the *first* modern UAP sighting, made on June 24, 1947, was by Kenneth Arnold, a veteran pilot, *while he was actually flying his plane.* But the *Wall Street Journal* editors saw fit to publish the opinion piece despite its basic factual inaccuracy.

If another debunking campaign is underway, entirely ignored will be the reality that, from the time of General Twining's memo in 1947 until now, thousands of objects with similar flight characteristics have been reported worldwide, and often by pilots and other trained observers. And there is a smattering of hard evidence that confrontations with them have been happening for a long time, still happen, and have caused injuries and deaths.

Given that the Department of Defense has such a long history of denial and cover-up, taking its statements at face value, as is done in the October 28 *Times* article, seems inappropriate. In that article, sources are not identified beyond vague phrases like "military officials." That might have been adequate before there were official admissions that there are objects of unknown origin in our skies, but given this, it no longer is. It is also stated that "efforts by the Pentagon or intelligence officials to stamp out theories about aliens have largely failed." The use of the phrase "stamp out" is chilling, to say the least, and may well presage a greater effort to turn back the clock.

In February of 2022, the Intelligence Community Experts Panel on Anomalous Health Incidents released a study showing that Havana syndrome may be "caused by pulsed electromagnetic energy, particularly in the radio frequency range." This was not denied by the March 2023 report, which states that "all agencies acknowledge the value of additional research on potential adversary capabilities in the RF field."

In its executive summary the experts panel specifically states that it did not investigate the possible origins of the Havana Syndrome attacks.

As revealed in a September 2022 CNN interview with Dr. Sanjay Gupta, a CIA doctor using the pseudonym of Dr. Paul Andrews (he is not Dr. Green) who was in Havana investigating the syndrome was himself attacked. Like others, he noticed a clicking sound in one ear. Because he could hear a sound that he already knew was related to the onset of the syndrome, he tried to defend against it by putting on earphones. Unfortunately, it turned out that sonic energy was not the cause of the injury, and a short time later he found himself struggling with confusion as he sought to escape the room. He is still dealing with long-term aftereffects of the attack and has been diagnosed with damage to his vestibular structures. As the clicking sound was not the cause of the damage but a sign of the attack, it is hard not to think that a weapon similar or identical to the cause of Havana syndrome has also damaged and destroyed the brains of individuals engaged in close contact and/or conflict with UAP.

We know from the Grand Central Parkway incident that our visitors will threaten people who make unwanted approaches. It is plausible that at least some of the personnel whose cases Drs. Green and Nolan have studied were injured such in situations, possibly when they gave chase under orders to repel some perceived intrusion.

The simple reason that the U.S. Air Force has probable history of attacking UAPs would be that, from the beginning, since nobody from presidents to privates understood what they were dealing with, they have been reacting like the Sentinelese islanders. This isn't their fault. Their responses have been induced by incursions into protected airspace. Unlike the Indian helicopter pilot, who obligingly flew off when the upset islander became aggressive, the visitors routinely penetrate into airspace that we are protecting and don't stop. The Oak Ridge overflights happened again and again, almost as if they were testing what it took to get us to react. The 1952 Washington overflights were even more provocative, as were the 1973 incidents. At first the visitors may not have known how we would respond, but by the time of the 2004 Afghanistan video, no matter how different our minds are, they must have understood that parking themselves in restricted airspace was going to mean that they would be shot at.

They were there, hanging over that firebase, to induce us to attack. And given what happened afterward, their motive is pretty obvious: They wanted to show us their invulnerability to our weapons. It was, in other words, a show of force.

While it seems clear that our military is being intentionally

provoked—one would assume to test its responses and capabilities—
it is not clear that our responses are based on best practices.

Our program of responses needs to be based on as clear an
assessment of the motives of the visitors as we can generate. This
means that it has to begin with a study of how their minds work.

Because the reality of the UAP/alien issue is just now—and very
erratically—being exposed to the public, how officials hidden deep
within the Department of Defense may be evolving policy is
unknown. From what little is in the public record, reactions such as
opening fire if the intrusions are sufficiently provocative seem to have
been the rule of the day as recently as 2004.

If so, why have we failed to generate a more subtle response—one
that enables us to predict their actions and react in ways that are
effective? Shooting missiles that don't hit and don't kill is not being
effective, it's revealing weakness.

Our response may or may not be based on logic. It is possible that
it emerges as much out of our mythologies as it does out of more
objective evaluation of the visitors' capabilities, tactics, and strategy.

Lue Elizondo made a statement on his blog on the To The Stars
Academy website (since moved or removed) to the effect that there
are religious zealots in the government and the defense industry
whose beliefs color their policymaking decisions.

It would be easy to scorn such people and bemoan the fact that
they have influence at a policy level. It's not that simple, though. I've
had enough personal contact with the visitors to know that they are
an extremely complex entity, and appear to be deeply divided about
us. In part, they are hostile toward us in ways so intricately horrible
and bizarre that they could understandably be believed by intellectu-
ally unprepared observers to have a supernatural and thus demonic
origin.

But to base policy on the idea that their unwanted behaviors
means that they are supernatural beings is a serious mistake. One has
only to remember the eerily human quality of their reaction to Bruce
Lee and to the man who encountered them in the Queens bookstore
to realize that they are probably not supernatural at all but living

creatures. That doesn't mean that they don't have the ability to seem demonic. My own early experiences with them might easily have led me to that belief, had I not had the intellectual resources to enable me to more fully dimensionalize the situation. Specifically, when Anne began to contextualize it in terms of past human experience with anomalous entities, I realized that there was much nuance to be considered. A black-and-white "demons-vs-angels" approach was not adequate for me as a single individual trying to understand, and it certainly is not an adequate basis upon which to build official policy.

Is policy actually being made based on such assumptions, though?

Traditionally, high-ranking military officers have been private about their personal religious beliefs and careful not to allow them to influence their work. General Twining had been converted to Catholicism by the legendary Padre Pio, now Saint Pio, in 1946. So when he was dealing with the Roswell material, his new Catholicism was very fresh in mind and heart and the result of conversion by a notably charismatic man. Did he share his knowledge and experiences with his confessor and receive religious advice about how to think about the visitors? We cannot know that, but we can know that in 1947, the idea of aliens from other planets was an abstraction, present in a few works of fiction and just beginning to enter mainstream thought. The only flying beings recognized by religion were angels and demons. Even if he did not consult any religious authorities, Twining, upon viewing the bodies that had been brought to Wright, might well have feared that they were demons. General Exon said that the concern was that they were "scouts" who would be followed by an invasion. The soldiers who were being exposed to them as a reality would have had no context in which to place them.

At present, the Catholic church takes a much more sophisticated approach to the whole question of an alien presence than does the fundamentalist Christian community, which, like most religious communities in the world, still has not separated the idea of such a presence from the mythological pantheon that is already part of their belief system. This means that, even today, Christian fundamentalists are going to believe that aliens are either demons or angels. As they are not "clothed in light," the conclusion will be that they are demons.

It therefore also means that policymakers who are fundamentalists would have to go against their religious beliefs to deal with the visitors on the terms of their own presentation of themselves: as a complex, enigmatic, and fairly aggressive society that operates from an experience of reality different from ours.

It is important for the public to know whether or not senior officials see the visitors through the lens of their religious beliefs because, if so, then they cannot be seeing them with enough dimensionality to form meaningful policy. If you assume that the visitors are a uniformly evil presence, you simply are not going to succeed because your policy toward them will not reflect reality. The reality is that they present us with a vast array of motives that we need to first understand before we decide how we want to react.

General Bruce Carlson, a member of the board of directors of Lockheed-Martin, is one officer who could have been involved in making policy toward the visitors who makes no secret of his religious beliefs. A video of him delivering an address at the 180th General Conference of the Church of Latter-Day Saints in April of 2010 can be found on YouTube. In it, he asserts that "strict obedience to God's laws brings His blessings, and failure to abide by His laws leads to foreseeable consequences."

At the end of his sermon, he affirms his belief in Mormonism. Therefore, it can be concluded that he lives by what he believes to be the laws of God as they are interpreted by the Church of Latter-Day Saints. Among Mormon teachings, coming from the writings of founder Joseph Smith, is the belief that the ten lost tribes of Israel were transported into outer space and will someday return. This idea is also the central theme of the stellar science fiction series *Battlestar Galactica*, which was created by a Mormon, Glen A. Larson. But is this a belief based on anything real, and if so, should it form the basis of official policy toward actual otherworldly entities?

General Carlson would probably say that he doesn't know a thing

about off-world materials, UAPs, or aliens. He served in a number of
roles, however, where others are on the record as having been
concerned about these issues. Like General Twining, he was
commanding officer at the Air Materiel Command. He also headed
the National Reconnaissance Office between 2009 and 2012 and has
had much exposure over the course of his career to areas of the military and the intelligence community that require access to extremely
sensitive material, quite likely including information on UAPs, visitors, and what has been learned about their activities. Does he therefore believe that they are the ten lost tribes in the process of
returning? I have no idea. But I do know that, when it comes to such
an extraordinarily important policy issue as how to respond to an
unknown presence in our skies, the public has an absolutely fundamental right not only to participate in the conversation but to know
exactly who all the principal players are and how they view the situation. The reason for this is simple: every single human being on
Earth has as deeply personal a stake in contact as it is possible to
imagine.

That said, I am not in any way criticizing General Carlson.
Despite his background, I cannot know if he is involved in making
policy in this area or whether or not he would bring his beliefs to the
table if he was. My point is only this: we the people need to know
who is making such policy and what they base their decisions on.
(We also need to know what they believe that they are dealing with.)

To me, relating the visitors as they now appear to past myths and
beliefs is a complex and potentially dangerous business that clearly
belongs in the hands of philosophers, specialists in religion and
mythology, and anthropologists, perhaps even to neurologists and
physicists. The fact that it is now, as it has been from our earliest
awareness of their presence in the 1940s, in the hands of the military
and is held secret is troubling.

We need the most objective approaches we can manage and must
not jump to conclusions based on myths, prophecies, and beliefs. I
think that people untrained in the appropriate disciplines are likely
to do just that. But I do not think that experts in those areas have ever

been included in any stream of information about UAPs and aliens that originates in the Department of Defense. Perhaps they have been consulted behind closed doors, but we cannot know that, and therefore the public is once again left on the sidelines, not allowed to even think about this most important of all subjects.

The responsibility for involved officials to disclose whether or not they look to their religious beliefs in their efforts to understand our visitors doesn't end with government. It extends into the private defense community, which has precisely the same moral requirement in this regard that attaches to government. I think there is enough evidence that we are fighting a secret war here for our representatives to demand of the military and the defense industry that they disclose whether or not such a conflict exists, how it started and why it continues, how it is managed, and what it is costing both in money and lives.

Every time government acts against the visitors without acknowledging the massive implications, that action emerges from a failure of policy—which, as I cannot emphasize enough, was caused by the way they engaged with the military in the first place.

Nevertheless, we need more than the release of UAP videos that are later called into question by nameless Pentagon officials. We need to be exposed, finally and at last, to the truth, awful though it may be. If ever there has been a truly universal and inalienable human right, it is this.

CHAPTER 16
THE UNKNOWN KNOWN

The world around us looks real, and our vision of it appears to be completely reliable and profoundly true. When you reach toward an apple in a bowl, your hand closes around an apple. You take it to your mouth, crunch into it, and are rewarded with an expected taste and texture. You have definitely eaten a bite out of a real thing. Your store of information tells you that it grew on a tree that was also a physical reality and that it was transported to your mouth by a hand that is part of your body and is commanded by you.

These assumptions are the foundation of a philosophical concept called physicalism. Another concept, called idealism, asserts that you cannot actually tell whether or not these things are absolutely real because the only way you can be aware of them is through the perceptual input being provided by your senses and interpreted by your brain. Idealism doesn't assert that what is out there is an idea and not physical but rather that all we can *know* is our own perceptions and therefore that the question is essentially unanswerable.

So how does this matter for strange experiences such as close encounters, UAP sightings, and even battles between unknown objects and military aircraft?

It is absolutely crucial. In fact, we can know only what our brains

interpret the impressions our senses are receiving to mean. Therefore, we never come into direct contact with the world around us.

This means that our understanding of the world around us is
absolutely dependent on how our senses and our brains work, and even
among the creatures of this one planet, there are as many different
perceptual systems as there are species, and significant variations
even within similar species. As a basic example of just how profound
these differences can be, the eyes of creatures that move fast (by our
standards) process more frames per second than we do. At a British
Ecological Society meeting in December of 2022, a study was
presented showing that dragonflies can detect 300 flashes of light per
second. By contrast, we can detect around 60 flashes per second. This
means that, while both species see the same wavelengths of light, our
brains cannot interpret what we see in the same way at all. In addition, we *cannot know* what a dragonfly's perceptual experience is like.

If the visitors are indeed from another planet or some other
manifestation of reality, how can we possibly expect that they are
going to see the world as we do?

To complicate matters further, memories are files of perceptions,
not of some final, absolute reality. As perceptions come in, the brain
does much more work looking into those files for comparisons than it
does actually processing them. If it has nothing in the files to match
up with the new sense data, it will choose something similar or, in the
most extreme cases, simply make a guess.

Because of this, in a case like contact, when there is high stress
and also high strangeness, the memory the brain makes of the experience is unlikely to test well for reliability—if it can be tested at all.
The only tool we would have would be memories of similar experiences we may have had or heard about, and they are apt to be just as
unreliable.

Our visitors must obviously be in a similar situation, with the
difference that they may know somewhat more about how the
perceptual gap works. One reason for stealing sexual material might
have been, as I have previously suggested, to create human beings
that they could study under controlled conditions. (Of course, if this

has been done, it suggests that their moral compass is far different from ours. If so, not too surprising.)

Memories are pliant, like clay, and may not only be formed incorrectly, especially when dealing with something that has never been encountered before, but also may be distorted by the conditions under which the perceptions happen.

Memory can also be changed by outside forces such as the sorts of frequencies discussed in the Condign Report, hypnosis, missing time, and the implantation of false memories.

Therefore, although we can reliably crunch down on an apple, when it comes to remembering exactly what we did even a moment ago, we can have no certainty—and how much less so when somebody is there who can apparently interfere with and even control the process, as the visitors can.

So how are we to think about the whole, vast experience of contact?

The answer to that question, at least, is straightforward: very, very carefully and with a large helping of considered and probing skepticism.

Let's take a brief stroll through an imaginary room full of different animals, just to get a sense of how complex this problem really is. It is a fundamental reality of perception that what a creature's senses cannot detect does not, for that creature, exist. Not only that, but the way the creature understands what the world is depends absolutely on the structure of its brain. This means that two creatures with similar senses but different brains will also not share the same vision of the world around them.

In his *What Kind of Creatures are We?* Noam Chomsky points out that what we can understand is dependent on the way the brain works, and comments that "some differently structured intelligence might regard human mysteries as simple problems and wonder that we cannot find the answers." I think it might go further than that. Judging from the overall way miscommunication with the visitors unfolds, I think they may not understand that we don't know things that they do.

Here's why: A mouse literally cannot hear the deep thundering cries of an elephant, nor an elephant the squeaks of a mouse. Your dog's eyes are only rough guides. His hearing is his primary means of orientation, and his nose is, for him, the source of the meaning of the world.

In other words, although he lives his life with you, he can never know what the world means to you, nor can you know what it means to him. Different senses, different meanings, and yet the same world.

If your dog had come from an entirely different world and had senses that were evolved in a different environment, possibly even some that no animal in this world has, the gulf would be even greater. Just as we and our familiar canine friends cannot have any idea of what the other makes of reality, we and our visitors must share the same quandary. Neither side is going to know how the other understands the world.

The various types of encounter that we have explored in this book include abductions with and without missing time, multiple witness close encounters, otherworldly assaults, and military encounters. They all have one thing in common: they started with what look to us like *penetrations* into our lives. Did they see these as efforts to build relationship, only to be thwarted by what to them looked like crazy, inappropriate panic?

This failure to see us as we see ourselves is, I think, clear from what we have seen in this book, which is that contact is as poorly handled by their side as it is by ours. The appearance of penetration rather than dialog might thus be a misapprehension on both sides. They may view their activities that we see as invasive as earnest attempts to communicate. They may see our fear as a sign of confusion. If you happen upon a raccoon in the forest who, for whatever reason, cannot simply run away, your attempts to communicate your friendliness and appreciation are going to be greeted with fear, suspicion, and, if you get too close, violent self-defense. This is exactly what happens when the visitors penetrate restricted military areas or when people who have been abducted wake up during the experience.

They must view our violent response with impatience and probably anger, especially if they are not, in their view, attempting to attack us at all. Judging from some of the contact stories, they may have a better understanding of the communications problems than we do, but it cannot be perfect. If it was, the relationship wouldn't be so difficult.

As it would seem that we do not share a common vision of reality, they are not going to be able to achieve contact by, say, sending conventional ambassadors to our governments. They might not even know what an ambassador is, let alone be able to provide one who can communicate with us successfully.

There is every evidence that dolphins and other cetaceans have significant intelligence, possibly close to ours, but the idea of sending an ambassador to them is absurd. We can't because we don't share the same vision of the world. Our sensory inputs and brains are simply too different.

I have been face to face with the huge, penetrant eyes of the visitors. That anatomical feature alone tells me that their senses and therefore their brains are different from ours. So the same communication problem that exists with the dolphins exists with them, but it's even worse because we have no idea at all about the environment they came from, how their societies work, or even what the world means to them.

We can teach a dolphin to learn sign language, to play ball with us, and all sorts of more complex communication—but only on *our terms*. We can't share meaning on their terms. We cannot express our sense of personal meaning to a dolphin or explain our ideas of nationhood or our political or religious beliefs, and neither can dolphins explain themselves to us on any terms that we can understand.

I would submit that our culture has not yet, at any level, grasped the significance of this when it comes to communication with our visitors. The military certainly hasn't, or they wouldn't be bothering to broadcast warnings on radio frequencies in whatever native language that particular military happens to speak when the visitors approach its restricted areas.

Also, we cannot go to them. They can only come to us. This means that we cannot know what their origin point is like and therefore, even if we were able to examine one of their bodies, might or might not be able to deduce the function of their organs. Because we cannot enter and study their environment, we also cannot know how they fit into the ecology of wherever they come from. This is crucially important, because culture is so connected to environment. The rhythm and meaning of Egyptian religion, for example, was profoundly influenced by a wish to control the annual Nile flood. And this is just one obvious example. Because we cannot go to our visitors' places, we also cannot know how their experience of their world affects their logic, their morality, their social structures.

We don't know how their biology works, or if they even have biology as we understand the term. We don't know how their environments have influenced their cultures and therefore how they understand themselves and, ultimately, what sort of sense we make to them. We don't know if they experience themselves as individuals like we do, or if they are more of a colony such as we see on Earth among species like ants and bees.

While we cannot go to them, they can enter our spaces, study our environment and our biology, our languages and cultures—whatever they care to do. Even so, it probably isn't enough to enable them to communicate with us on terms that make sense to both sides. A scientist can tranquilize a monkey, abduct him, study his biology, and perhaps tag him. His semen can be taken for breeding purposes and injected into a captive female in order to breed offspring for zoos or laboratory use. No matter what is done though, the monkey cannot understand what has been done to him, let alone that he is being tracked by a scientist ten thousand miles away. The reason is simple: the monkey's brain cannot process the information needed for him to understand what has been done to him. He sees any intrusion into his personal space, whether beneficial to him or not, as a threat. He cannot do otherwise, and the scientist cannot explain himself.

If we are not in a similar situation with our visitors, I would be very surprised. The difference between us and the monkey is that, because of our higher level of intelligence, we can detect and attempt to understand much more detail and nuance and speculate, perhaps even usefully, about the meaning of what is being done to us.

Even though we cannot observe the ecology out of which our visitors emerged or study their bodies, we can analyze their goals and intentions by looking carefully at what happens to us, albeit always with the caveat that perceptual issues may distort our recollections.

The result of both the secrecy and the perceptual issues has been that elaborate alien races' folklore has sprung up. Is any of it real? I often interview believers in various of these, attempting to see if anything definite can be found that might suggest that they are true. When people have experiences, especially strange encounters, that they cannot understand, they will contextualize them in terms of whatever the current consensus reality may be. Dr. Jacques Vallée illustrates this effect in his *Passport to Magonia,* and more recently George M. Eberhart has published a paper (May 31, 2022) entitled "UFOs and Intelligence: A Timeline" that compiles cases from 822 CE to the present. Both of these efforts illustrate the same point: conclusions about what is being observed depend on what the observer believes about reality at the time of the observation.

Unknown presences have a vast number of different identities in the West, from angels and gods to sylphs and fairies, and on to the aliens of today. In non-Western cultures, we see beings like the star people of some Native American traditions, the *djinn* of the Islamic world, and many others.

The fact that the visions are so inconsistent suggests either that we don't have the biological equipment to determine what is actually causing our perceptions or that whatever is out there has been disguising its own reality for eons, and may still be doing so. The visitors of today could easily be yesterday's fairy folk or sylphs. As author Terrence McKenna put it, "We are part of a symbiotic relationship with something which disguises itself as an extraterrestrial invasion so as not to alarm us." It is only a speculation, but it is surely one that points toward some unseen truth.

Does that truth actually even involve physical ships, and if so, is there any connection between them and the close encounters?

Direct evidence may be lacking, but there are strong suggestions of a connection. The best piece of UAP footage in my possession shows one operating in a clear blue sky over British Columbia on a fall day in 2004. It was taken during the same week and in the same area that the Corina Saebels abduction took place. Because that abduction involved two witnesses and resulted in documented physical injuries that were quite unusual, it is accurate to say that something unexplained happened to Ms. Saebels and her friend. And the fact that UAP sightings were being reported and recorded in the area at the time does suggest that there could be a connection. But that's all there is: a suggestion, not proof. It may be that proof of such a connection is concealed behind the wall of classification, but I have no way of knowing that.

Given all this uncertainty, the question must be asked: Are there physical nonhuman beings here at all?

The answer is that, on a societal level, we don't know. Again, perhaps the answer *is* known and hidden from the public eye. Hopefully, we'll one day be told what is kept behind the veil of secrecy, especially since it so intimately involves our own lives and safety. On a personal basis, of course, I would assert that our visitors are physical nonhuman beings and that their presence is associated with UAPs. The reason is that they took me into one and raped me there, leaving diagnosable physical injuries. But this, like all the other accounts, is my subjective recollection. It is not proof of anything.

Also the fact that I have experienced and described physical events does not mean that I also think that my perceptions are accurate beyond a doubt, and that goes for the entire body of witness testimony, not just my own. The reason for this is that we are dealing with something that has an ability to influence and distort memory, and probably has motive for doing so.

Let's look briefly at the process as it is presently understood. False memories can be created. In *Psychological Science*, Julia Shaw and Stephen Porter published a paper entitled "Constructing Rich False Memories of Committing Crime" that detailed how innocent people can be implanted with memories of committing crimes of which they are completely innocent. If we can do this, our visitors, who can induce effects like missing time, may be able to actually design our memories of contacts with them that may or may not have happened.

Studies using functional MRI scanning, which observes neural activity in real time, reveal that the brain assembles memories of actual sensory events differently than it does of imaginary material. The reason is that memory that originates with sensory input is stored differently from memory that starts in the imagination. The brain stores a memory of a car accident, for example, in a different way than it stores the memory of a nightmare about one.

A study called "Neural correlates of true and false memories" by K. A. Paller, published in *Neuron* in 2000, found that when people were experiencing memories of actual events, the activity in the left hippocampus and the right parahippocampal gyrus was greater than when they were experiencing imaginary memories they believed to be true. The study's conclusion was that the right parahippocampal gyrus and the left hippocampus are differentially engaged by true and false recognition.

This technique might be used to determine whether a memory concerns an actual, physical event or is imaginary, which parts of a memory are imagined, and which parts of real events.

Our visitors are elusive, even ghostly, but they do seem to be possessed of a very real physical presence. The messages they have embedded in our culture about environmental peril and nuclear danger mean that they want us to survive. But if so, then why do they hide the way they do, never publicly revealing their physical presence and leaving us with confusing and contradictory memories? Why have they apparently led our military into conflict with them instead of avoiding confrontation?

They have left us to argue among ourselves about what they are and whether or not they even exist. We are doomed, therefore, to never really explore their presence deeply, and thus also to fail to heed their warnings. If their warnings about nuclear peril and environmental upheaval are to be heeded, they have to come reveal themselves. But they would appear to be doing everything they can to avoid that.

Why? Is it that they have no clear, single policy toward us? It certainly looks as if they are themselves in a state of conflict or indecision about us, so perhaps there is some truth to the stories of the wars in space told in the *Upanishads* and the modern stories of conflicting alien species.

We just don't know, although it is possible that at the very deepest level of the Department of Defense, something more of their final reality, state of internal conflict, and true motives is known. However, of what use is that to those of us on the outside who are trying to think seriously about this subject? What is especially worrying is that at least some of the people who are most fully informed hold strong religious beliefs that may color their interpretations of what they experience. In addition, our visitors may themselves lie, and if there are factions among them, the combination of our side seeing them through a distorting filter of beliefs and their side presenting a tangled web of contradictions is bound to be causing chaos.

And that, I believe, is exactly where we are. The question must be asked, then, is there a way out?

Of course there is, and it doesn't involve breaking the will of those who are keeping the secrets. In fact, it cannot be broken, not by pressure from the public or its elected authorities, not even from a president. The reason for this is that revealing the secrets is an existential threat to the community that is keeping them. By carrying out abductions and other provocative forms of contact, the visitors have placed those who know about this and cannot stop it in a position where they must keep it secret in order to protect their own validity. The mission of the Air Force is to protect us from threats from above. If the abductions are real, then they are failing. Therefore they do the visitors' bidding and keep it all secret. Without realizing it, our own insiders are therefore following the policy of the very entity that they seek to oppose.

This started in 1947. Whatever happened at Roswell, it was not a straightforward crash. As it was preceded by the conflict situation discussed previously, it was almost certainly not random. It was an intentional provocation. The reason I say this is that it took place just thirty miles from what was then the most sensitive military site in the Western world, the Roswell Army Air Field, where the 509th Bomb Wing was then stationed.

At that time, the 509th was the only nuclear strike force on Earth, and as such it was also the only existential threat to Joseph Stalin and his ambitions. He had millions of soldiers stationed along the border that was becoming known as the Iron Curtain, and would certainly have swept across Europe to the English Channel if he'd felt that he could win. By contrast, allied armies were in the process of standing down, the great majority of American and British soldiers already mustered out by 1947.

Those bombers were the primary reason that he was unwilling to commit his troops. He did not possess air defenses sufficiently robust to stop them, and they could have annihilated his cities and, quite possibly, him.

Western governments were well aware of the peril, and here comes an unknown aircraft crashing just a few miles from where the bombers that were keeping the peace were based. Did the craft contain Geiger counters and radios, perhaps, that could send back to Stalin some idea of the bombers' state of readiness? Did it contain some sort of weapon that could destroy them?

The inability to answer these questions was what induced the military to drop a blanket of secrecy over the whole affair, even though—as General Exon told me—everyone from the White House right down to Brigadier General Roger Ramey, then commanding the Eighth Air Force, knew that "what we had found was not of this world within twenty-four hours of our finding it."

That certainly did not suggest to a very frightened president that the public should be told. On the contrary, it suggested a completely unknown situation, even more likely to spin out of control than if it had been a Russian spy plane.

The debris was flown on a specially allocated plane from Roswell to Wright Field in Dayton and the Air Materiel Command. Unless this debris was extremely important and believed to be highly sensitive, it would never have been handled in this way. According to the record, General Ramey knew that it was a radar target before sending it to Wright. So why put it on a special plane and fly it to Air Materiel to find out what it was?

When he and Major Jesse Marcel gave their press conference in Dallas, calling it a radar target, both men were almost certainly lying, which is exactly what Marcel later admitted in a video made by Stanton Friedman that is readily available on YouTube.

Even if the crash was an accident—and as we are dealing here with a very complex mind about which we know little, we cannot draw that or any other conclusion about the cause of the event—the fact that it occurred in such a sensitive area was certain to cause the imposition of a level of extraordinary secrecy. Over time, this secrecy has become like a lie that is too dangerous to admit. It has built on itself to the point that revealing the truth threatens the most fundamental bonds of trust between the official world and the public. Because the media has repeated the falsehoods for generations, it now has an almost equal stake in maintaining them and is willing to bend its own rules to do so, as was seen in the insufficiently precise attributions in the October 28 *Times* article.

There is something about the situation that is not generally understood and needs to be made clear. This is that we didn't make the decision to drop the mantle of secrecy over the subject. Our visitors did that. They made it inevitable by what they did in 1947, attacking extremely sensitive rocket launches and then crashing the object so close to Roswell AAF and its nuclear strike force.

When I think of what those soldiers must have gone through, facing such a powerful and bizarrely menacing mystery with weapons that must have seemed quite weak, my heart goes out to them. I don't fault the government for keeping this secret, either.

They had no choice then, and with all that has happened since, they still don't.

It is time for the defense community to realize this and to think very, very seriously about the power our policy of secrecy gives the visitors.

On the good side, mentioned in the introduction, secrecy has prevented cultural colonization, which is the process of a more technologically powerful culture causing a less powerful one to come to seem irrelevant to its own participants.

So here we are, trapped on our struggling planet, face to face with something very strange and at once very powerful and very vulnerable that, despite the lie that was told to General Twining, has an intense interest in us.

Our visitors are skilled at keeping us off balance. The secrecy that our authorities have been tricked into upholding may be protecting us from the destruction of our culture, but it is also corroding trust between us and our leadership. I have recently witnessed this method of manipulating us in my personal life, where a number of attempts were made to corrode trust between me and people I work with and people I love.

I would like to turn, now, to these events and to ask the question, *are* we dealing with demons, after all?

CHAPTER 17
FEAR COMES KNOCKING

The events I am about to describe are extremely strange and among the most terrifying things I have ever known. I am not speaking of the sort of panic I experienced during my abduction but rather of a kind of creeping fear that ate at me until, to continue to concentrate on writing this book, I had to leave home. At this time, I am working from a small flat far from there.

The events involved were physical. They may have involved some sort of official locomotion or been perpetrated by private individuals. I don't know. Had I not been living the life I am living, I am certain that they would not have happened.

Even as they were unfolding, the positive aspect of my experience continued. The nonphysical aspect of my experience is, for the most part, teacherly, gentle, and loving. It will become insistent if I ignore it when it wants to communicate with me. Even then, the various physical effects (waking me up for the early morning meditation, for example) tend to be as gentle as possible and usually have a loving or humorous side to them, or both. (I have described them in *Afterlife Revolution* and discussed them in *A New World*. To briefly recap, they started a couple of months after Anne passed away and initially involved fairly intense wakeups, but once I got used to getting up in the early hours to meditate, they became much gentler. Currently, they only happen if I don't get up for a night or so. The wee-hours meditations are the time of day I look forward to the most. The give-and-take that goes on is useful in my work. It turns out that this time of day is well known in Yoga traditions as the best time to meditate, as the mind is quietest and most open.

At the time the events I am about to describe happened, I saw them for what they were, an attack, and yet what happened was not purely evil. I was also being challenged by what was being done to me, and I think that I have come to understand a little better how that challenge works, and how to meet it. But this is still very much a work in progress, as will become evident.

When I started to get awakened for the early morning meditation, I was delighted. I felt that Anne was involved, and it was all very wonderful. I didn't mind having my sleep interrupted. Since childhood, I've only slept four or five hours a night, usually in a three-hour stretch, then a two-hour one, so the meditation fit in very comfortably.

My side of my relationship with the visitors began when I started going out into the woods at night back in the late '80s. I got to know them as tough and fierce, also brilliant and possessed of an ability to communicate mind to mind. What I am about to describe, though, is not about them, and it is not about supportive presences that meditate with me in the wee hours.

It is about people.

In late January of 2021, shortly after I had discussed with some friends some indications I'd had that my apartment was being entered, I was doing my 11:00 p.m. meditation when there was a flash of sparks and an explosion on my deck, which I face when I meditate. Shocked and frightened, I jumped up. But then I thought that it must have been firecrackers, as New Year's was just a few weeks past. Perhaps someone had tossed a leftover firecracker that happened to land on my deck—or maybe it had been somebody who knew about my 11:00 p.m. meditation and wanted to annoy me. In either case, I thought no more of the incident.

As matters have turned out, it marked the beginning of one of the most difficult times in my life.

On July 21, 2021, at 3:56 a.m. I was once again meditating when there was an absolutely terrific double explosion outside. It resulted in car alarms going off, and it also happened while the cameras were on, so I got a record of it. I talked about it on my show and posted the video to my YouTube channel. In addition, there were comments on the Neighborhoods app that indicated that it had been heard across an area of at least a square mile. Obviously not a firecracker.

After I posted the video, nothing more seemed to happen. But then, nearly a year later, things got darker. Much.

On April 21, 2022, I was coming in from exercise at about 8:00 a.m. I opened the door, which was locked with a key lock in the door handle. When I walked in, and found that drawers had been opened in my bedroom. I rushed through the house, but nothing was missing. I called the police, but as nothing had been stolen and there was no evidence of a break-in, there seemed to be no point in making a report.

I was even more upset about this incident than I would normally have been. This was because of the seeming coincidence that it had taken place on the one morning in at least a year when my router had been turned off. Something had been done the day before to cause a warning that a new computer was trying to get onto my network. I'd decided to get a new, more secure router and had turned off internet access until I could do so. Obviously, whoever had been testing its security had known that it was off and taken the opportunity to break in.

But why not steal? Because they weren't robbers, as would shortly become evident.

On Saturday morning, April 23, I was sitting in a park when I had a sudden, odd urge to check the technical integrity of my website. When the urge came, my mind was far from thoughts about the website, and yet I felt compelled to look at it at once.

When I entered the site's backend on my phone, I was appalled to see that somebody was trying to brute force their way in by opening various administrator usernames and then using a program to rapid-fire test different passwords. This had started just before I logged on.

I called my webmaster, and we played a game of cat and mouse as the intruder raced from one IP address to another and we chased them, blocking each one as soon as they tried to use it. Meanwhile, the webmaster closed all the admin usernames and began controlling the site from the code level.

When the attack stopped, I rushed home and opened my laptop to examine the site and see if anything had been damaged. In the meantime, the webmaster had a new admin login for me in the backend of the site, then sent it to me via a secure protocol. There was no way anybody could know it, and yet the instant I logged in, the intruders had it and began at once damaging the site.

I was on the phone with the webmaster when this happened, and he was able to stop it after a few seconds, but in the meantime the site's bookstore had been half erased.

It meant only one thing: the purpose of the break-in had been to put a keylogger on my laptop and the opening of drawers had been a diversion. (We eventually located the keylogger and neutralized it.)

But the motive was not to wreck the site. It would have taken only a moment to simply scrape it off the server. We would have restored it from one of the backups, of course, but totally erasing it obviously wasn't the point. It was actually much more of a pain in the neck to restore the books than it would have been to repost the whole site.

It was immediately obvious to me that they could have come into the apartment, installed the keylogger ,and then left without my noticing a thing.

So why do it like this? It could be intimidation, but it also could be something more subtle, which would be an effort to get me to increase my security.

I did just that, of course, and we also discovered how they'd found the admin usernames in the first place and closed down that avenue of access.

But despite our efforts, more happened. A friend contacted me to say that the emails she had sent to all of her friends over the past few months were reappearing in her inbox. Then her email address showed up in the backend of the site that made it look as if *she* was hacking it. But we have extensive monitoring capabilities, and while this was happening, she was not on the website. She also did not have any admin access.

After that, the attacks stopped. Home and site security were once again increased. Among other things, more cameras were installed outside the apartment. On July 20, 2022, at 8:26 a.m. a man appeared at the door. He didn't knock, but the new doorbell camera recorded him as he briefly examined the recent installations. I sent the video of his movements to a security expert who analyzed the stranger's every glance and movement. He replied that the man had carefully observed all visible aspects of the system and that he was "a thief or worse." He has not returned. So far. I gaze at his photo and I wonder, who am I looking at? Or what?

By this time, I had understood that this was no normal attack. It had started with the odd explosions. Then I had been tricked into turning off my router by somebody who had gained access to my network.

Things went from bad to—well, terrible.

I left to spend some time with old friends in another state. One evening we went to dinner and returned at about nine. I have stayed with them many times over the years, so everything was very familiar to me. When I went to brush my teeth and take my evening pills (a Lipitor and a vitamin), I was horrified to discover that two extra pills had appeared in my pill planner. I noticed them immediately, of course, and set about finding them on a pill identification site on the internet. I discovered that they were an antiseizure medication and an antidepressant. I have never taken either, and nobody in the house would have had any reason at all to slip them in among my pills.

I was terrified.

There was obviously no way that I could stay in the house another minute, so I booked a hotel room, quietly packed my things, and left. Everyone else was asleep, and nobody saw me go.

I got to the hotel, which was your usual roadside Hilton, nothing special. I checked in, went to my room, brushed my teeth and put on my pajamas. The room was completely normal and there was absolutely not a soul in it but me.

After lying in bed for a moment, I noticed movement and opened my eyes. To my utter horror, there was a short man, almost a dwarf, in a red shirt jumping up and down at the bedside. The naked, bound body of a woman lay on the floor at the foot of the bed. She was young. Her eyes were glazed with death.

As the room had been empty when I walked in and I had locked the door behind me, I thought that this had to be some sort of hallucination. And yet, if I closed my eyes, it would disappear. When I opened them, there it was again. So not a normal one. But there was no sound connected with it. In other words, as the grinning gnome hopped up and down, there was no thudding. No matter how real it appeared, it remained obvious to me that it was not.

I decided that, despite the fact that I hadn't taken the pills, I had somehow been drugged. I experienced great fear, knowing that what I was seeing was not real but not knowing how in the name of God I had been drugged or what damage the drugs might do to me. My heart started racing. I felt sick with fear. But what could I do? Unsure of my ability to navigate the space, I dared not move an inch. I looked over at the dwarf then down at the dead girl with her glassy eyes and did the only thing I could do, which was wait.

It seemed like one hell of a long time before it stopped, but when it did, I think just a few minutes had passed. While it was going on, I feared that maybe I would never get out of it. Maybe psychosis had been induced. But when? How?

When it ended, I started for the emergency room. But I didn't know the laws in that state, and I wasn't sure of what might happen if they found evidence of a controlled substance in my bloodstream. Would I be arrested? Would my friends be investigated?

The next morning, I stopped by their house and said goodbye, then returned home. The next day wrote Dr. Green, describing what had happened. He wrote back that he thought that, had I taken the two drugs that had ended up in my pill planner I would probably have slept very deeply. I would then have been asleep when the hallucination took place and unable to wake up. Would I have been driven insane? Had a heart attack from the terror?

The most recent incident took place on September 9, 2022, at 11:37 p.m. I was meditating in my living room when I noticed that the cameras had turned themselves off. (This is often a precursor to odd incidents.) A moment later, another explosion. Security in the apartment is now divided among a number of systems, and the one that covers the den and bedroom had not been affected, so the sound was recorded but not the flash that I saw from where I was sitting.

At this point, I became too stressed to work in the apartment and moved to another location. In fact, I left the country altogether and was grateful to find friends abroad to put me up. I wrote most of this book at their kitchen table.

All of these events were attacks, some more serious than others. Two of them were similar to others that have taken place in the past, which involve attempts to destroy my relationships with people I love. The explosions were there to frighten and intimidate me. The attack on the computer was probably a result of the fact that my website has recently had some new safeguards installed. I'm sure that they could be defeated by a skilled hacker, but whomever had the motive to harm it chose another way that, because it involved a break-in, was meant to also threaten my person.

It's the sort of vindictiveness that happens when somebody you thought loved you gives you pain. You want to hurt them back, and what better way to do it than to ruin their work and their relationships with people they love?

And there the story ends. Unfinished, as always. I hope that I will one day understand what this is about and who is doing it, but that day has not yet come. I do not know the degree to which, if at all, these attacks involve the visitors or conceivably people who are connected to them in unusual ways, and, given the fact that they have taken human sexual material, I think that such people could exist. As I have recounted in chapter 4 of *Solving the Communion Enigma* and elsewhere, Anne and I may have encountered one of them in the woods behind our cabin back in the 1990s. He was young, obviously profoundly disturbed, seemed capable of reading minds, and when we lost the cabin, followed us to Texas and tried to hide outside our condo. I drove him off by installing a motion-sensitive light in the cul-de-sac where he would conceal himself at night. When he was there, he was four feet away from me. We were separated only by a flimsy wall. I could feel him entering my mind, and it was quite disturbing. He could not speak, but he was proficient at mental communication. We reached out to him but were unable to develop any sort of a normal relationship with him. Whether he or others like him are responsible for these intimidating events or not I cannot say.

There's no question that these things happened. They weren't done by ghosts. Could it be intelligence agents? I suppose, but what possible motive could they have to torment me and corrode my friendships. Frankly, it seems more like the work of somebody living on a shadow line between normal reality and—well—something else.

Perhaps somebody hidden deep in the labyrinth of the secret world knows, but I doubt that they'll ever tell me.

Even though the official world is going to continue denying that this hidden reality even exists, and most of us don't realize that it does, I think that we all have a place in it. Some of us, such as the people whose letters are analyzed in part 1, do remember and do a surprisingly good job of it.

If it's true that the military has engaged in the lonely and dangerous struggle that it appears they have, I feel for those who have died in it or been maimed and must hold their silence. Despite all the denials, I do think that there is reason to believe that the hidden war is real. It is important, therefore, to understand the reasons, both good and bad, that the visitors' presence inspired our soldiers to seek to protect us from them. Just as the Sentinelese islander, alone on the beach facing a monster, was a man of courage, so are our soldiers. Perhaps neither fight was necessary for the reasons the warriors may think, but if modern civilization landed on North Sentinel Island, all that the members of the little tribe love and value and cherish about themselves and the world would vanish into the past. They would be humbled and, even if the invaders were loving and supportive and kind, degraded into the same sense of irrelevance that has impacted and in some cases destroyed most of the indigenous cultures around the world. Thus the warrior was indeed fighting a monster, even though it was not the one he imagined, and he certainly saved his people with his arrows.

Our military is in exactly the same position, and the evidence suggests that the visitors have understood this from the beginning. This is what all the incursions were about. Our soldiers were being goaded into the fight so that they would end up keeping the secret that, if it came out too early, would strip the entire human species of its sense of self-worth, its belief that it is important in the greater scheme of things and that each fate is cherished in the many heavens of our many faiths, including the intellectual faith, which holds that our mind is a fine one, and our ideas have significance.

Our visitors have been ghosts in our world, but now that time seems to be growing short, they may well be bringing themselves more into focus. It is to be hoped that we have gotten sufficiently used to them that we will not be so overawed by their different abilities that we lose faith in ourselves.

Where are we, then? As our planet's ability to support us declines, I think that they have a decision to make. Either they become more openly present (if they can) and engage with us, or let us go through whatever upheaval may await. If they do finally reveal themselves as a concrete reality, then I hope this and my other books will help us adapt. I want a good outcome for everybody, us and them.

Earth lives by cycles of extinction and rebirth. Before history began—not so very long ago, really—we were struggling to survive similar changes on this ever-heaving planet of ours. Worldwide flood stories dating back to earliest times likely reflect the sudden end of the last ice age. The tale of Isis freeing the Egyptians from cannibalism by teaching them to farm is a memory of the fact that the women, the gatherers, in a land where all the animals had gone, discovered how to turn plants collected into plants cultivated. (Societies without a cannibal tradition will often turn to cannibalism if their protein intake drops too low and they have no other way of restoring it.)

History with its counting and its kings followed the discovery of farming, and now, as another extinction event shadows the future, the long, ungainly poem of life on Earth comes to the singing of what could be the final stanzas of this latest verse. Many of us are looking up into the stars and out into the shadows that are gathering around us, seeking help from anyone who might linger there. The worse things get, the more will join them, and more and still more, and the refusal of the authorities to reveal what they know to these desperate seekers will become more than a social irritant. In the end, it will become a storm of anger, and as nature sweeps the world we have come to know away, this and other sources of distrust will turn us against our authorities in fundamental and finally irrevocable ways.

This could be what we face, and all we face, if the visitors prove to be a will-o'-the-wisp of this strange, mysterious mind of ours and are blown away in the rising of the storms. But if not, if they are something that is not us, then—well—despite all the trouble there has been, we have a charge before us: we need them and therefore need to do all we can to make the relationship work.

CHAPTER 18
IN CONCLUSION

From my years of experience with our visitors and the research I have done for this book and so many others, I have come to think that there are two key differences between us and them that are making it hard for us to develop a relationship. This does not mean that I have decided that I know what they are. I think that the most likely possibility is that, even though they do present physical appearances that would lead us to believe that they were creatures from other worlds, when (if ever) we are face to face with them, we are going to come to know that there are things about them that we may never understand. But this isn't because they are somehow our superiors. It is for the same reason that we can never fully understand a dolphin, a monkey or, for that matter, any other sentient creature. The gulf between us will be wide, and I would think it foolish to assume that either side can truly and deeply understand the other.

The first thing that enforces the gulf between us is the fact that they communicate mind to mind while we use physical voice. The second is that they are active both in physical and nonphysical realms of reality, while in our species, communication is physical and contact with the nonphysical—and even its existence—is an open question.

Because of these differences, the way we see and understand the world, the way our societies work, how we understand life and reality —all of this must be very different. We are also bound to have radically different histories.

Because they have joined minds, inevitably they are going to be less developed as individuals than we are. We are many bodies, many minds, but if I am right, they are many bodies, one mind.

How do they govern themselves—by some sort of consensus, or is there an organized hierarchy? Perhaps, as with insect colonies on Earth, the different forms that we see are not different races at all but have different roles in the community. And what about individuality? What does it mean to them, and, therefore, what do we?

The fact that we slip so readily into telepathic communication when with them suggests that this is an ability that we have, too, but that is normally dormant. Is it something we lost, then, and if so, why and how? Could it be that the beginning of systems like writing, the appearance of beliefs and gods and the rising prayer of a desperate humankind is really a response to the collapse of a community of mind that left us a fractured society of isolated individuals?

If so, is this something that happened to us or that was done to us? Could it be why we are surrounded by ancient structures that we can no longer build—because the power of mind needed for their construction has been lost to us? Many of us believe that there was an actual, physical civilization that disappeared in the distant past— Atlantis or whatever it might be called. But what if it wasn't a civilization at all but a capability so vastly more powerful and radically different from what we know now that we can hardly even begin to understand it, let alone recover it? If Dr. Somé's account of the pots rising from the floor and gravity turned topsy-turvy at his grandfather's funeral is accurate, did he witness the last fluttering sigh of this lost power?

Judging from the confusion and the conflicts, and our visitors' reputation among close encounter witnesses of being harsh, it would seem that they display as much of a lack of understanding of us as we do of them. The way they have communicated their military warnings, for example, is superficially not at all the way we would do it. Look deeper, though, and it's exactly the same.

If we were trying to prevent somebody who spoke another language from, say, wading out into surf where rip current warnings were posted, when they failed to understand our spoken warnings and kept on, we would finally drag them back. Not understanding, they'd probably think they were being mugged and put up a fight.

I suspect that the conflict we are in has been caused by something like this. Is it that we had been ignoring telepathic warnings, probably all through World War II and possibly before, with the result that they finally started trying to warn us by demonstrating the danger through interruption of our weapons tests and missiles? We reacted, quite naturally, as if we were under attack.

While I cannot speculate about why they ended up with telepathy while we use voice, or why among us there is a barrier between the living and, as my wife used to put it, "what we call the dead," I feel sure that this is another core reason that the relationship is so poorly developed. The fact that our best minds, having no experience of either telepathy or afterlife communication and no ability to confirm either's existence, reject these possibilities out of hand is unfortunate but also inevitable. We have no scientific tools that would enable us to bring them into our canon of knowledge. One promising sign is that being close to the visitors seems to unlock telepathic abilities that are normally dormant in us, so it seems conceivable that, if they draw closer in a more public way, this ability will awaken in more of us.

Their familiarity with telepathy probably means that their technology is radically different from ours. They may not use radio, for example. They might not even know about it. They may or may not have books, and in a society where it is impossible to hide one's thoughts, social structures are going to be completely different from ours. Would there be crime? And what of privacy, or wealth? Add to this that the physical and nonphysical aspects of their race are not separated as ours are, and it becomes obvious that the gulf between us must be very wide indeed.

If telepathy is their fundamental means of communication, it could also be integral to their technology. How that would work, of course, I cannot speculate, but it could be the reason that our gravitic propulsion research has not had enough success to be moved out of the classification system like, say, stealth technology.

Researcher Grant Cameron, who has been in the field for fifty years, has published a book called *UFO Sky Pilots* in which over three dozen close encounter witnesses report that flying UAP involves the use of the mind, not technology as we understand it. One would assume that this testimony would be dismissed as worthless, but I would argue that what we are facing in the overall phenomenon is too new and too little understood for anything to be dismissed at this point.

Both British Aerospace and NASA are working on gravitic propulsion, and there is reputedly a program underway in Boeing's Phantom Works, their equivalent to Lockheed's Skunkworks. A defense contractor called Radiance Technologies is also rumored to be involved. Unfortunately, I have been unable to follow up these rumors. My efforts have been thwarted by official secrecy

Perhaps there is another level to the business of their mysterious propulsion system that involves the use of energies that only someone familiar with the physics of telepathy can understand. If so, then no matter how hard we try, we are not going to gain a full understanding of the principles and energies involved—at least, not until we face the fact that telepathy does happen and that nonphysical consciousness is real and begin to explore ways of understanding both phenomena in ways that are useful to us, which means the detection of relevant energies and the experimental repeatability that goes with this.

The last, and probably the most important, problem is that our brains do not assemble reality in the same way as those of our visitors. Our different physiologies mean different sensory input, and that is going to generate different meanings and therefore different ways of understanding literally everything.

The "Visitors in the Trees" story illustrates just how difficult it is going to be to overcome the differences between us, but also that it's not impossible. Hopefully it also suggests how they may help us and how to detect their efforts.

Whether their intention in conducting the abductions was to preserve some record of humankind against the danger of catastrophe or to take something of ourselves from us, or both, there is no way to know. If we are able to establish functional communications of some kind, perhaps we can get them to explain this. The fact that they stopped the abductions suggests that it wasn't some sort of feeding process, at least, and it certainly looks more like an effort to create a seed bank of our and possibly other species. If it was any sort of feeding or harvesting process, it would continue.

Judging from the tremendous variety of experiences we have with them, I think it's probable that they have many different ways of approaching us, maybe because more than one type of being, and therefore more than one type of perceptual system, is involved. Forms that are most commonly reported are five: tall light-complexioned humanoids, dark blue troll-like creatures, willowy ones with big dark eyes, creatures with a reptile-like appearance, and something like a giant praying mantis, which is what General Exon said they had found at Roswell and Jacques Vallée and Paola Harris maintain in their book *Trinity* was seen inside a crashed UAP by two young witnesses in 1945.

If these represent different races from different worlds, they are all likely to have different perceptual biology and brains, but if they all share some sort of universal telepathy, they might nevertheless be able to work together. Witnesses who experience telepathy during close encounters generally report, as did our correspondent in the "Where Did That Time Go?" letter, that it seems perfectly natural when it is happening and is always in one's native language—unless it unfolds at a level of mind that is deeper than language, where there is a universality of consciousness that we do not yet understand.

During a contact experience, perceptions are distorted and thought processes changed. Large swaths of time routinely go missing. We assume that this is because "they" are distorting our perceptions, but I think it just as likely that it is caused by our brains' difficulty with novel experience, and I think that it's perfectly possible that they would be having difficulties, also.

Because of their different experience of life (the ability to function in a nonphysical state and to communicate mind to mind) we cannot assume that their understanding of what reality is—and thus also what we are—is the same as our own.

We have reached almost to the borders of the physical universe with our telescopes. They seem to be seeking a border, also, but one that is within.

We need to learn how to share these two journeys, ours toward the limits of physical reality, which they probably already know, and the other toward the depths of the mind, which might well be the only frontier left to them. If I am correct about what they are, then they need us to help them more than we need them. Given time, we are going to come to final understanding of the outer, physical world, and perhaps reach depths of the inner world far beyond what we can now imagine. We can do this because we are a vast collection of complex, highly intelligent, and creative minds that are independent of each other. If they are linked telepathically, then they may have, in essence, only one even more complex and intelligent mind.

This difference is profoundly important, and recognizing it and using it could be the foundation (at last!) of a functional relationship between us that works for both species.

A great Hindu wisdom-keeper, Sri Nisargadatta Maharaj, sounded the note upon which such a relationship must rest:

"The seeker is he who is in search of himself. Give up all questions except one: 'Who am I?' After all, the only fact that you are sure of is that you are. The 'I am' is certain. The 'I am this' is not. Struggle to find out who you are in reality."

As we probe into the universe, its physics will continue to disclose new knowledge to us and, with it, new insights into ourselves and what we mean in and to the vast ocean of stars that is our home. Similarly, as they probe into the boundless labyrinth of inner life, they will also make new discoveries. If we are calm in our hearts with one another, and open each to the other's quest, we will be able to share our discoveries.

They seek insight into what we in our community of individuals can find—the self. We can do this because we can see our reflections in others. For example, each of us can, on their own and in the privacy of their own life, see the wisdom and with it the challenge in Sri Nisargadatta's words. They can see it, too, but in a very different way. If I am right and all of them feed into a collective mind, then, while they will undoubtedly see the question very well, they will see it only once. No matter how big a mind may be, that question will always be bigger.

Our coming together will be something entirely new in this universe, and I think—hope—that it is what they seek with us.

If so and we manage to make the other's aim fundamental to our own journey, everything is going to change. If our relationship evolves into one of mutual search, we will be able to share the one question that is universally present in all of us, whether we are exploring the outer universe or the inner. It is summed up by Master Nisargadatta's question: "Who am I?"

That they have found us—when and how is no matter—offers both sides an absolutely transcendent opportunity to discover ourselves in the mirror of the other. Their eyes seek with fierce urgency into our depths, ours through telescopes and other tools into the wonderful stars.

The two journeys fit like puzzle pieces.

Face to face, naked to each other's quest—that is the deepest place we can go together. This is because our two questions are actually one, perhaps too deep for words, that has to do with the reason for being and its nature. Such a question is truly the testing ground of truth, where contact becomes communion.

Before that happens though, they will continue to face the tremendous loneliness that I suspect has driven them to search the great darkness of the universe. Meanwhile, riding this little speck of matter called Earth, we will feel more and more the truth of how lost we are in the vastness of space, our skies flecked here and there with secret signs that never seem to come quite clear, but which suggest to us that other lives with other histories roam the desert of the universe.

As huge as it is, it is also for the most part completely empty, an infinity whose trillions of galaxies amount to only the barest dusting of matter. And then there is us—all the intelligent creatures, those who can know—scattered here and there in those galaxies, so few and so very, very rare that what signals we may send out must almost inevitably be fated to fade unheeded into the tremendous night.

Still, we are here, all of us, children of different stars and living in ways that seem so very strange to one another. But all intelligent races are in this sense united: we all know that we drift in the ocean of space and are alone. Because of this, the most essential journey we can take is to find one another so that we can come together and light its dark with companionship, and at last call it not "the universe" but "our universe," and call it home.

AFTERWORD
THE ME WITHIN THEE

by Jeffrey J. Kripal

I remember well the lived context of this book. Whitley had basically fled from his own home, and for some time. The place was haunted. Or under surveillance. It was impossible to tell which. I remember the text-messages. Whitley was genuinely afraid, and so he got out of there. He actually flew across an ocean and stayed with some friends to escape from the whatever-it-was. I remember him writing me in distress, in flight, and in protection. I felt as I always feel in these situations—hopeless, inadequate, at a loss.

Still, these events speak directly to one of the central messages of this book, a message that Jacques stresses in his own opening words —*this is real*. And it is there that Whitley begins, not with yet another tired debate about whether these things happen or not. They happen. Get over it. And then move on to the much deeper and more productive questions that Whitley asks in the present pages over and over again: *How* does this communication work? How *should* it work? Should we trust it? If so, when. If not, why not? What are these appearances and apparitions? Epiphanies of other dimensions of the human?

What that presence is, of course, we cannot say, not at least clearly, and certainly not with our sciences, logics, sense-based rationalities, and secular institutions. That is the other message of this book. Whoever these presences are, they are speaking to us in ways that we cannot understand, not because someone knows the truth and is not saying (that's the simplistic story, or conspiracy theory, which has done endless damage to this inquiry), but because there is some kind of cross-species or cross-mind communication gap— because there is an inevitable problem in communication between different life-forms.

William James, the Harvard psychologist and philosopher, long ago noted a related gap, this time with respect to paradoxical findings of psychical research. He suggested that we are like cats sleeping in the library: we have no idea what is in the books of the room, and most of us do not care. We sleep on them. We do not read them, much less understand and act on them.

Still, we try. Not all of us sleep. Some of us listen, and read. A lot. I am deeply heartened by how much this book relies on the Archives of the Impossible, an immense repository of various anomalous or paranormal experiences, including the contact experience and UFO phenomenon, that we have been collecting and organizing for almost a decade now at Rice University. Whitley suggests that this may be one of the most important archives in the world, leaving himself the out that it might otherwise be one of the largest collections of modern folklore in the world. I would just remove the subjunctive and observe that folklore can express a particular set of truths that, apparently, can be passed on to the next generation in no other way. Not yet anyway. Hence Jacques Vallée's long interest in mythology and folklore as the true target of the ufological event. They are ultimately after our cultural imaginations and unconscious mythologies, not only our skies or bodies (although they may be after those, too).

There is almost endless data in the Archives of the Impossible, although to call it "data" is already to misunderstand it, to scientize it, as it were. What there really is are thousands upon thousands of human descriptions of experiences of contact with what, or whom,

Whitley calls simply the visitors. As the letters quoted and analyzed in these pages give ample witness, the archives possess such concretized experiences in great abundance, indeed in greater abundance than any single researcher can read, much less interpret and understand. It is not, then, that we do not have enough evidence. We have too much evidence. What we need now is a way to organize and, above all, theorize it.

Still, there is a problem. Conventional intellectuals are generally very good at studying and analyzing cross-cultural contact between living human beings (which usually does not go so well, too put it mildly). But they are generally very bad at studying and analyzing cross-species contact, much less contact between living human beings and invisible entities that may, or may not, be our own "dead." Then they resort to endless refusals to take the experiences as they clearly represent themselves—as contact with other forms of super-human intelligence. The intellectuals read these experiences instead in terms that they themselves can accept—as projections of various social processes, as bad politics, as escape, as evidence of emotional need, and so on. As a result, intellectuals have not actually dealt with what Whitley is saying here, that there is, to put it bluntly, a Them there.

That is really the central message of the book—Them. That's it. Great title. Everything else follows. If there is a Them there, though, then what? What should we do? What should we say? We call this sense of a Them "otherness" or "alterity" in the academy. But we do not generally mean it in the radical ways that Whitley means it. We generally mean some kind of human otherness or alterity, or perhaps now an ecological or species one. If we are really brave, we might even mean the otherness or alterity of "God." But even that way of speaking and thinking is respectable, acceptable.

Whitley complexly understands this presence as an offer of a relationship. They want something from us, or perhaps about us, or perhaps us. It looks very much like they want us to change, even to become "what amounts to a new species." This, of course, has long been the promise of religion—to change us into something else, or to recognize that we have long been something else, something super-human. Wisely, Whitley locates this relationship in the long history of contact with entities who can be as threatening, fearful, and controlling as redemptive, loving, and ecstatic. They may be saving something of us. They may also be eating something of us.

Whitley also insists—again, quite rightly, in my opinion—that this contact is always a both-and, always in the mirror of us. This is why it looks so much like us (or a bad science fiction movie from the 1950s). It is us. This is also why it does not look like us. It is not us. This is the Me within the Thee, a paradoxical relationship through and through.

Jeffrey J. Kripal
J. Newton Rayzor Professor of Philosophy and Religious Thought
Archives of the Impossible
Rice University

BIBLIOGRAPHY

"Anomalous Acute and Subacute Field Effects on Human Biological Tissues." Washington, DC: Defense Intelligence Agency, March 11, 2010. https://docu ments2.theblackvault.com/documents/dia/AAWSAP-DIRDs/DIRD_26- DIRD_Anomalous_Acute_and_Subacute_Field_Effects_on_Human_Biologi cal_Tissues.pdf

Arnold, Matthew. "Dover Beach." *New Poems*. London: Macmillan & Co., 1867.

Au, Jacky, et al. "Improving Fluid Intelligence with Training on Working Memory: A Meta-Analysis." *Psychonomic Bulletin and Review*. 22, 366–77, 2015.

Bain, Donald. *The Control of Candy Jones*. Playboy Press, 1976.

Barnes, Julian E. "Many Military UFO Reports are Just Foreign Spying or Airborne Trash." *The New York Times*, October 28, 2022. https://www.nytimes.com/2022/10/ 28/us/politics/ufo-military-reports.html

Beckwith, Robert W. "Levitation, Teleportation, and Time Travel." Largo, FL: Beck- with Electric Co., 2002. http://stealthskater.com/Documents/Beckwith_02.pdf

Beckwith, Robert W., and Drew Craig. *Hypotheses: Superatoms, Neutrinos & Extrater- restrials*. Independently published, 1998. https://web.archive.org/web/ 20170225055655/https://beckwithelectric.com/ber/downloads/Hypotheses.PDF

Blum, Howard. *Out There: The Government's Secret Quest for Extraterrestrials*. New York: Simon & Schuster, 1990.

Blumenthal, Ralph, and Leslie Kean. "'Project Blue Book' is Based on a True UFO Story. Here It Is." *New York Times*, January 15, 2019. https://www.nytimes.com/2019/ 01/15/arts/television/project-blue-book-history-true-story.html

Brannen, Peter. *The Ends of the World: Volcanic Apocalypses, Lethal Oceans, and Our Quest to Understand Earth's Past Mass Extinctions*. New York: Ecco, 2017.

Brest, Mike. "National Intelligence Director Avril Haines Admits Possibility of Aliens." *Washington Examiner*, November 11, 2021. https://www.washingtonexam iner.com/policy/defense-national-security/national-intelligence-director-avril- haines-admits-possibility-of-aliens

Campion, Thobey. "Stanford Professor Garry Nolan Is Analyzing Anomalous Mate- rials from UFO Crashes." *Vice* Motherboard, December 10, 2021. https://www.vice. com/en/article/n7nzkq/stanford-professor-garry-nolan-analyzing-anomalous- materials-from-ufo-crashes

Carlotto, Mark. "Anomalous Phenomena in Space Shuttle STS-80 Video." *New Fron- tiers in Science*. 4, no.4, Summer 2005. http://www.carlotto.us/newfrontiersin science/Papers/v04n04a/v04n04a.pdf

Carlson, Bruce. "When the Lord Commands." Address to the 180th General Conference of the Church of Jesus Christ of Latter-Day Saints. April 3, 2010. https://www.youtube.com/watch?v=KXJZPKnOHMo

Chomsky, Noam. *What Kind of Creatures Are We?* New York: Columbia University Press, 2016.

Cinone, Danielle. "Hidden Sightings: US Navy 'Admits It Has Unseen UFO Videos but Refuses to Release Footage That Could Harm National Security,' Report Says." *The U.S. Sun*, September 11, 2022. https://www.the-sun.com/news/6194612/us-navy-unseen-ufo-videos-national-security/

Communion Letter. Edited by Anne Strieber. http://beyondcommunion.com/newsletter.html

Condon, Edward U. *The Condon Report: Scientific Study of Unidentified Flying Objects.* New York: E. P. Dutton, 1969.

Condon, Edward U., and Walter Sullivan. "Scientific Study of Unidentified Flying Objects." October 31, 1968. https://drive.google.com/file/d/1Gu75p6N-HU888f G8BU-T5_pqm-TofsFo/view [Google Drive] https://archive.org/details/pdfy-4vyHjooOJagoGAwN/mode/2up [Internet Archive]

Corso, Philip J., and William J. Birnes. *The Day After Roswell*. New York: Pocket Books, 1997.

Cory, Caroline, director. *A Tear in the Sky*. Documentary film, 2022. https://www.atearinthesky.com

Delgado, Jose M., et al. "Intracerebral Radio Stimulation and Recording in Completely Free Patients." *Journal of Nervous and Mental Disease.* 147, no. 4: 329–40, 1968. https://docs.google.com/viewer?a=v&pid=sites&srcid= ZGVmYXVsdGRvbWFpbnxjb25sZW1lbnRhbHxneDoiZTQyNWVlYjMx MGFlZjVl

Dimri, Bipin. "Where is Magonia, the Hidden Cloud Realm?" Historic Mysteries, 2022. https://www.historicmysteries.com/magonia/

Eberhart, George M. "UFOs and Intelligence: A Timeline." May 31, 2022. https://www.academia.edu/43868466/UFOs_and_Intelligence_A_Timeline_By_George_M_Eberhart

Eno, Paul. *Dancing Past the Graveyard: Poltergeists, Parasites, Parallel Worlds, and God.* Atglen, PA: Red Feather / Schiffer Publishing, 2019.

"Establishment of Unidentified Aerospace-Undersea Phenomena Joint Program." Sec. 1683 (amended) of S. 4503, Intelligence Authorization Act for Fiscal Year 2023. In: Heberlein, Todd. "The US Government mobilizes to address UAPs." July 30, 2022. https://www.toddheberlein.com/blog/2022/7/30/the-us-government-mobilizes-to-address-uaps

Excerpts from "Project Blue Book | Unidentified Flying Objects – UFO." *Matrix Disclosure* Science & History News Magazine, October 17, 2022. https://matrixdisclosure.com/project-blue-book-unidentified-flying-objects-ufo/

EWD Notes: Eric Davis meeting with Admiral Thomas Wilson. October 16, 2002.

https://imgur.com/a/ggIFTfQ?fbclid=IwAR3I7aes386_CrObJBe4AQrqK6mokXz
Cgd2YiSwOGURPiORQTA-wyLuiR3A

Executive Summary, Report of IC Experts Panel on Anomalous Health Incidents
(AHIs). Office of the Director of National Intelligence. https://www.dni.gov/files/
ODNI/documents/assessments/
2022_02_01_AHI_Executive_Summary_FINAL_Redacted.pdf

Feschino, Frank. *Shoot Them Down!: The Flying Saucer Air Wars of 1952*. Independently
published, 2007.

Finney, Jack. *Time and Again*. New York: Simon & Schuster, 1970.

Fleming, Lan. "A New Look at the Evidence Supporting a Prosaic Explanation of the
STS-48 'UFO' Video."

New Frontiers in Science. 2, no. 2, Winter 2003. http://www.carlotto.us/newfrontiersin
science/Papers/v02n02a/v02n02a.pdf

Fort, Charles. *The Book of the Damned*. New York: H. Liveright, 1919. https://archive.
org/details/bookofdamnedbychoofortrich/page/8/mode/2up

Fox, James, director. *The Phenomenon*. Documentary film, 2020. https://
thephenomenonfilm.com

Green, Christopher. "Clinical Medical Acute and Subacute Field Effects on Human
Dermal and Neurological Tissues." Austin, TX: EarthTech International Institute
for Advanced Studies at Austin. https://www.theblackvault.com/docu
mentarchive/wp-content/uploads/2020/01/kitgreen-dird.pdf

Greenewald, John. "Project Condign – The Full Condign Report." The Black Vault,
November 27, 2020. https://www.theblackvault.com/documentarchive/project-
condign-the-full-condign-report/ Text: Defence Intelligence Analysis Staff.
"Unidentified Aerial Phenomena in the UK Air Defence Region: Executive
Summary." Scientific & Technical Memorandum – No. 55/2/00. London: Ministry
of Defence, December 2000. https://documents2.theblackvault.com/documents/
ufos/projectcondignreport-full.pdf

Haines, Avril, Director of National Intelligence. Interview by David Ignatius. "Our
Future in Space," Ignatius Forum, Washington National Cathedral, November 10,
2021. https://www.youtube.com/watch?v=67KZfeZyw_U 8:50 [interview begins],
22:46 [statement on extraterrestrials].

Hastings, Robert. *UFOs and Nukes: Extraordinary Encounters at Nuclear Weapons Sites*.
Independently published, 2008, 2017.

Jane's All the World's Aircraft. Coulsdon, Surrey, UK: Jane's Information Group Ltd.

Jaynes, Julian. *The Origin of Consciousness in the Breakdown of the Bicameral Mind*.
Boston: Houghton Mifflin, 1976.

Johnson, Leland, and Daniel Schaffer. *Oak Ridge National Laboratory: The First Fifty
Years*. Knoxville: The University of Tennessee Press, 1994. https://archive.org/
details/oakridgenationaloojohn

Kasher, Jack. "A Scientific Analysis of the Videotape Taken by Space Shuttle *Discovery* on Shuttle Flight STS-48." In *MUFON 1994 International UFO Symposium Proceedings*, edited by Walter H. Andrus Jr., 108–36. Cincinnati, OH: Mutual UFO Network (MUFON), 1994. https://www.nicap.org/papers/kasher/muj_kasher_sts48.pdf

Kissner, J. Andrew. *Peculiar Phenomenon: Early United States Efforts to Collect and Analyze Flying Disks, 1994–95.* Earthfiles, October 14, 2022. https://www.earthfiles.com/2022/10/14/part-1-peculiar-phenomenon-early-united-states-efforts-to-collect-and-analyze-flying-discs-2/

Kuiper, D. B. H., and M. Morris. "Searching for Extraterrestrial Civilizations." *Science* (n.s.) 196: 616–21, 1977.

Lacatski, James T., Colm A. Kelleher, and George Knapp. *Skinwalkers at the Pentagon: An Insiders' Account of the Secret Government UFO Program.* Lacatski, Henderson, NC: RTMA, LLC, 2021.

Lander, Paul W. *Tapping into the Total Power of the Universe: Time and Gravity Control Technologies for the 21st Century and Beyond.* Independently published. Outskirts Press, 2019.

Library of Congress, Science Policy Research Division. "United States Civilian Space Programs: an Overview." Report prepared for the Subcommittee on Space Science and Applications of the Committee on Science and Technology, U.S. House of Representatives, Ninety-fifth Congress, second session. Washington, DC: U.S. G.P.O., 1979–1983.

Lillis, Katie Bo. "CIA Doctor Hit by Havana Syndrome Says He Was in 'Disbelief' as He Suffered What He Was Investigating." *CNN*, September 25, 2022. https://www.cnn.com/2022/09/25/politics/havana-syndrome-cia-doctor-cnn-special/index.html

Montgomery, Ruth. *Strangers Among Us: Enlightened Beings from a World to Come.* New York: Coward, McCann & Geoghegan, 1979.

National Defense Authorization Act for Fiscal Year 2023, H.R. 7900. "About Unidentified Aerospace-Undersea Phenomena." U.A.P.S.G. – G.E.F.A.I., August 27, 2022. https://www.uapsg.net/2022/08/about-unidentified-aerospace-undersea.html

National Intelligence Council. "Updated Assessment of Anomalous Health Incidents." Intelligence Community Assessment 2023-02286-B. March 1, 2023. https://files.constantcontact.com/fab49a91901/6925ff67-6e1f-4688-838c-f18dbe15c5a1.pdf

O'Brien, Cathy, and Mark Phillips. *TRANCE Formation of America: The True Life Story of a CIA Mind Control Slave.* Reality Marketing, 1995.

Office of the Director of National Intelligence. "Preliminary Assessment: Unidentified Aerial Phenomena." Washington, DC: ODNI, June 25, 2021. https://www.dni.gov/files/ODNI/documents/assessments/Prelimary-Assessment-UAP-20210625.pdf

Paller, K. A. (2000). Neural correlates of true and false memories. *Neuron*, 28, no. 2, 305–313. doi:10.1016/S0896-6273(00)00104-5

Pasulka, D. W. *American Cosmic: UFOs, Religion, Technology.* Oxford and New York: Oxford University Press, 2019.

Redfern, Nick. "UFOs: Invasion at Oak Ridge." Mysterious Universe, November 25, 2015. https://mysteriousuniverse.org/2015/11/ufos-invasion-at-oak-ridge/

Ruppelt, Edward J. *The Report on Unidentified Flying Objects*. New York: Doubleday, 1956.

Saboski, Art. "A Pilot Explains UFO Sightings—for the Last Time." *Wall Street Journal*, November 1, 2022. https://www.wsj.com/articles/pilot-ufo-sightings-unexplained-unidentified-11667256792

Sauder, Richard. *Underwater and Underground Bases: Surprising Facts the Government Does Not Want You to Know!* Kempton, IL: Adventures Unlimited Press, 2001, 2014.

Schindele, Captain David D. (USAF, retired). *It Never Happened: U.S. Air Force UFO. Cover-up Revealed*. Vol. I. Naches, WA: EdgarRock Publishing, 2017.

Seppi, Sheila. *Walk-Ins: The Cosmology of the Soul*. Independently published, 2020.

Shaw, Julia, and Stephen Porter. "Constructing Rich False Memories of Committing Crime." *Psychological Science*. 26, no. 3: 291–301, 2015.

Sniekers, Suzanne, et al. "Genome-Wide Association Meta-Analysis of 78,308 Individuals Identifies New Loci and Genes Influencing Human Intelligence." *Nature Genetics* 49: 1107–12, 2017.

Them, filmscript, 1954. https://www.stockq.org/moviescript/T/them.php

Twining, N. F. "AMC [Air Materiel Command] Opinion Concerning 'Flying Discs'" (the Twining memo). Wright Field, Dayton, Ohio, September 23, 1947. https://imgur.com/gallery/uDLKPN3

"UFO." 1947–1954. FBI Records: The Vault. https://vault.fbi.gov/UFO

U.S. Department of Defense. "DoD Announces the Establishment of the Airborne Object Identification and Management Synchronization Group, (AOIMSG)." Washington, DC: Department of Defense, November 23, 2021. https://www.defense.gov/News/Releases/Release/Article/2853121/dod-announces-the-establishment-of-the-airborne-object-identification-and-manag/

Vallée, Jacques, and Paola Leopizzi Harris. *Trinity: The Best-Kept Secret*. Starworks-USA, 2021.

Vallée, Jacques. *Passport to Magonia: From Folklore to Flying Saucers*. New York: McGraw-Hill, 1969, repr. 1974; Chicago, IL: Contemporary Books, 1993; Brisbane, Australia: Daily Grail Publishing, 2014.

White, Harold "Sonny." Interviewed by Anne-Marie Corley. "Meet the NASA scientist devising a starship warp drive." *New Scientist*, August 13, 2013. https://www.newscientist.com/article/mg21929300-300-meet-the-nasa-scientist-devising-a-starship-warp-drive/

Wu, Xiang, et al. "Tether-free Photothermal Deep-brain Stimulation in Freely Behaving Mice via Wide-field Illumination in the Near-infrared-II Window." *Nature Biological Engineering*. 6, 754–70, 2022. https://www.nature.com/articles/s41551-022-00862-w

Printed in Great Britain
by Amazon

35767197R00169